THE
Consequences
of Consent

THE
Consequences
of Consent

ELECTIONS, CITIZEN CONTROL
AND POPULAR ACQUIESCENCE

★★

BENJAMIN GINSBERG

Cornell University

▲
▼▼

ADDISON-WESLEY PUBLISHING COMPANY

Reading, Massachusetts ★ Menlo Park, California
London ★ Amsterdam ★ Don Mills, Ontario ★ Sydney

Library of Congress Cataloging in Publication Data

Ginsberg, Benjamin.
    The consequences of consent.

    Includes index.
    1. General will. 2. Representative government and
representation. 3. Consensus (Social sciences)
4. Elections. 5. Pressure groups. 6. Consent (Law)
I. Title.
JC328.2.G56   320'.01'1   81-3581
ISBN 0-201-04079-4   AACR2

ISBN 0-201-04079-4
ABCDEFGHIJ-DO-8987654321

For Sandy

PREFACE

✦✦

The Consequences of Consent presents both an inquiry into and an argument about the history, character, and significance of democratic electoral institutions. My use of the phrase "electoral institutions" rather than "voting" or "voting behavior" is deliberate. This is a book about elections as political institutions rather than a more conventional discussion of voting behavior. This difference of emphasis is sufficiently important that even those who may later decide to reject some portion of my argument may still be interested in the terms of the inquiry.

Studies of voting behavior are centrally concerned with the character and causes of voters' choices and, more important, with the implications for leadership and policy of alternative voting patterns and election outcomes. Even those voting studies that have an historical or institutional dimension deal essentially with the etiology and effects of variations in voting patterns and electoral decisions.

My central concerns, by contrast, are the broader and intellectually prior questions of why individuals may choose to participate electorally rather than engage in other forms of political action and, more important, the implications for government and politics of the very existence of democratic electoral institutions. I freely acknowledge that voting choices and electoral outcomes can be quite consequential. Those who deny that elections in the democratic context can have significant implications for the makeup of a nation's ruling circle and the character of its policies are merely being foolish.

Nevertheless, to observe that there are relationships between voting choices, leadership composition, and policy outputs is only to begin to understand the importance of democratic elections rather than to exhaust the possibilities. If we go beyond the implications of variations in voting behavior to consider the significance of the existence of democratic elections, we find ourselves at the very foundations of government. For elections are among the principal mechanisms through which contemporary governments regulate mass political action and maintain their own power and authority. Stated succinctly, the chief consequence of consent is the modern liberal state itself.

I am indebted to a number of individuals for their assistance. My principal obligation is to Theodore Lowi, who has been a teacher, a colleague, a friend, and a source of interesting ideas for nearly twenty years. Many other colleagues offered suggestions and criticisms during the course of this project. I benefited particularly from conversations with E. W. Kelley, T. J. Pempel, Martin Shefter, Alan Stone, and, most especially, Robert Weissberg. In addition, I would like to thank David Brady, William Keech, Michael King, and John Wahlke for their careful reading and evaluation of the entire manuscript. Several present and former Cornell graduate students and undergraduates provided valuable research assistance. Among the graduate students the most important to this project were Peter Galderisi, John Green, Susan Grogan, and Paul Pescatello; among the undergraduates, Judith Esman and Charles Honart. Essential financial support for my research came from Cornell's Jonathan Meigs Fund. Michael Busch and Gertrude Fitzpatrick were tireless manuscript typists. My thanks also to Arline Blaker and Karen Spencer.

A section of Chapter 4 of the book is based on an article of mine that was originally published in the *American Political Science Review;* a section of Chapter 5 is slightly revised from a portion of an article that I wrote with Robert Weissberg and that originally appeared in the *American Journal of Political Science*. Both pieces are reprinted here with the permission of these journals. Unless otherwise indicated, the source of all American opinion survey data used in this study is the Center for Political Studies of the Institute for Social Research, University of Michigan. Data were made available through the Inter-University Consortium for Political and Social Research. Other types of data were either collected by me or acquired from sources cited in the text.

Finally, I would like to thank Stanley Evans and Stuart Johnson of Addison-Wesley, the former for his prescience and the latter for his patience.

Cosmos Hill, New York   B. G.
May 1981

CONTENTS

✱✱✱

ELECTIONS AS INSTITUTIONS OF GOVERNANCE

****

1

Some 150 years after its publication, de Tocqueville's *Democracy in America* must still be considered the single most important work dealing with American democratic institutions. It is enormously ironic, however, that de Tocqueville came to the United States to observe its innovations in the area of social control, particularly the prison, before turning his attention instead to America's novel institutions of popular control and mass participation, particularly the election. The irony, as de Tocqueville came to see, is that whatever its potential for popular control of the state, the election is simultaneously one of the most important instruments of social control available to the modern state. The election and the prison, along with mass education and the factory, were the great institutions of social control introduced in the eighteenth and nineteenth centuries to deal with the entry of the masses onto the political and economic stage. Since the nineteenth century, governments have ruled through electoral mechanisms even when they sometimes have been ruled by them.[1]

The central questions of democratic politics have always concerned the relationship between the citizen and the state. But with the great expansion of the state's role during the course of the twentieth century, the problem of the use and control of governmental powers has become particularly critical. Are there means by which citizens can continue to use government to improve their lot, or is the state's power, like that of the genie, beyond control once released? Having allowed their rulers sufficient power to do good, can citizens exert sufficient influence over public officials' use of power to prevent them from doing evil?

---

[1] Alexis de Tocqueville, *Democracy in America*, 2 vols. (New York: Random House, Vintage Books, 1945). De Tocqueville's study of the American penal system is Gustave de Beaumont and Alexis de Tocqueville, *On the Penitentiary System in the United States and Its Application in France* (Carbondale: Southern Illinois University Press, 1964). There exists, of course, a fascinating literature on the "invention" of the penitentiary, the factory, and mass education during the nineteenth century and their implications for social order. On the prison, see Michel Foucault, *Discipline and Punish* (New York: Pantheon, 1977); Kai T. Erikson, *Wayward Puritans* (New York: Wiley, 1966); and David Rothman, *The Discovery of the Asylum* (Boston: Little, Brown, 1971). On

In the Western democracies elections are conceived to be the most important institution of popular control of governments' conduct. On a formal and routine basis, elections allow mass publics the opportunity to influence their rulers' actions. It is largely because of the availability of the electoral sanction that the possibility of popular control of the state is taken seriously by Americans and the citizens of the other democracies.

But rather than present a simple solution to the problem of the state's power, the election poses a fundamental and complex dilemma. The democratic election, the most important means yet devised to enable citizens to exercise a measure of formal control over their governments' actions, is at the same time one of the most important means by which contemporary governments maintain a measure of control over their citizens. However real the possibilities of popular control through the ballot box, the election is at the same time an institution of governance. As though a single pedal controlled both an automobile's brake and its accelerator, the principal mechanism by which citizens attempt to control the state simultaneously helps both to limit popular intervention in the governmental process and to increase the state's authority and power.

VOTING

The study of elections, particularly in the United States, has for the most part meant the study of voting behavior. The principal focus of analysis has been the question of how voters reach their decisions.

---

the factory, see Harry Braverman, *Labor and Monopoly Capital* (New York: Monthly Review Press, 1974); Samuel Haber, *Efficiency and Uplift* (Chicago: University of Chicago Press, 1964); and Alfred D. Chandler, Jr., *The Visible Hand* (Cambridge, Mass.: Harvard University Press, 1977). On mass education, see Michael B. Katz, *The Irony of Early School Reform* (Cambridge, Mass.: Harvard University Press, 1968); Marvin Lazerson, *Origins of the Urban School* (Cambridge, Mass.: Harvard University Press, 1971); and David Nasaw, *Schooled to Order* (New York: Oxford University Press, 1979).

Two key works that set the agenda for modern electoral research, *Voting,* by Berelson, Lazersfeld, and McPhee, and *The American Voter,* by Campbell *et al.,* stated the question succinctly. *The American Voter* sought to "account for variation in whether a given individual voter is going to vote and which candidate he will choose."[2] Similarly, *Voting* aimed to determine "how people come to vote as they do."[3]

To study how voters decide presumes that what voters decide is important. And, indeed, voting behavior is not analyzed simply for its own sake. *The American Voter* noted that, whatever voting behavior might suggest about the nature of human choice, voting was important chiefly "for the decisions to which it leads."[4] The presumption underlying the study of voting behavior is, of course, that voting is significant because of the decisions that voters collectively make about who will govern and because of the impact that these decisions, in turn, have upon governments' actions. As *The American Voter* stated, "what the electorate decides may determine which actors will have the power of decision, and the outcomes of past and future elections generate important influences to which these actors respond."[5]

The American Voter and *Voting* obviously had an enormous effect upon the character of subsequent electoral research. In the years since the publication of these volumes, social scientists' answers to the seemingly simple question of how voters come to vote as they do have become complex enough to tax the powers of our most sophisticated computers, to say nothing of the credulity of our undergraduates.

To ask a question is always to limit the range of possible answers. But to answer, especially to answer well, is often to foreclose exam-

---

[2] Angus Campbell *et al., The American Voter* (New York: Wiley, 1960), p. 19.

[3] Bernard R. Berelson, Paul F. Lazersfeld, and William N. McPhee, *Voting* (Chicago: University of Chicago Press, 1954), p. vii.

[4] Campbell *et al., The American Voter,* p. 4.

[5] *Ibid.,* p. 5.

ination of the assumptions upon which the question was initially based. Although the study of voting behavior generally assumes rather than examines the importance of electoral decisions, the enormous attention and often excellent scholarship devoted to the analysis of voting behavior have tended to inhibit discussion of this central assumption. Even when, rightly or wrongly, the study of voting seemed to suggest that what voters decided was unlikely to have much significance for a government's actions, students of voting continued to think that somehow it should. For example, after finding that most voters appeared to exhibit little of the interest, awareness, or understanding of public issues that was thought to be required if the electorate was to influence policy, Berelson, Lazersfeld, and McPhee proceeded to redefine their criteria for appropriate electoral decisions.[6]

It is precisely this tendency to foreclose examination of its basic assumption that can make the study of voting so misleading. And what is most misleading about the study of voting behavior is precisely the assumption that the significance of elections is mainly a function of what voters decide.

What voters decide is not at all the most significant aspect of the electoral process. Voters' decisions can sometimes be important. But in many respects, what voters decide, and thus how they come to vote as they do, is far less consequential for government and politics than the simple fact of voting itself. The impact of electoral decisions upon the governmental process is analogous to the impact made upon organized religion by individuals who obey the injunction to worship at the church of their choice. The fact of worship can be more important than the choice. The fact of mass electoral participation is generally far more significant for the state than what or how citizens decide once they participate. It is the institution of the election rather than any particular pattern of voting that is critical, even for those regimes that can sometimes be affected by what voters decide.

---

[6] Berelson, Lazersfeld, and McPhee, *Voting,* ch. 14.

THE ELECTION AS AN INSTITUTION

First, democratic elections socialize political activity. Voting is not a natural or spontaneous phenomenon. It is an institutionalized and routinized form of mass political involvement. However low voter turnout may be in the state of Mississippi, as far as can be determined no one votes in the state of nature. That individuals vote rather than engage in some other form of political behavior is a result of national policies that create the opportunity to vote and encourage voting relative to other political activities. Elections transform what might otherwise consist of sporadic, citizen-initiated acts into a routine public function. With the advent of the election, control over the agenda for mass political action passes from the citizen to the state. Elections make 'how, when, where, and which citizens take part in political life a question of public policy rather than simply a matter of individual choice. This transformation, as we shall see, expands and democratizes mass political involvement. At the same time, however, elections help to preserve governments' stability by containing and channeling away potentially more disruptive or dangerous forms of mass political activity. By establishing formal avenues for mass participation and habituating citizens to their use, governments reduce the threat that mass involvement in politics can pose to the established order.

Second, elections institutionalize mass influence in political life. Democratic elections are sometimes conceived to be synonymous with popular influence in government and politics. But, obviously, elections are hardly the only means through which citizens can convince those in power to heed their views and listen to their grievances. The behavior of even the most rigid autocrat can be influenced by the threat of popular disobedience, riot, or insurrection. Elections substitute an institutional mechanism for the informal sources of influence that might be available to a mass public. This substitution means, on the one hand, that even rulers whose power could not easily be threatened by popular unrest or violence are vulnerable to a formal public sanction. But at the same time, elections delimit mass intervention into policymaking processes and permit governments a measure of formal control over citizens' ability to control them. As we shall see, the substitution of elections—even democratic elections—for more spontaneous modes of mass political action can have the effect of diminishing mass influence in political life. Indeed, elections are often introduced, or the suffrage expanded, precisely in order to reduce the impact of mass political action upon government and policy.

Third, elections institutionalize access to political power. The democratic election serves as a formal means through which groups outside the existing ruling circle can displace those in power. Elections, in effect, permit the state's power to be acquired without having to be overcome. Elections, moreover, permit ordinary citizens to play an important role in the leadership selection process. At the same time, however, elections permit governments to set formal conditions for legitimate access to power. Precisely because they formalize access to power as well as popular influence over the acquisition of power, elections can constrain and delimit both.

Fourth, elections bolster the state's power and authority. Elections help to increase popular support for political leaders and for the regime itself. The formal opportunity to participate in elections serves to convince citizens that the government is responsive to their needs and wishes. Moreover, elections help to persuade citizens to obey. Electoral participation increases popular cooperation with a government's programs and policies, particularly popular acquiescence to the taxes and military service upon which the state's power depends. Even if popular voting can influence the behavior of those in power, voting serves simultaneously as a form of cooptation. Elections—particularly democratic elections—substitute consent for coercion as the foundation of the state's power.

It is for these four reasons that the election is the most important governmental innovation of the modern era. However, and to an extent, whatever voters decide, elections help to confine mass political action to routine, peaceful channels and to transform its potentially dangerous force into a principal source of the modern state's power and authority.

THE SUFFRAGE

The election's role as an institution of governance is brought into particularly sharp focus by the factors associated with the introduction and expansion of the suffrage. The history of the suffrage is often written in such a way as to suggest that the opportunity to vote was only wrung from unwilling rulers after long and bitter popular struggles. This interpretation of the suffrage's development is, of course, consistent with a view of elections as simply instruments of popular control—something to which governments certainly accede reluctantly, if at all. It is certainly true that at least some citizens of every nation obtained the right to vote only after a protracted period of strife. And, indeed, it is also true that some ruling groups embarked upon the electoral path hesitantly, conceiving elections to be, at best, the least objectionable alternative available to them.

Yet, as Schattschneider once noted, the difficulty with which voting rights were secured, particularly over the past 150 years, has frequently been overstated.[7] Especially in the nineteenth and twentieth centuries, those in power have often seemed quite ready to extend the suffrage to their subjects. In a number of instances, ruling groups have been much more anxious to grant voting rights to their subjects than those subjects have been to receive or to exercise them. Although the opportunity to vote was difficult to secure, especially in the eighteenth and sometimes into the nineteenth century, by the twentieth century governments as diverse as Albania and Italy had made voting compulsory.[8] In some instances, failure to vote has been considered a serious offense. The Pinochet government in Chile, for example, declared failure to vote in its 1980 referendum on the continuation of military rule to be an offense punishable by three months in prison and the equivalent of a $150 fine.[9] In the twentieth

---

[7] E.E. Schattschneider, *The Semi-Sovereign People* (New York: Holt, Rinehart and Winston, 1960), p. 100.

[8] On compulsory voting in Western Europe, see Harold F. Gosnell, *Why Europe Votes* (Chicago: University of Chicago Press, 1930). Voting was compulsory in several of the American colonies in the seventeenth and eighteenth centuries. See Cortlandt F. Bishop, *History of Elections in the American Colonies* (New York: Columbia College, 1893), pp. 190-192.

[9] On the Chilean referendum, see Edward Schumacher, "Chile Votes on Referendum that Tightens Pinochet's Grip," *New York Times,* September 11, 1980. For the referendum's results, see Edward Schumacher, "Chilean Leader, Winner of Vote, Attacks U.S." *New York Times,* September 13, 1980.

century, governments not only have accepted the concept of mass electoral participation, but they also have obviously come to embrace the idea with considerable enthusiasm.

The explanation for this change of attitude toward the suffrage is that rulers had come to see the potential value of elections first as a means of channeling and controlling mass political activity and second as a means of mobilizing popular support for the regime. These two factors have played key roles in prompting the introduction and expansion of the suffrage, especially after the nineteenth century.

SUFFRAGE EXPANSION
AND POLITICAL DISARRAY

The suffrage is often conceived by governments to be a means of curbing or preventing political disorder. By providing routine electoral channels for political expression, governments attempt to discourage more violent or disruptive forms of mass political activity. It might be noted that this strategy also became popular among university administrators during the 1960s. Many universities established formal mechanisms of student participation in university affairs during this period as a means of curbing campus disorder.

Far from intending to increase popular influence, those in power often introduce or expand the suffrage precisely when citizens have too much influence over their actions. The purpose of suffrage expansion in this context is to bring political activity under control and to diminish mass intervention into governmental processes.

In some instances, of course, the relationship between political disorder and suffrage expansion requires little explanation. Citizens' desire for the suffrage may be a cause of riot or unrest, and expansion of the suffrage may be a direct governmental concession to popular demand. For example, the federal voting rights legislation of the 1960s, which made black suffrage in the southern United States a reality, was obviously hastened by demonstrations, sit-ins, and protest marches in which blacks demanded, among other things, the opportunity to vote.

Probably more often, however, the relationship between the suffrage and political disorder involves more than a simple case of a government succumbing to an irresistible demand for the right to vote. Whatever demand exists for the suffrage is as often unresisted as it is irresistible. Indeed, expansion of the suffrage often takes place only after the popular agitation for it has been suppressed.

For example, Dorr's Rebellion during the late 1830s grew out of an attempt to enlarge the Rhode Island suffrage by substituting a tax-paying requirement for property restrictions on voting. After some violence, including an unsuccessful attempt to seize the state arsenal in 1842, Dorr's followers were forcibly dispersed and Dorr arrested. In 1843, after the suppression of the insurrection, however, a new state constitution that liberalized voting requirements by the introduction of a minimal tax-paying alternative to property ownership was enacted.[10]

Similarly, the British Reform Act of 1832 came at a time when popular agitation for suffrage liberalization was relatively minimal. Demands for suffrage reform had been suppressed in the 1790s and again in the 1820s. During both periods, the government suspended the right of *habeas corpus,* tried advocates of reform for sedition, and employed military force, culminating in the Peterloo massacre of 1819. By the late 1820s the demand for suffrage reform had all but disappeared.[11]

In neither of these instances were authorities forced to succumb to popular demand for suffrage reform. Instead, the political violence that they had suppressed appears to have convinced those in power of the desirability of opening formal channels for the expression of whatever political demands might arise in the future. Indeed, the

---

[10] An account of the relationship between Dorr's Rebellion and Rhode Island suffrage reform may be found in Jacob Frieze, *A Concise History of the Efforts to Obtain an Extension of Suffrage in Rhode Island* (Providence: Thomas S. Hammon, 1842). See also Kirk H. Porter, *A History of Suffrage in the United States* (Chicago: University of Chicago Press, 1918), p. 100; and Chilton Williamson, *American Suffrage from Property to Democracy* (Princeton, N.J.: Princeton University Press, 1960), ch. 13.

[11] John Cannon, *Parliamentary Reform 1640-1832* (Cambridge: At the University Press, 1973), is an excellent history of British suffrage reform.

most important threat that suffrage reform was intended to avert in the American case was the possibility of lower-class insurrection, and in the British case, middle-class support for lower-class revolt. The revolution that Lord Grey thought to prevent by his policies in 1832 was not believed likely to limit its aims to liberalization of the suffrage. As Macaulay, a supporter of reform, remarked in the House of Commons, "If this bill should be rejected, I pray to God, that none of those who concur in rejecting may ever remember their votes with unavailing regret, amidst the wreck of laws, the confusion of ranks, the spoilation of property, and the dissolution of social order."[12]

Even more interesting, however, than suffrage expansion following the forcible suppression of demands for the vote are those cases in which the suffrage was not a major focus of the popular agitation that seemed to lead to its expansion. Perhaps the most clear-cut example is the lowering of the voting age to 18 in the United States. This expansion of the suffrage occurred during a period of civil strife and disorder. But what is fascinating is that little or no demand for voting rights had been expressed by their eventual recipients. Student discontent was focused upon the Vietnam war, race relations, social policy, institutions of higher education, almost every aspect of American society but the suffrage. Yet, despite this apparent lack of student interest in the question of voting, many political leaders seemed quite anxious to lower the voting age. Senate Judiciary Committee hearings on the subject, for instance, indicated a widespread belief among public officials that reduction of the voting age to permit college-age students the opportunity to vote would help to discourage their participation in disruptive forms of political action. Statements and testimony before the Judiciary Committee are quite revealing.

United States Senator Birch Bayh:

No longer are young Americans content to sit idly by and watch the passing scene from the grandstand. They want to be down on the field. They have made it abundantly clear that they intend to participate in the game. No longer should older Americans be content to leave this

---

[12] Quoted in Cannon, *Parliamentary Reform*, p. 216.

vigorous and exciting force on the sidelines. This force, this energy, is going to continue to build and grow. The only question is whether we should ignore it, perhaps leaving this energy to dam up and burst and follow less-than-wholesome channels, or whether we should let this force be utilized by society through the pressure valve of the franchise.[13]

United States Senator Jacob Javits:

We all realize that only a tiny minority of college students on these campuses engaged in unlawful acts. But these deplorable incidents make a point. There is really no excuse for such acts of civil disobedience at any time in a nation that guarantees the right of orderly protest and redress of grievances through the ballot box. I am convinced that self-styled student leaders who urged such acts of civil disobedience would find themselves with little or no support if students were given a more meaningful role in the political process. In short, political activism of our college-age youth today — whether it be in demonstrations or working in behalf of candidates like Senator McCarthy — is all happening outside the existing political framework. Passage of the resolution before this Committee would give us the means, sort of the famous carrot and the stick, to channel this energy into our major political parties on all levels, national, state and local.[14]

United States Senator James B. Pearson:

While some of our campuses may be torn by dissent, the fact remains that the great, indeed, the overwhelming majority of our youths are responsible, hard-working, dedicated citizens with faith in our demo-cratic process. They want to vote. They want to participate. They want to make our country a better place to live. Many of them join demon-strations simply because they feel it is the only way they can be heard. This is not to excuse the violence and complete disrespect for authority that some demonstrators employ. But the fact remains that many of the

---

[13] United States Senate, Committee on the Judiciary, *Hearings before the Subcommittee on Constitutional Amendments on S. J. Res. 8, S. J. Res. 14, and S. J. Res. 78 Relating to Lowering the Voting Age to 18,* May 14, 15, and 16, 1968 (Washington, D.C.: U.S. Government Printing Office, 1968), p. 3.

[14] *Ibid.,* p. 12.

participants are involved because of their inability to find meaningful political outlets elsewhere to express their concern. For them, certainly, the right to vote is an opportunity for rewarding involvement in public affairs. [15]

United States Senator William Proxmire:

The situations on many of our college campuses today, alarming as they are, raise this question: Why not allow students the right to make a positive choice as an alternative to a negative protest? [16]

United States Representative Ken Hechler:

Many people who reflect on the disgraceful episodes on our college campuses, with the ransacking of the offices of college officials, the defiance of authority, the outbreaks of violence, the use of drugs, and the draft-card burnings—many people conclude that America's youth are irresponsible iconoclasts. Many older people yearn for the good old days of the 1950s when grey-flanneled youth declined to be identified with civic issues lest the corporate recruiters would regard overactive participation as a blemish on student records. I favored the eighteen year old vote then in order to blast some students out of their complacence. Today the eighteen year old vote is needed to harness the energy of young people and direct it into useful and constructive channels, not simply for their benefit, but for the benefit of the entire nation. . . . At this crucial point, if we deny the right to vote to those young people between the ages of eighteen and twenty, it is entirely possible that they will join the more militant minority of their fellow students and engage in destructive activities of a dangerous nature. [17]

Even taking into account the rhetorical excess sometimes occasioned by Senate hearings, the perceptions of these and other public officials of the period seem quite clear. The opportunity to vote was not given to citizens between the ages of 18 and 20 because they demanded it. Rather, public officials believed suffrage expansion

---

[15] *Ibid.,* p. 36.

[16] *Ibid.,* p. 39.

[17] *Ibid.,* p. 74.

to be a means of institutionalizing youths' participation in politics, which would, in turn, curb disorder. Though somewhat less clear-cut, a parallel case can be made for the federal government's efforts on behalf of voting rights for blacks during the 1960s. Piven and Cloward, for example, argue that the Kennedy administration's concentration on voting rights for blacks was, in part, an attempt to divert civil rights activists away from their campaign for desegregation of schools and public facilities.[18] Indeed, a number of black activists of the period resisted participating in the voting rights effort precisely because they perceived it to be little more than an attempt to divert their energies from more important goals. One faction, for example, of the Student Non-Violent Coordinating Committee (SNCC), at that time an important civil rights group, refused to take part in voter registration efforts on the ground that voter registration was simply an attempt by the national government "to cool the militancy of the student movement."[19]

Whatever the aims of those in power, the introduction or expansion of the suffrage certainly does not guarantee the prevention of disorder. In several instances in recent years, the suffrage has been extended to politically quiescent Third World populations in anticipation of the possibility of the emergence of political activity. Heeding the example of the West, leaders sought to establish formal avenues of mass political participation to channel and confine whatever popular demands might eventually emerge.[20] The system of "basic democracies" established by Pakistan's Ayub Khan in the 1950s is an example. The subsequent history of these attempts indicates that the mere availability of institutional channels of participation by no means guarantees their use. In the West, the availability of the suffrage has been coupled with a socialization process that, albeit

---

[18] Frances Fox Piven and Richard A. Cloward, *Poor People's Movements* (New York: Random House, Vintage Books, 1979), pp. 231-235.

[19] *Ibid.*, p. 233.

[20] Myron Weiner, "Political Participation: Crisis of the Political Process," in Leonard Binder *et al.* (eds.), *Crises and Sequences in Political Development* (Princeton, N.J.: Princeton University Press, 1971), p. 196.

imperfectly, teaches citizens to want to use formal electoral channels when they attempt to take part in political life. "Civic education" and the other mechanisms that encourage citizens to vote rather than engage in other forms of political activity will be discussed in more detail in Chapter 2. But in the absence of appropriate training and incentives, citizens may certainly choose to ignore the opportunity to vote and opt instead for informal modes of political action if they have grievances to express or demands to assert.

It is, moreover, obvious that the suffrage is not governments' only means of dealing with chaotic or disorderly forms of political activity. Probably no government in history has not had some occasion to suppress political protest by force. It may well be that political leaders are most likely to turn to suffrage expansion when they are unable to muster sufficient force to suppress disorder or, for one or another reason, cannot use the force ostensibly available to them. Governments' inability to muster sufficient force to stifle unrest was certainly a factor behind liberalization of the suffrage in the defeated nations of post–World War I Europe. The United States government's lack of the legal and political capacity to fully employ the forces it commanded to suppress disorder in the 1960s contributed to its inclination to turn to a policy of suffrage expansion.

But even many governments that have clearly possessed the capacity to suppress unwelcome political agitation have often preferred not to do so in order to avoid alienating subjects whose support they might subsequently require. From the perspective of political leaders, suffrage expansion not only discourages rioting and unrest but also serves to maintain or increase popular support for the regime.

SUFFRAGE EXPANSION AND POPULAR CONSENT

Since the eighteenth and nineteenth centuries, rulers have conceived mass electoral participation to be an important means of mobilizing popular support for the regime, its leaders, and national policies.[21] This use of suffrage expansion becomes especially evident during periods when a regime is confronted by some external threat.

Efforts to induce a population to rally to the nation's defense and willingly bear the cost and sacrifice of war probably account for more instances of suffrage expansion than any other single proximate cause. This relationship between the suffrage and mass mobilization for war is well illustrated by the slogan coined during the nineteenth-century Swedish suffrage debates, "One man, one vote, one gun."

Among the most obvious examples of the use of suffrage expansion to bolster support for a war effort are the Canadian Military Voters' Act of 1917 and the Canadian Wartime Elections Act, also of 1917.[22] Under the terms of the first piece of legislation, military personnel of both sexes and all ages were granted the right to vote in general elections so long as the war continued and they remained on active duty. The second act was designed specifically to bolster support for military conscription. Under its terms women with close relatives in the armed services were granted the suffrage—*for the duration of the war.* The effects of mass mobilization for war sometimes carry over into the postwar period. The impetus for the introduction of women's suffrage in both Britain and the United States, for example, came during World War I, even though the actual enfranchisement of women in both nations did not occur until shortly after the war.[23]

---

[21] An interesting treatment of the relationship between expansion of the suffrage and elite efforts to increase governments' legitimacy is offered in John Freeman and Duncan Snidal, "Diffusion, Development and Democratization: Enfranchisement in Western Europe," paper presented at the Annual Meeting of the Midwest Political Science Association, Chicago, Illinois, April 23-26, 1980.

[22] Both pieces of Canadian legislation are discussed by Catherine Lyle Cleverdon, *The Woman Suffrage Movement in Canada* (Toronto: University of Toronto Press, 1950), ch. 5.

[23] The British case is discussed in Homer L. Morris, *Parliamentary Franchise Reform in England from 1885 to 1918* (New York: Columbia University Press, 1921), especially ch. 9. See also Harold F. Gosnell, *Democracy, the Threshold of Freedom* (New York: Ronald Press, 1948), pp. 22-25. The impact of World War I on the suffrage is treated in Goran Therborn, "The Rule of Capitalism and the Rise of Democracy," *New Left*

Though mobilization for war provides the most clear-cut examples of the use of the suffrage to bolster mass support, similar processes can be seen even in the absence of any direct external threat to the regime. In nations that permit open competition for office, suffrage expansion has been used to increase electoral support for the groups in power vis-a-vis their rivals. Examples range from the British Reform Act of 1867 to the Fifteenth Amendment to the U.S. Constitution. In the latter case, northern Republicans sought black enfranchisement mainly in the North to strengthen their own grip on national power.[24] As Sigler notes, blacks had not actively sought expanded voting opportunities prior to the amendment's adoption.[25]

Even more interesting is the introduction or expansion of the suffrage by authoritarian governments seeking both to build a mass base of support for themselves and to demonstrate their popular support to potential foes. In the nineteenth century, Napoleon III favored universal suffrage for these reasons. In the twentieth century, European communist governments introduced not only universal suffrage but compulsory voting soon after coming into power. Voting appears to be taken very seriously by these regimes. As one Soviet writer stated, "Elections raise the consciousness of the masses, heighten the activity of the people, and attract millions of workers to participate in State construction and direction."[26]

Creation of mass support through the introduction or expansion of the suffrage has, on a number of occasions, been designed to facilitate the centralization of national authority. The purpose of suffrage expansion in this context is to subvert local or regional popular allegiances by linking citizens directly to the central govern-

---

Review, no. 103 (May 1977): 3-41. See also Charles Seymour and Donald Paige Frary, *How the World Votes* (Springfield, Mass.: C.A. Nichols, 1918), ch. 8.

[24] William Gillette, *The Right to Vote: Politics and the Passage of the 15th Amendment* (Baltimore: Johns Hopkins University Press, 1965), especially ch. 2. The most powerful general treatment of this period of American history is C. Vann Woodward, *Reunion and Reaction* (Boston: Little, Brown, 1951).

[25] Jay A. Sigler, *American Rights Policies* (Homewood, Ill.: Dorsey Press, 1975), p. 114.

[26] Quoted in Howard Swearer, "The Function of Soviet Local Elections," *Midwest Journal of Political Science* 5 (1961): 147.

ment via the ballot box. Bismarck, for example, liberalized the suffrage in the German Reich in order to undermine citizens' traditional identifications and tie them directly to the imperial government.[27] Similarly, in "new nations" in the twentieth century, efforts of governments to induce citizens to participate in national elections were often designed to erode the authority of local elites and create popular ties with the central government. Weiner suggests the example of India, where suffrage expansion and liberalization were aimed in part at reducing the influence of the maharajas and creating a measure of loyalty to state and local governments.[28]

Finally, suffrage expansion has been regarded with particular favor by those governments whose policy aims have been sufficiently ambitious to require them to increase taxes or call for other forms of popular sacrifice. As in the case of wartime mobilization, such governments sometimes feel compelled to increase citizens' support to a level commensurate with the sacrifices and exertions that will be demanded of them.[29] The Soviet Union, the People's Republic of China, and a variety of Third World nations with ambitious development goals serve as illustrations. Not altogether different is an example from recent American history. The now-famous plan for "maximum feasible participation," associated with Lyndon Johnson's poverty program, was strictly speaking not an expansion of the suffrage. Yet the principle involved is quite similar to those associated with expansion of electoral participation. Involvement of the poor in the "War on Poverty" was conceived, in part, as a means of coopting their support for federal initiatives and diminishing their distrust of the government's intentions.[30]

---

[27] Theodore S. Hamerow, *The Social Foundations of German Unification* (Princeton, N.J.: Princeton University Press, 1972), vol. 2, especially pp. 244-245; also pp. 183-190 and 331-333. See also Stein Rokkan, *Citizens, Elections, Parties* (New York: David McKay, 1970), pp. 31, 150; and Weiner, "Political Participation," p. 170.

[28] Weiner, "Political Participation," p. 177.

[29] *Ibid.*, p. 197.

[30] Frances Fox Piven and Richard A. Cloward, *Regulating the Poor* (New York: Pantheon, 1971), pp. 265-266. See also J. David Greenstone and Paul E. Peterson, *Race*

The theme that emerges very clearly in all these cases is that permitting citizens the opportunity to participate in elections is conceived by governments to be a source of increased authority and stability. Expansion of the suffrage is often designed to control the potentially disruptive power of mass participation in politics and to convert it into support for the state. This conception of the role of elections, moreover, is by no means alien to American political history. Indeed, the framers of the U.S. Constitution seemed fully aware of the potential role of elections in generating popular support for the government. James Wilson, for example, arguing in favor of the popular election of members of the House of Representatives, asserted that he favored "raising the federal pyramid to considerable altitude," and for that reason wished to give it "as broad a base as possible."[31] This sentiment was echoed by other delegates to the convention. Delegates like Elbridge Gerry, for example, who was distrustful of popular influence in government, believed nonetheless that the establishment of a strong and stable central government required a regular means of obtaining popular consent through elections.[32] Some delegates, to be sure, favored direct popular election of national leaders in order to give citizens a voice in the new government. Virtually all the delegates, however, conceived direct popular election of national leaders to be a means of increasing the authority and influence of the new national government. Direct popular election of national leaders, it was thought, would increase the influence of the federal government vis-a-vis the states and would give citizens the necessary "confidence" in government to enable the new regime to function effectively.

During the eighteenth and nineteenth centuries suffrage expansion was not necessarily permanent. Once the factors that had prompted a government to liberalize voting rights had diminished in

---

and Authority in Urban Politics (New York: Russell Sage Foundation, 1973); and Theodore J. Lowi, *The End of Liberalism* (New York: Norton, 1969), ch. 8.

[31] Max Farrand (ed.), *The Records of the Federal Convention of 1787* (New Haven, Conn.: Yale University Press, 1966), vol. 1, p. 49.

[32] *Ibid.*, p. 132.

importance, political leaders sometimes found reason to revoke or ignore the privileges they had granted. Thus, for example, at the successful conclusion of the Revolutionary War, Massachusetts imposed additional restrictions on voting, its leaders apparently finding the logic of "One man, one vote, one gun" no longer as compelling as it had been.[33] The most notorious American example is, of course, that of post–Civil War black suffrage in the South.[34] For reasons that are fairly well-known, the Republican national leadership found it expedient to overlook the disenfranchisement of Southern black voters after the 1870s. But this pattern of suffrage expansion and contraction is perhaps best illustrated by the World War I Canadian legislation cited earlier. Ultimately, many of the provisions of these acts were retained after the war's end. But the intention of the Military Voters and Wartime Elections acts was to liberalize the suffrage for the duration of the war. Once the state's need for mobilization of support passed, there would presumably be less need for mass voting participation.

Though this Canadian legislation was enacted at the beginning of the twentieth century, the pattern that it illustrates is more typical of the eighteenth and nineteenth centuries. Suffrage contraction has been unusual in the twentieth century because electoral participation is too important to the modern state to permit governments to abridge voting rights. For it is particularly in the context of the modern state that elections are critical to governments' capacity to control citizens. First, the modern state routinely requires considerable support and cooperation from its citizens in forms ranging from military service and large tax payments to popular adherence to a multitude of rules and regulations. Moreover, the scope and technical complexity of the twentieth-century state's sphere of activities renders it extremely sensitive to violent or disorderly forms of political activity. In recent years we have seen many examples of the extra-

---

[33] Elisha P. Douglass, *Rebels and Democrats* (New York: Da Capo Press, 1971), ch. 11.

[34] For an analysis of the mechanisms of suffrage contraction, see J. Morgan Kousser, *The Shaping of Southern Politics: Suffrage Restriction and the Establishment of the One-Party South* (New Haven, Conn.: Yale University Press, 1974). See also V.O. Key,

ordinary amount of damage and destruction that can be produced by even a handful of disgruntled individuals. Yet at the same time, the enlarged sphere of the contemporary state itself has a "politicizing effect"—the effect of stimulating a variety of forms of political activity, as citizens seek to influence the government's actions in areas that once would have been considered purely private matters. In the short run, of course, disorder and disruption can be forcibly suppressed. But over longer periods, even many of those governments commanding both the requisite armed forces and appropriate lack of scruples have come to appreciate the wisdom of the Napoleonic dictum that one may "do anything with a bayonet but sit on it."

DEMOCRATIC VERSUS AUTHORITARIAN ELECTORAL FORMS

Suffrage introduction or expansion can involve any of a number of alternative electoral arrangements and institutions. Conventionally, the most important distinction drawn among electoral systems is that between democratic and authoritarian forms. The key difference between those electoral processes normally characterized as democratic and those generally considered authoritarian is the opportunity for opposition within the formal electoral framework. The central feature of a democratic electoral process is usually conceived to be the possibility that public officials can be deposed and replaced through electoral means. An electoral process that, by contrast, provides no legal opportunity for opposition and thus no possibility for the electoral defeat of those in power would normally be classified as authoritarian.

Whether national electoral systems come closer to the democratic or the authoritarian model when first introduced or in the early stages

---

Southern Politics (New York: Random House, Vintage Books, 1949), chs. 25-28; and Jerrold G. Rusk and John J. Stucker, "The Effect of the Southern System of Election Laws on Voting Participation," paper presented at the Mathematical Social Science Board's Conference on the History of Popular Voting Behavior, Cornell University, June 11-13, 1973.

of their development depends largely upon ruling groups' ability to stifle opposition. It is, no doubt, the case that aspects of political history and tradition have the effect of making some nations' rulers more willing to tolerate opposition than others. For example, a measure of tolerance for political diversity and opposition seems to have developed in the Netherlands as early as the sixteenth century. No doubt, too, the character of early oppositions has had an effect upon rulers' tolerance. That the parliamentary opposition in eighteenth-century Britain, for example, consisted mainly of other "gentlemen" certainly increased the government's forbearance.[35]

Nevertheless, seldom did the ruling groups that first introduced electoral institutions to their nations intend thereby to pave the way for their own removal from power. On the contrary, the removal of those in power was often precisely what the introduction of elections was designed to prevent. Where rulers had the option of thwarting or suppressing electoral opposition, they generally did so. Even in those nations whose initial electoral arrangements did not formally bar opposition, incumbents usually sought to suppress whatever electoral opponents presented themselves.[36] In the United States, for example, the Alien and Sedition Acts of 1798 were only one part of an attempt by the Federalists to outlaw the emergent Jeffersonian opposition and prevent their own displacement from office. Hamilton and other Federalist leaders even went so far as to urge that opposition be eliminated by force if necessary. The failure of the Federalists to suppress their Republican rivals was, in large measure, due simply to the military and political weakness of the federal government of that period. The military impotence of the national government precluded any serious Federalist effort to crush an opposition that controlled several state governments and their militias.[37]

---

[35] For a discussion of the significance of different patterns of opposition, see Robert A. Dahl (ed.), *Political Oppositions in Western Democracies* (New Haven, Conn.: Yale University Press, 1966), especially ch. 12 and epilogue.

[36] *Ibid.*, p. xiv.

[37] Richard Hofstadter, *The Idea of a Party System* (Berkeley and Los Angeles: University of California Press, 1969), pp. 102-121. See also Dahl, *Political Oppositions*, p. 51; and Martin Shefter, *The Business of Politics* (New York: Basic Books, in press).

The American case is not atypical. Generally speaking, democratic electoral forms emerged only in those nations in which ruling groups were not in a position either to prevent the emergence of electoral opposition or to forcibly suppress such opposition as did develop. It is very likely for this reason that many of the same governments that were compelled to turn to suffrage expansion rather than force to reduce political disorder also found it necessary to introduce democratic electoral forms. Lacking the force necessary to suppress disorder, they also lacked the force necessary to suppress electoral opposition.

Obviously, conditions may change over time. Authoritarian regimes have introduced elections simply as means of control only to discover that they could not restrain the forces they unleashed. Democratic electoral forms, especially in the developing nations, have often been short-lived. As a rule, however, the longer a democratic electoral pattern remains intact, the less the likelihood that incumbents can or will use force to stifle opposition. Given sufficient time to develop, norms and beliefs supporting the legitimacy of electoral opposition can become strong enough to mean that attempts by groups in power to suppress their adversaries not only will result in popular disaffection, but also that the very military and internal security forces required for suppression may not allow themselves to be used for such a purpose. Preparations apparently made by the Secretary of Defense during the "final days" of the Nixon administration are instructive in this regard. Given sufficient time, moreover, elites themselves tend to internalize the rules of the electoral game to the extent that forcible suppression of the electoral opposition does not usually occur to them as an option. Also, over time, contending groups of elites often learn to accommodate themselves to electoral competition and to the principle of rotation in office. Often, in fact, competing elites' accommodation to the electoral process and to one another reaches the point that competition among them takes on many of the same oligopolistic characteristics of collusion and cooperation that often occur in the marketplace. The formal agreement on rotation of national offices, the Pact of Stiges, signed by the two major Colombian parties in 1958 is merely the most obvious and blatant example of such collusive practices. A measure of cooperation and collusion among ostensibly competitive groups is a fairly common tendency within democratic electoral systems.

DEMOCRATIC ELECTIONS, RULERS, AND THE RULED

The emergence and persistence of democratic electoral forms has the potential to substantially alter the relationship between citizens and their rulers. In particular, democratic electoral processes can transform the nature of the association between popular influence and rulers' power.

Even in the absence of elections or other formal mechanisms for their expression, citizens' wishes almost always have some impact on rulers' conduct. Routine voting is hardly the only way that citizens can reward or punish public officials for their behavior. Even the most autocratic regime must beware lest its actions provoke popular disobedience, riot, or insurrection.

But in the absence of formal mechanisms for its expression and enforcement, popular influence tends to be inversely related to rulers' power. That is, rulers tend to be most concerned with their subjects' wishes when their own power to govern is weakest or most insecure and least interested in citizens' views when their own power is most secure.

For example, European monarchs were traditionally most solicitous of their subjects' opinions when they lacked the military power to collect taxes by force. When monarchs' military forces were greatest, their interest in citizens' views about the kingdom's affairs were accordingly diminished.

The advent of the democratic election, however, meant that even when rulers had the military and administrative capacity to compel obedience, citizens' influence was no longer necessarily reduced. Citizens' capacity to influence their rulers' conduct had become at least partially independent of rulers' military and administrative power. The effectiveness of the electoral sanction, unlike the threat of riot, revolution, or insurrection, does not necessarily vary with the regime's power. With the advent of the election, popular influence and rulers' power were no longer inversely related but could instead coexist.

It is because of this possibility for coexistence between popular influence and governmental power that democratic electoral forms potentially transform the relationship between rulers and the ruled. For, given a formal electoral means of influencing their rulers' actions, a means independent of rulers' military and administrative power, citizens potentially stand to benefit from rulers' power rather than from their weakness. It is the advent of the democratic election that opens the possibility of citizens using governments' power for their own benefit rather than simply benefiting from rulers' inability to muster sufficient power to compel citizens to obey their commands. It is largely because of this characteristic of democratic electoral processes that the enormous expansion of the state's power in the twentieth century has not seemed entirely to foreclose the possibility of popular influence over governmental conduct.

Unfortunately, however, the story does not end with this felicitous concurrence between popular influence and the state's power. Precisely because they erode the adversary relationship between rulers and ruled, democratic elections facilitate expansion of the state's powers. Democratic elections encourage citizens to believe that expansion of the state's power means only an increase in government's capacity to serve. Electoral participation in the United States and other Western democracies has been a key factor in persuading citizens to accept the taxation, labor, and military service associated with the construction of the modern state, as well as to reconcile them to the loss of individual liberties that sometimes results. Elections, moreover, have helped to create public support for enlargement of the state's role vis-a-vis that of other social and political institutions, as well as to sustain the popular impression that ordinary citizens may somehow affect the behavior of the vast bureaucracies that this substitution brings into being.

It is the very fact that they do allow the masses some degree of influence over their rulers' conduct that makes democratic elections such effective catalysts for the state's expansion. If citizens' belief in influence via the ballot box were utterly without foundation, it could not be sustained for long. It is, moreover, precisely when those in power appear to be most responsive to the electorate's interests and views that the opportunity for the state's expansion is most enhanced. The public becomes especially receptive to governmental intervention in economy and society when its elected rulers are clearly committed to courses of action that citizens favor. As de Tocqueville observed, "If this [central power] faithfully represents their own interests and exactly copies their own inclinations, the confidence they place in it knows no bounds, and they think that whatever they bestow upon it is bestowed upon themselves."[38]

In time, unfortunately, expansion of the powers of even the most democratic regime not only poses a threat to its citizens' liberties, but may also create a vast and complex governmental apparatus whose behavior is not easily affected by the electoral fortunes and misfortunes of a handful of officials. Indeed, not only does the state's expansion diminish governments' vulnerability to electoral intervention, but also the growth of governmental powers inevitably feeds back into the electoral process itself. In time, as we shall see, modern democratic governments tend to increase their control over the public's putative means of controlling their actions.

Though democratic elections initially promise to eliminate the adversary relationship between rulers and ruled, growth of the state's powers can, nonetheless, erode the possibility of popular influence through the ballot box. One of the ironies of democratic electoral politics is that by helping to reconcile citizens to the desirability of "big government," elections help to fuel processes that undermine their own potential as instruments of popular control.

---

[38] De Tocqueville, *Democracy in America,* vol. 2, p. 318.

ELECTIONS AND THE SOCIALIZATION OF MASS POLITICAL ACTIVITY

2

In the twentieth century, voting has come to be seen as the normal or typical form of mass political activity. Yet the masses took part in politics long before the advent of the election or any other formal mechanism of popular involvement in political life. If there is any natural or spontaneous form of mass political participation, it is the riot rather than the election. Indeed, the urban riot and the rural peasant uprising were endemic to Western Europe prior to the nineteenth century and Eastern Europe until the twentieth.

In the countryside, peasant uprisings were usually precipitated by grievances against the aristocracy. Disputes over pasturage, hunting privileges, the injustices of the lord's court, and compulsory labor could lead to rural unrest and violence. Occasionally, such outbursts involved large areas and thousands of peasants. A peasant uprising that began on one estate in Bohemia in 1775, for example, eventually required the imperial government to mobilize 40,000 infantrymen and four regiments of cavalry before order could be restored.[1] Similarly, the state's policies, particularly tax increases and military conscription, often provoked peasant violence. During periods when famine or disease exacerbated peasant discontent, riot and violence were especially likely to occur. Peasant violence, though sporadic, was hardly unusual. Soviet authorities, according to Blum, have counted 1904 peasant disturbances between 1826 and 1849, with troops mobilized to restore order 381 times. Between 1857 and 1861 alone, some 3800 disturbances occurred in Russia and led to 903 instances of the use of troops.[2]

In the preindustrial cities of Europe, food shortages, demands for better wages, or unpopular government policies could often incite demonstrations, riots, and looting. In eighteenth-century Paris and London, even before the events of the French Revolution, political disturbances were not uncommon. According to Rudé, for example,

---

[1] Jerome Blum, *The End of the Old Order in Rural Europe* (Princeton, N.J.: Princeton University Press, 1978), p. 337. See also A. P. Donaljgrodzki (ed.), *Social Control in 19th Century Britain* (London: Croon Helm, 1977); and John Stevenson and Roland Quinalt (eds.), *Popular Protest and Public Order* (London: Allen and Unwin, 1974).

[2] Blum, *Rural Europe*, p. 333.

disturbances were sparked in Paris in 1720 by John Law's financial speculations. Riots occurred in 1743 and 1752 over the balloting for the militia. In 1720 and 1750 rumors concerning the abduction of children by the police provoked violent protests. In 1752 there were riots against the Archbishop of Paris. Disturbances in support of the Parlement of Paris occurred in 1753, 1757, 1758, 1768, 1771, and 1786. Similarly in London, riots against Nonconformists occurred in 1709, 1715, and 1716; against the excise tax in 1733; against the Gin Bill and Irish in 1736 and 1753. The Wilksite disturbances of the 1760s and the Gordon riots of the 1780s are, of course, even more well-known examples of eighteenth-century urban unrest.[3] The advent of the Industrial Revolution brought changes in the composition of riot participants and in the focuses of the disturbances, but did not immediately end the role of the riot as the major vehicle for the assertion of popular demands and grievances.

Political activity and conflict in one form or another is probably an inherent feature of social life. Politics or political behavior, in the sense used by Easton and by Lasswell, may well be a phenomenon stemming from natural human drives and needs.[4] Political behavior can, however, take any number of different forms. The urban riot, the peasant uprising, and the national election are all species of the genus, mass political activity.

The fundamental difference between voting on the one hand and the riot or uprising on the other is that voting is a socialized and institutionalized form of mass political action. The peasant uprising or urban riot is usually a spontaneous affair sparked by some

---

[3] George Rudé, *Paris and London in the 18th Century* (New York: Viking Press, 1970), pp. 35-60. See also George Rudé, *The Crowd in the French Revolution* (Oxford: Oxford University Press, 1959), especially ch. 15. On tax riots, see Gabriel Ardant, "Financial Policy and Economic Infrastructure of Modern States and Nations," in Charles Tilly (ed.), *The Formation of National States in Western Europe* (Princeton, N.J.: Princeton University Press, 1975). On food riots, see Charles Tilly, "Food Supply and Public Order in Modern Europe," in Tilly, *Western Europe.*

[4] See David Easton, *The Political System* (New York: Knopf, 1966), especially ch. 5, and Harold Lasswell, *Politics: Who Gets What, When, How* (New York: Meridian Books, 1958).

particular event or grievance. Though riots may have been common-place, each riot was itself a unique event. Where and when distur-bances occurred and who took part in them usually depended upon a unique pattern of circumstances and spontaneous individual choices.

Voting, however, is far from spontaneous. Elections provide a routine institutional channel for the expression of demands and grievances. Elections, thereby, transmute what might otherwise take the form of sporadic, citizen-initiated activity into a routine public function. When, where, how, and which individuals participate in elections are matters of public policy rather than questions of spon-taneous individual choice. With the advent of the election, control over the agenda for political action passes from the citizen to the state.

The introduction of the election had a number of vitally important consequences. The most obvious of these was a diminution of the like-lihood of disruption and disorder. By establishing an institutional channel of political activity and habituating citizens to its use, governments reduced the danger that mass political action posed to the established political and social order. Elections contain and channel away potentially violent and disruptive activities and protect the regime's stability.

Elections also affect the character of mass political involvement in at least two other crucial respects. On the one hand, elections expand and democratize citizen involvement. In the absence of public mechanisms for its organization, political activity is almost certain to distort the popular will. Left to their own devices, only relatively small and unrepresentative segments of the public normally attempt to take part in public affairs. At the same time, however, elections help to limit mass political involvement by prescribing conditions for acceptable participation in political life.

First, elections limit the frequency of citizen participation in politics. In the United States elections occur at fixed points in time and grant elected officials the freedom and authority to govern, without fear of citizen intervention, for a defined term. So long as participation is confined to periodic voting, officials have an oppor-tunity to overlook public sentiment about the conduct of public affairs much of the time.

Second, elections limit the scope of mass political participation. Elections permit citizens to take part only in the selection of leaders. The mass public does not directly participate in subsequent policy-making. Though there may be links between citizens' choices among candidates for office and choices about the government's actions, elections do not usually function as referenda on issues or policies. Indeed, as we shall see, elections in the United States tend for the most part to focus mass attention exclusively on the question of who shall govern and to divert it away from questions of how and what the government shall do.

Third, elections limit the intensity of political activity by converting it from a means of asserting demands to a collective statement of permission. In the absence of formal avenues, participation serves almost exclusively as a device for the expression of strongly held beliefs and preferences. So long as political involvement is difficult, only those individuals with intense, often extreme, views will normally be sufficiently motivated to seek to become involved. Elections, however, facilitate participation sufficiently that large numbers of citizens take part despite their relative indifference or apathy about most public questions. Elections usually submerge those participants with strongly held views in a generally apathetic mass electorate.

In this chapter we shall examine the factors that induce individuals to vote and the role of elections both in democratizing political activity and inhibiting unrest and disorder. The role of elections in limiting the scope, frequency, and intensity of mass political action will be among the principal subjects of Chapter 3.

WHY VOTE?

In principle, Americans to an even greater extent than the citizens of other democracies are free to assert whatever demands, views, and grievances they might have through a variety of different means. Citizens may, if they wish, lobby, petition, demonstrate, file suit in court, and so on. Although there are some legal impediments to many of these forms of participation, relatively few modes of political expression are directly barred by law.

Despite the hypothetical availability of an array of alternatives, in practice, citizen participation in American politics is generally limited to voting and a small number of other electoral activities. It is true that voter turnout in the United States is relatively low. However, when, for one reason or another, Americans do seek to participate, their participation generally takes the form of voting. Relatively few individuals choose to engage in types of political action not formally a part of the electoral process. A large number of citizens have never engaged in any form of political action but voting.[5]

The preeminent position of voting and other forms of electoral involvement in the American political process is not surprising. The hypothetical availability of any number of alternatives notwithstanding, the American legal and political environment is overwhelmingly weighted in favor of electoral participation generally and voting in particular. Though Americans may in principle do as they wish, they are strongly encouraged to participate electorally and to ignore the potential alternatives.

Probably the most influential among the forces helping to channel participants into the electoral arena are law, civic education, and the party system. The institution of the election and the availability of the suffrage are, of course, questions of law. But the simple existence of the suffrage does not guarantee that citizens will use it in preference to other possible forms of political action. Beyond making the ballot available, state legislation in the United States prescribes the creation of an elaborate and costly public machinery that makes voting a rather simple task for individuals. Civic education, to a large extent legally mandated, encourages citizens to believe that electoral participation is *the* appropriate way to express opinions and grievances. The major parties are legally charged with staffing and giving effect to the

---

[5] Verba and Nie's summary of twelve "participatory acts," for example, indicates that voting in presidential elections is the only act performed by more than half the respondents. Thirty-one percent of all respondents had never performed any political act but voting. The participatory acts in question include such simple matters as attempting to persuade others to vote in a particular way and contacting local government officials about a problem. Sidney Verba and Norman Nie, *Participation in America* (New York: Harper and Row, 1972), pp. 31-34.

formal machinery of elections and in a number of vital ways help directly to induce citizens to participate.

Unlike many other nations, the United States neither obligates its citizens to vote nor prohibits them from engaging in other political activities. Nevertheless, systemic influences facilitate electoral participation, particularly voting, to the near exclusion of other possible forms of political activity. The prevalence of voting relative to other forms of popular political action in the United States is by no means accidental.

THE IMPACT OF LAW

Voting is among the least demanding forms of political involvement. Despite complicating factors such as registration, the time, energy, and effort needed to vote are considerably less than are required by all but a few other political activities. It is, indeed, usually assumed that the relative ease of voting is one of the major reasons why it is more common in the United States than any other mode of participation.

The relatively low degree of individual effort required to vote, however, is somewhat deceptive. Voting is a simple way for large numbers of citizens to participate only because it is made simple by an elaborate and costly electoral system. The ease with which citizens can vote is a function of law and public policy rather than an inherent attribute of voting itself. The costs of voting are paid mainly by the state.[6]

In the United States electoral contests are administered principally by states and localities. Though the Constitution, federal law, and federal court decisions have an obvious bearing on the conduct of elections, the creation of the necessary administrative machinery

---

[6] In some respects, the cost of voting is quite literally paid by the state. Recently, for example, the New York City Board of Elections incurred a cost of approximately $50 per individual to register some 40,000 new voters. See Maurice Carroll, "Cost of Registering Voters Raises Issue," *New York Times*, October 7, 1979.

and the management of electoral procedures remain largely state and local tasks.

Though state law is sometimes conceived only to regulate and limit the suffrage, the bulk of state action in the area of voting is in fact permissive. Whatever limits states impose on voting must be set against a backdrop or baseline of facilitation. States must and do create the opportunity to vote before they can begin to regulate it.

States and localities legally require themselves to invest considerable effort in the facilitation of voting. In the state of New York, for example, the steps needed to conduct an election fill well over 200 pages of statutes. At the state, county, and municipal levels, boards of elections must be established to supervise the electoral process. For every several hundred voters, in each state, special political units—precincts or election districts—are created and staffed exclusively for the administration of elections. During each electoral period, polling places must be set up, equipped with voting machines or ballots, and staffed by voting inspectors. Prior to an election, its date, the locations of polling places, and the names of candidates must be publicized. After each election, returns must be canvassed, tallied, reported, and often recounted.

Because virtually all of it is borne by municipal governments, the total annual cost of American elections is not known. Even the very spotty evidence that is available, however, suggests that election administration is quite expensive. The state of Ohio, for example, reported a total expenditure of over 14.5 million dollars for voter registration and elections in 1970. Los Angeles County spent over 11 million dollars for just two elections in 1971. The state of New York estimated that its 1976 presidential primary cost approximately 14 million dollars to administer.[7] It would appear not at all unreasonable to assume that the total annual cost of election administration in the United States is well over one billion dollars. This, of course, does not include the enormous cost of campaigns, which until recently has been borne by parties, candidates for office, and the organized interests.

---

[7] Richard Smolka, *The Costs of Administering American Elections* (New York: National Municipal League, 1973).

Though every state facilitates voting by providing for the creation and funding of election machinery, states obviously vary in the precise extent to which they encourage electoral participation. Indeed, until the 1970s states varied enormously in their voter residence requirements, registration procedures, absentee voting rules, and the hours that polls remained open. Until recent years, literacy tests and poll taxes, often employed in a deliberately discriminatory manner, were also important in producing interstate differences in the ease of voting. The impact of these variations in state electoral procedures helps to underline the significance of legal facilitation of voting.

Table 2.1 ranks the 50 states on the basis of the extent to which their election laws facilitated voting.[8] It can be seen that on the whole the most facilitative states report higher rates of voting participation than those states with less encouraging election laws.

A more revealing portrait of the impact of legal facilitation, however, can be derived from the relationship between rates of participation and the resources and attitudes of participants. In the less facilitative states, personal resources and beliefs play a large role in determining who will vote. Where voting is relatively difficult, the wealthy, for example, vote with considerably greater frequency than the poor. Similarly, those who are convinced that voting is important

---

[8] Both the rankings of the states and voter turnout figures are based on 1960 data. While more contemporary data are certainly available, the effect of three decades of intervention by the federal courts has been to reduce substantially the extent of interstate variation in voting requirements. The importance of electoral law is not diminished merely because of a lack of interstate variation. However, in the absence of such variation, interstate comparisons, which in all other respects are ideal means of assessing and demonstrating the significance of legal requirements, lose much of their value. Since my purpose in this section is to analyze the effects of legal facilitation rather than to discuss contemporary patterns of voter turnout in the United States, 1960 data would seem to be perfectly appropriate. State election law data were drawn from Lester W. Milbrath, "Political Participation in the States," in Herbert Jacob and Kenneth Vines (eds.), *Politics in the American States* (Boston: Little, Brown, 1965), p. 46. Rankings are based simply on the number of facilitative features Milbrath found in each state's statutes. For an interesting analysis of the relationship between election law and contemporary American voting patterns, see Raymond E. Wolfinger and Steven J. Rosenstone, *Who Votes?* (New Haven, Conn.: Yale University Press, 1980), especially ch. 4.

TABLE 2.1 *Percentage of voter turnout in the 1960 presidential election by states ranked according to degree to which voting was legally facilitated.*

Idaho	(11)*	80.6	Florida	(6)	50.0
Oregon	(10)	72.4	New Hampshire	(6)	80.2
Illinois	(9)	76.5	Maryland	(6)	58.3
Michigan	(9)	72.7	Massachusetts	(6)	76.9
Nebraska	(9)	72.1	N. Carolina	(6)	54.1
New Jersey	(9)	71.8	Ohio	(6)	71.3
Utah	(9)	78.9	Pennsylvania	(6)	70.7
Arizona	(8)	53.8	South Dakota	(6)	78.8
Colorado	(8)	71.7	Tennessee	(6)	50.4
Connecticut	(8)	77.1	Wyoming	(6)	73.9
Iowa	(8)	76.8	Georgia	(5)	32.9
Kansas	(8)	71.8	Louisiana	(5)	45.1
Maine	(8)	74.0	New Mexico	(5)	64.5
Minnesota	(8)	77.1	Oklahoma	(5)	64.3
Virginia	(8)	34.4	North Dakota	(5)	79.1
Wisconsin	(8)	73.5	Rhode Island	(5)	77.3
California	(7)	67.9	Vermont	(5)	72.9
Hawaii	(7)	58.9	Alabama	(4)	31.2
Indiana	(7)	76.9	Alaska	(4)	59.2
Missouri	(7)	72.6	Kentucky	(4)	60.5
Montana	(7)	71.7	New York	(4)	66.9
Nevada	(7)	61.0	Texas	(4)	42.4
Washington	(7)	74.1	Arkansas	(3)	41.1
W. Virginia	(7)	77.9	S. Carolina	(2)	31.4
Delaware	(6)	74.5	Mississippi	(2)	25.7

* The number in parentheses is the number of facilitative features found in the state's statutes.

appear at the polls far more regularly than individuals with doubts about the utility of voting. Legal facilitation, however, appears to considerably lessen both the motivation and resources needed to vote. In the more permissive states individual attitudes and social characteristics are less important correlates of voting. For example, differences in rates of turnout between upper- and lower-income voters are considerably more pronounced in the less facilitative states. Of course, even in the most permissive localities, lower-income persons are less likely to vote than their wealthier peers. But, as

TABLE 2.2 *Income, legal facilitation, and voter turnout in the 1960 presidential election.*

	Income		
	$0-2999	$3000-7499	$7500 and over
The 15 least facilitative states	50.0%* (N = 102)	77.8% (N = 167)	87.5% (N = 88)
The 35 more facilitative states	66.7% (N = 171)	80.4% (N = 423)	89.0% (N = 219)

* That is, 50 percent of the voters in the lowest income group voted in the least facilitative states.

Table 2.2 indicates, the more that voting is encouraged by electoral laws, the less that rates of participation vary among the income groups.

Because even the least permissive states expend large amounts of money and effort to promote voting, it is likely that in the complete absence of legal facilitation *only* those individuals with substantial personal resources or motivation would attempt to participate. This is, of course, what does occur in the case of modes of participation that are not facilitated by public policy. "Private" forms of political involvement are normally the province of the wealthy and the strongly committed.[9]

Obviously, in all the states there are selective legal impediments to voting. Age disqualifies some. Registration requirements have an important impact on specific sets of potential voters. Nevertheless, although the laws of every state discourage or disqualify some potential participants, law can diminish the likelihood that citizens will disqualify themselves from participating. Legal facilitation reduces the effort and motivation needed to participate to the point that individuals are less likely to be discouraged from voting than from engaging in alternative forms of political action.

---

[9] See, for example, Verba and Nie, *Participation in America,* p. 132. See also Lester Milbrath and M.L. Goel, *Political Participation* (Chicago: Rand McNally, 1977), ch. 4.

CIVIC EDUCATION

Legal facilitation, of course, cannot completely explain the prevalence of voting and the relative absence of alternative forms of mass participation in the United States. If public attitudes were completely unfavorable to elections, it is doubtful that legal facilitation alone would have much impact. The ubiquity of voting is, in large part, also a function of generally favorable public beliefs about the electoral process and perhaps a low regard for alternative forms. Most Americans seem at least ambivalent about "lobbying," "pressure groups," and "protest."

Public attitudes conducive to voting do not come into being in a completely spontaneous manner. As a matter of public policy, Americans are taught to equate participation in politics with electoral participation, and especially with voting. Civic training, designed to give students an appreciation for the American system of government, is a legally required part of the curriculum in every elementary and secondary school. Though it is not as often required by law, civic education usually manages to find its way into college curricula as well.

In the elementary and secondary schools, through formal instruction and, more subtly, through the frequent administration of class and school elections, students are taught the importance of the electoral process. By contrast, little attention is given lawsuits, direct action, organizing, parliamentary procedures, lobbying, or other possible modes of participation. For example, the techniques involved in organizing a sit-in or protest march are seldom part of an official school course of study.[10]

The New York State first grade social studies curriculum offers a fairly typical case study of the training in political participation given

---

[10] The question of civic education is discussed in Charles Merriam, *The Making of Citizens* (Chicago: University of Chicago Press, 1931), and Charles Merriam, *Civic Education in the United States.* See also Fred I. Greenstein, *Children and Politics* (New Haven, Conn.: Yale University Press, 1969); Robert D. Hess and Judith V. Torney, *The Development of Political Attitudes in Children* (Chicago: Aldine, 1967), ch. 5; and Robert Weissberg, *Political Learning, Political Choice and Democratic Citizenship* (Englewood Cliffs, N.J.: Prentice-Hall, 1974), ch. 8.

very young children. The State Education Department provides the following guidelines to teachers:

> *To illustrate the voting process, present a situation such as: Chuck and John would both like to be the captain of the kickball team. How will we decide which boy will be the captain? Help the children to understand that the fairest way to choose a captain is by voting.*
>
> *Write both candidates' names on the chalk board. Pass out slips of paper. Explain to the children that they are to write the name of the boy they would like to have as their captain. Collect and tabulate the results on the chalk board.*
>
> *Parallel this election to that of the election for the Presidency.*
>
> *Other situations which would illustrate the election procedure are voting for:*
>
> *a game*
> *an assignment choice*
> *classroom helpers.*[11]

Though secondary school students periodically elect student government representatives rather than classroom helpers and are given more sophisticated illustrations than kickball team elections, the same principle continues to be taught, in compliance with legal requirements. College students, it must be added, are also frequently given the opportunity to elect senators, representatives, and the like, to serve on the largely ornamental representative bodies that are to be found at most institutions of higher learning. Millions of college students believe this sort of experience is good preparation for life.[12]

The importance of voting is also given a good deal of emphasis in the citizenship training received by many foreign-born Americans prior to their naturalization. In the late nineteenth and early twentieth

---

[11] The University of the State of New York, The State Education Department, Bureau of Elementary Curriculum Development, *Social Studies — Grade 1, A Teaching System* (Albany, N.Y., 1971), p. 32.

[12] Civic training at the college level is discussed in Dean Jaros, *Socialization to Politics* (New York: Praeger, 1973), p. 115.

centuries, particularly, millions of newcomers were "Americanized" by lessons like the following:

The power of the ballot.

Why is each citizen's vote important?
Because by means of his vote each citizen has a share in making the government good or bad. If good men are elected to office by the people, all the people are benefited; if bad men are elected, all the people suffer.

The vote of each citizen counts as one and only one regardless of his birthplace, position in life, or wealth. Elections have sometimes been decided by the margin of a single vote. This shows how important it is for every citizen to use his privilege of voting.

Why should every citizen vote?
In order that our Government may continue truly representative, and that the laws may be what the people as a whole want them to be.

It is only the votes that are cast that count for or against a candidate or a law. It is not good citizenship to fail to express an opinion on public affairs.[13]

Obviously, civic education is not always completely successful. College students and graduates in sizable numbers demonstrated, sat-in, and picketed for various political causes in the late 1960s and early 1970s. Segments of the educational process clearly provide skills, resources, and ideas that enable their recipients to participate more readily in a variety of political contexts than those with lower levels of educational attainment. The state's civics curriculum is hardly all that students learn in school. Nevertheless, level of education is strongly associated with interest in elections, belief in the efficacy and importance of voting, and with voting itself.[14]

---

[13] Hanson Hart Webster, *Americanization and Citizenship* (Boston: Houghton Mifflin, 1919), p. 31.

[14] Milbrath and Goel, *Political Participation*, p. 98.

Civic education, of course, does not end with formal schooling. Early training is supplemented by a variety of mechanisms ranging from the official celebration of national holidays to the activities of private patriotic and political organizations. Election campaigns themselves are occasions for the reinforcement of training to vote. Campaigns include a good deal of oratory designed to remind citizens of the importance of voting and the democratic significance of elections. Parties and candidates, even if for selfish reasons, emphasize the value of participation, of "being counted," and the virtues of elections as instruments of popular government. Exposure to such campaign stimuli appears generally to heighten citizens' interest in and awareness of the electoral process. Though until recently campaigns were entirely private affairs, they have now in part become public functions. Under the terms of national campaign finance legislation enacted in the 1970s, the federal government pays a substantial share of the cost of national presidential campaigns. In the 1980 presidential races, for example, candidates received tens of millions of dollars in public funds to help them deliver their messages to the citizenry in the primary and general elections.

Exposure to the stimulus of a campaign not only heightens political interest, but also appears to exert considerable influence on citizens' attitudes toward the governmental process. As we shall see in more complete detail in Chapter 5, the occurrence of an election seems usually to increase citizens' faith in the legitimacy and the responsiveness of the government. We can observe something of this phenomenon below. Tables 2.3 and 2.4 report the patterns of attitude changes among respondents asked, in national surveys both before and after the 1968 presidential election, first, whether people like themselves have "much say" about what the government does, and second, whether they believe that public officials care what people like themselves think.

The data in Tables 2.3 and 2.4 indicate that a sizable proportion of respondents who expressed negative opinions prior to the election had come to feel that they indeed had some "say" after the election's conclusion. Though the data raise a number of questions, we shall postpone a fuller discussion until Chapter 5. What is important for our present purposes is that the stimulus of the campaign appears to strike an especially responsive chord among those citizens who, by

TABLE 2.3 *Changes in popular perceptions of "say" in government follow-ing the 1968 presidential election.*

	Level of Education		
	8 years or less	9 to 12 years	College
Percentage of respondents with negative preelection perceptions who became positive following the election	29.1 (N = 244)†	50.2 (N = 484)	68.6 (N = 236)
Percentage of respondents with positive preelection perceptions who became negative following the election	23.1 (N = 52)	16.4 (N = 152)	14.7 (N = 127)

* The question asked prior to the election was, "Would you say that people like you have quite a lot of say about what the government does, or that you don't have much say at all?" The postelection form of the question asked respondents to agree or disagree with the assertion, "People like me don't have any say about what the government does."

† The number in parentheses is the base on which the proportion of changes is calculated. For example, 244 voters had negative perceptions prior to the election. Twenty-nine percent of them became positive after the election; the others remained negative.

virtue of their years of schooling, likely received the most extensive civic training. As respondents' levels of education increase, so does the relative magnitude of positive changes in beliefs about the government.

This effect, which can be seen even more clearly from the 1972 presidential election data presented in Tables 2.5 and 2.6, seems to be independent of the other important forces, extent of participation in particular, which usually produce changes in beliefs about the quality of the regime during electoral contests. It appears to be the case that among the educated, prior conditioning to the value of elections creates sufficiently positive and persistent images that the stimulus of an election campaign evokes a sharply affirmative reaction. Thus, in addition to encouraging participation in elections, civic education

TABLE 2.4 *Changes in popular perceptions of whether or not public officials care following the 1968 presidential election.**

	Level of Education		
	8 years or less	9 to 12 years	College
Percentage of respondents with negative preelection perceptions who became positive following the election	19.6 (N = 143)	39.1 (N = 233)	49.5 (N = 109)
Percentage of respondents with positive preelection perceptions who became negative following the election	58.1 (N = 136)	32.2 (N = 379)	12.5 (N = 255)

* The question asked prior to the election was, "Would you say that most public officials care quite a lot about what people like you think, or that they don't care at all?" The postelection form of the question asked respondents to agree or disagree with the assertion, "I don't think public officials care much what people like me think."

also appears to contribute to making elections events that reinforce beliefs in the merits of the government holding them.

PARTY

Law and civic education do not directly stimulate voting so much as create a favorable legal and attitudinal climate for electoral participation. Within the context of this climate, the major parties, until recent years at least, have been the principal agents responsible for giving citizens the motivation and incentive to actually vote. The use of party for this purpose by authoritarian regimes is, of course, well-known. But even in the American context, party has served the state as an instrument of voter mobilization. By law in most American states, party workers staff the electoral machinery; major party candidates have automatic access to a place on the ballot; at one time the parties even printed the ballots. Though the parties have played a

TABLE 2.5 *Changes in popular perceptions of "say" in government following the 1972 presidential election.**

	Level of Education		
	8 years or less	9 to 12 years	College
Percentage of respondents with negative preelection perceptions who became positive following the election	23.6 (N = 127)	37.2 (N = 226)	45.5 (N = 77)
Percentage of respondents with positive preelection perceptions who became negative following the election	33.8 (N = 71)	20.1 (N = 314)	6.0 (N = 245)

* Both pre- and postelection respondents were asked to agree or disagree with the statement, "People like me don't have any say about what the government does."

TABLE 2.6 *Changes in popular perceptions of whether or not public officials care following the 1972 presidential election.**

	Level of Education		
	8 years or less	9 to 12 years	College
Percentage of respondents with negative preelection perceptions who became positive following the election	16.2 (N = 136)	22.0 (N = 261)	32.0 (N = 102)
Percentage of respondents with positive preelection perceptions who became negative following the election	45.5 (N = 55)	30.1 (N = 266)	15.0 (N = 215)

* Both pre- and postelection respondents were asked to agree or disagree with the statement, "I don't think public officials care much about what people like me think."

role in both civic education and legal facilitation of voting, their principal efforts have been aimed at the direct mobilization of voters. One of the most interesting pieces of testimony to the lengths to which parties have been willing to go to induce citizens to vote is a list, assembled by Gosnell, of Chicago precinct captains' activities in the 1920s and 1930s. Among other matters, precinct captains helped constituents obtain food, coal, and money for rent; gave advice in dealing with juvenile and domestic problems; helped constituents to obtain government and private jobs; adjusted taxes; aided with permits, zoning, and building-code problems; served as liaisons with social, relief, and medical agencies; provided legal assistance and help in dealing with government agencies; and in addition handed out Christmas baskets and attended weddings and funerals.[15] Though obviously their motives were not unselfish, the fact remains that in these and quite likely in a number of more direct ways, party functionaries literally paid citizens to come to the polls. Even though the forms have been changed, parties still spend tremendous time getting out the vote.

Party competition has long been known to be a key factor in stimulating voting. As Kelley, Ayres, and Bowen note, competition gives citizens an incentive to vote and politicians an incentive to get them to vote.[16] The origins of the American national electorate can be traced to the competitive organizing activities of the Jeffersonian Republicans and the Federalists. According to Fischer:

> *During the 1790s the Jeffersonians revolutionized electioneering. . . .*
> *Their opponents complained bitterly of endless "dinings," "drinkings,"*
> *and celebrations; of handbills "industriously posted along every road";*
> *of convoys of vehicles which brought voters to the polls by the cartload;*
> *of candidates "in perpetual motion."*[17]

---

[15] Harold F. Gosnell, *Machine Politics, Chicago Model,* rev. ed. (Chicago: University of Chicago Press, 1968), ch. 4.

[16] Stanley Kelley, Jr., Richard E. Ayres, and William G. Bowen, "Registration and Voting: Putting First Things First," *American Political Science Review* 61 (June 1967): 359-379.

[17] David H. Fischer, *The Revolution of American Conservatism* (New York: Harper and Row, 1965), p. 93.

The Federalists, though initially reluctant, soon learned the techniques of mobilizing voters: "mass meetings, barbecues, stump-speaking, festivals of many kinds, processions and parades, runners and riders, door-to-door canvassing, the distribution of tickets and ballots, electioneering tours by candidates, free transportation to the polls, outright bribery and corruption of other kinds."[18]

The result of this competition for votes was described by Henry Jones Ford in his classic *Rise and Growth of American Politics.*[19] Ford examined the popular clamor against John Adams and Federalist policies in the 1790s that made government a "weak, shaky affair" and appeared to contemporary observers to mark the beginnings of a popular insurrection against the government.[20] Attempts by the Federalists initially to suppress mass discontent, Ford observed, might have "caused an explosion of force which would have blown up the government."[21] What intervened to prevent rebellion was Jefferson's "great unconscious achievement," the creation of an opposition party that served to "open constitutional channels of political agitation."[22] The creation of the Jeffersonian party diverted opposition to the administration into electoral channels. Party competition gave citizens a sense that their votes were valuable and that it was thus not necessary to take to the streets to have an impact upon political affairs.

Whether or not Ford was correct in crediting party competition with an ability to curb civil unrest, it is clear that competition between the parties promotes voting. A large number of empirical studies have indicated that competitive areas tend to show higher rates of voter turnout than noncompetitive areas. Moreover, partisan competition, which eases the difficulty of choice by offering voters a choice among recognizable party labels, stimulates voting more effectively than nonpartisan competition.[23]

---

[18] *Ibid.,* p. 109.

[19] Henry Jones Ford, *The Rise and Growth of American Politics* (New York: Da Capo Press, 1967, reprint of the 1898 edition), ch. 9.

[20] *Ibid.,* p. 125.

[21] *Ibid.*

[22] *Ibid.,* p. 126.

[23] Milbrath and Goel, *Political Participation,* pp. 132-136.

The parties' competitive efforts to attract citizens to the polls are not their only source of influence on voting. The propensity of individuals to form psychological ties with parties has of course been intensively studied.[24] Though the strength of partisan ties in the United States has declined in recent years, a majority of Americans continue to identify with one or the other major party. Partisan loyalty gives citizens a stake in election outcomes that encourages them to take part with considerably greater regularity than those lacking partisan ties.[25] Even where both legal facilitation and competitiveness are weak, partisans vote with great regularity.[26] This routinizing effect is important. Any number of factors can induce citizens to participate some of the time, but partisanship imposes what Sir Henry Sumner Maine called "civil discipline."[27] Partisanship induces large numbers of individuals to vote routinely and predictably regardless of other external stimuli.

In recent decades, the importance of party as a political force in the United States has diminished considerably.[28] The decline of party

---

[24] Beginning with Angus Campbell *et al.*, *The American Voter* (New York: Wiley, 1960), chs. 6 and 7.

[25] *Ibid.*

[26] In 1960, for example, in the states that ranked in the upper third in both competition and legal facilitation, 86 percent of the strong partisans and 92 percent of the independents voted. In the least competitive and facilitative states, by contrast, though only 40 percent of the independents voted, more than 75 percent of the strong partisans went to the polls.

[27] Sir Henry Sumner Maine, *Popular Government* (New York: Henry Holt, 1886).

[28] The decline of party raises the most profound questions about the future of American electoral processes. The most provocative discussions are Walter Dean Burnham, "Party Systems and the Political Process," in William N. Chambers and Walter Dean Burnham (eds.), *The American Party System* (New York: Oxford University Press, 1975); Walter Dean Burnham, *Critical Elections and the Mainsprings of American Electoral Politics* (New York: Norton, 1970); and Walter Dean Burnham, "The Changing Shape of the American Political Universe," *American Political Science Review* 59 (1965): 7-28. See also Norman H. Nie, Sidney Verba, and John R. Petrocik, *The Changing American Voter* (Cambridge, Mass.: Harvard University Press, 1976); Warren E. Miller and Teresa E. Levitin, *Leadership and Change* (Cambridge, Mass.: Winthrop, 1976); and Everett Carl Ladd with Charles Hadley, *Transformations of the American Party System* (New York: Norton, 1978).

is undoubtedly one of the factors responsible for the relatively low rates of voter turnout that characterize American national elections. To an extent, the federal and state governments have directly assumed some of the burden of voter mobilization once assigned to the parties. Voter registration drives and public funding of electoral campaigns are two obvious ways in which government helps to induce citizens to go to the polls. Another more subtle public mechanism for voter moblization is the primary election, which can increase voter interest and involvement in the electoral process.[29] It remains to be seen, however whether governmental mechanisms of voter mobilization can be as effective as party.

THE DEMOCRATIZATION OF POLITICAL ACTIVITY

Taken together, law, civic education, and interparty competition help to make mass participation more democratic. Though citizen involvement is often conceived to be synonymous with democratic government, left to itself participation is virtually certain to distort rather than reflect the popular will. In the absence of compensatory mechanisms, individual differences in motivation, economic status, social background, and a number of other factors that affect individuals' ability and propensity to participate would almost certainly mean that participants in politics would be quite unrepresentative of the public at large. Economic status, for example, has an obvious and important bearing upon the ability to participate in politics. Economic status affects the time, resources, interest, and effort individuals are likely to be able to devote to politics or, for that matter, to any but the most essential activities. As we saw earlier, if political participation were solely a private activity, dependent exclusively upon individual

---

[29] The relationship between primary elections and voter involvement is discussed in Benjamin Ginsberg and Robert Weissberg, "Participation and Party Survival," paper presented at the Annual Meeting of the Southwest Political Science Association, Houston, Texas, April 12-15, 1978.

efforts, rates of participation on the part of the economically well-off would usually greatly exceed those of the poor. Indeed, as Table 2.7 suggests, most forms of political activity that are not publicly facilitated are dominated by upper-income groups.

In the case of voting, the gulf between rich and poor is not nearly so wide. It is not that voting is somehow inherently easier for lower-income persons than other political activities. Rather, facilitation of voting, through election law, civic education, and party, tends especially to help those persons who have fewest resources of their own. Stated simply, the rich have the capacity to participate with or without assistance; when assistance is given it is primarily the poor who benefit. In essence, it is the poor who most require state assistance to pay the costs of participation.

The compensatory effect of legal facilitation was evident from Table 2.2, which examined the relationship between voter turnout and economic status in states grouped according to the extent to which voting was legally facilitated. It was apparent from Table 2.2 that upper-income individuals are considerably less affected by the degree to which voting is legally facilitated than lower-income persons

TABLE 2.7 *Voting and participation in nonelectoral forms of political action in 1976.**

	Political Actions			
Annual income	Voting only	1 nonelectoral form of action	2 nonelectoral forms of action	3 nonelectoral forms of action
$0-5,999	28.8%†	12.3%	4.5%	7.7%
$6,000-10,999	23.2	20.6	20.5	15.4
$11,000-16,999	23.6	25.8	21.4	7.7
$17,000 and over	25.2	41.3	53.6	69.2
	(N = 1523)	(N = 431)	(N = 112)	(N = 13)

* The nonelectoral forms of political action are participation in a protest march, writing a letter to the editor of a newspaper, and contacting a public official.

† Percentages are the proportion of each type of participant falling into the specified income category. Thus 28 percent of those respondents who only voted reported incomes of $5,999 or less.

are. Participation on the part of the wealthy varies little with state law. Individuals of lower economic status, however, vote with considerably greater frequency in the more facilitative states than they do in the less permissive states.

Like legal facilitation, party also has a markedly compensatory effect on participation. Both partisan competition and partisan identification tend to diminish the disparity in rates of turnout between the rich and the poor. Verba and Nie have very skillfully shown that while the effect of partisan identification is to increase rates of voting for both upper and lower socioeconomic groups, the increase is much more pronounced among lower socioeconomic strata. The net impact of party identification is to reduce considerably the gulf between voting rates among the two groups.[30]

Similarly, the parties' competitive organizing activities are likely to have the greatest impact upon the lower economic strata. The sorts of material inducements described by Gosnell were quite clearly designed specifically to attract lower-income citizens to the polls. But in a more general sense, party efforts to induce citizens to vote are more important sources of motivation to lower-income groups than they are to upper-income groups. Party competition has a compensatory effect much like that of legal facilitation. It is, in fact, when Table 2.8 compares states that are both legally facilitative and competitive with those that are neither that the importance of these compensatory factors stands out most clearly.

Quite likely, legally mandated civic education in the public school system also has a compensatory effect upon electoral participation. Working-class children are less likely to be exposed to familial and environmental influences outside the classroom that would train them to vote than are middle- and upper-income children. Classroom civic lessons to all children may well help to offset the inherent advantage of the better-off.[31] This type of compensatory effect is at

---

[30] Verba and Nie, *Participation in America,* p. 223.

[31] For discussions of the potentially compensatory effects of civic education, see Hess and Torney, *Development of Political Attitudes,* p. 154; Greenstein, *Children and Politics,* p. 98; and Weissberg, *Political Learning,* p. 100.

TABLE 2.8 *The effects of legal facilitation and party competition on voter turnout in the 1960 presidential election.*

	Income		
	S0-2999	S3000-7499	S7500 and over
States that rank in the upper third in terms of both legal facilitation and interparty competition *	61.4%† (N = 44)	79.6% (N = 152)	88.7% (N = 97)
States that rank in the lowest third in terms of both legal facilitation and interparty competition	44.4% (N = 36)	74.4% (N = 39)	88.9% (N = 18)

* Party competition is defined simply as the difference between the Democratic and Republican shares of the presidential vote. The less the difference, the more competitive the state is said to be.

† Each percentage indicates the proportion of individuals falling in the defined income group who voted. The total number of individuals in that income group living in the specified set of states is indicated by *N.*

least suggested by the fact that the relationship between income and voter turnout is considerably reduced when controlled for level of educational attainment. Among those individuals whose level of education is relatively high, income and participation are not strongly associated. By contrast, among those whose level of education is low, the wealthy are much more likely to vote than individuals of more modest means.[32]

---

[32] In 1976, for example, among respondents with an eighth-grade education or less, though 81 percent of those earning an annual salary greater than S17,000 voted, only 49 percent of the respondents earning less than S6,000 appeared at the polls. Among those with high school educations, however, the comparable figures were 78 percent and 61 percent. Among respondents with some college, 72 percent of even the lowest income group voted.

All in all, public facilitation democratizes political activity and helps to make the universe of participants more nearly resemble the public at large. Socialization of mass political activity transforms it into a democratic force in political affairs.

ELECTIONS AS ALTERNATIVES TO POLITICAL DISORDER

While elections democratize citizen involvement and offer millions of individuals a routine opportunity to participate in political affairs, they also limit mass participation and cushion its likely impact upon the regime. Elections facilitate participation in much the same way that floodgates can be said to facilitate the flow of water. Elections direct mass involvement into formal channels, thus removing many potential impediments to participation, but at the same time diverting it from courses that may be hazardous to the established political order.

Given the proper circumstances, of course, even those who normally value the vote and regularly participate at the polls can turn to protest and violence. Elections themselves can sometimes be sufficiently divisive that the losers withdraw from the electorate, or worse. European, Latin American, and even United States history provide any number of examples of voluntary and violent withdrawals from the electorate. However, a good bit of intriguing, though fragmentary, evidence suggests that when formal electoral channels of participation are available and citizens habituated to their use, the attractiveness of violent and disorderly mechanisms for the assertion of popular grievances is indeed diminished.

The first piece of evidence concerns the impact of adverse changes in economic conditions upon mass political activity. The stimulus of economic distress has historically been among the most important proximate causes of mass political violence and disorder. Pre-nineteenth-century urban riots and peasant uprisings, for example, were often responses to one form or another of economic distress. The relationship between increases in the price of bread and popular agitation during the French Revolution will always be remembered, in part because it was so carefully studied by Rudé, but even more because of the famous solution to the problem of high bread prices usually attributed to Marie Antoinette.[33] Similarly, in the twentieth century, adverse economic conditions have often led to popular disturbances. Even Eastern European Communist governments have been shaken by mass protest over economic conditions upon several occasions in recent years.

Though economic distress can spark popular agitation in any nation, the form of the political activity so stimulated can vary. What is important for our present concerns is that the form of the political activity associated with economic downturns seems to vary considerably depending upon whether or not electoral channels of political action are open and available.

Table 2.9 reports the lagged relationship between the incidence of riots and demonstrations, on the one hand, and percentage changes in the gross national product, on the other, for two groups of nations during the 1960s. The first group is composed of all those nations for which data were available that either held no regular elections or were classified as holding only "rigged" elections by the *World Handbook of Political and Social Indicators.* "Rigged" is defined as meaning that no opposition or competition is permitted and the electoral outcome is foreordained. The second group of nations consists of all those for which data were available that routinely held free and competitive elections as determined by the *World Handbook.*[34]

The differences revealed by Table 2.9 between the relationship of changes in economic conditions to subsequent incidence of riots in these two groups of nations are quite striking. In those nations that do not hold regular elections or where elections are purely symbolic affairs without the possibility of opposition, changes in the gross national product are negatively associated with the subsequent incidence of riots and demonstrations. That is, in these nations, economic downturns, as measured by drops in the gross national product, seem correlated with an increased incidence of protest.

---

[33] Rudé, *Paris and London,* p. 163.
[34] Charles Lewis Taylor and Michael C. Hudson, *World Handbook of Political and Social Indicators,* 2d ed. (New Haven, Conn.: Yale University Press, 1972).

TABLE 2.9 *The relationship between economic change and political disorder in dictatorships and democracies—Pearson correlation coefficients.*

	Incidence of riots in 1965	Incidence of demonstrations in 1965
Change in GNP between 1963 and 1965 for nations with "rigged" elections (N = 33)	−0.28	−0.16
Change in GNP between 1963 and 1965 for nations with "competitive" elections (N = 35)	−0.08	0.09

In those nations that, by contrast, have institutionalized electoral forms of political activity to the extent of holding regular and competitive elections, there appears to be no relationship between adverse economic changes and the incidence of protest activity. In this group of nations, virtually no relationship whatsoever between change in gross national product and riots or demonstrations is evident.

Conclusions based upon gross comparisons of whole nations and, at that, based upon a small number of cases during a short period of time, must be considered tentative. Nevertheless, the findings are consistent with the argument that the availability of electoral channels of political agitation diminishes the likelihood that attempts by citizens to assert their grievances will take disorderly or disruptive forms. That economic downturns are associated with riots and demonstrations only where electoral channels of political activity are not available seems to suggest that elections can indeed contain and channel away the effects of stimuli that would otherwise create political disorder. This conclusion is further supported by the fact that in the second group of nations, those with open and competitive elections, the incidence of riot and protest is negatively correlated with voter turnout. The relationship across all these nations is −0.13. This negative association suggests that in electorally competitive nations, voting and protest activity are somewhat mutually exclusive alternatives. That is, the greater the number of individuals who vote, the smaller the incidence of riots and demonstrations.[35]

It is apparent, moreover, that economic fluctuations do have an impact upon mass political activity in this second group of nations. This impact appears more likely, however, to take the form of changes in electoral behavior than variations in the incidence of popular riot and disorder. In the United States, for example, economic downturns appear to result in shifts of electoral support away from the incumbent party.[36] During periods of severe economic distress, moreover, electoral support for minor-party candidacies tends to increase substantially.[37] In short, adverse changes in the economy do have an impact upon mass political activity in nations where electoral channels are available. But the political activity that results appears to take mainly an electoral form.

SUPPORT FOR PROTEST

Of course, even where electoral channels are available, political violence can and does occur. But some additional evidence suggests that, even when political activity is not completely diverted into the electoral arena, the availability of elections still tends to reduce the potential mass base of support for disorderly or violent forms of political action. One case in point is the period of the late 1960s and early 1970s, when the United States experienced a good deal of

---

[35] A similar implication emerges from Adam Przeworski, "Institutionalization of Voting Patterns," *American Political Science Review* 69 (March 1975): 49-67.

[36] Recent analyses of the effects of changes in economic conditions upon voting behavior include Gerald Kramer, "Short-Term Fluctuations in U.S. Voting Behavior, 1896-1964," *American Political Science Review* 65 (March 1971): 131-143; Edward R. Tufte, "Determinants of the Outcomes of Midterm Congressional Elections," *American Political Science Review* 69 (September 1975): 812-826; and Edward R. Tufte, *Political Control of the Economy* (Princeton, N.J.: Princeton University Press, 1978), chs. 4 and 5.

[37] Parties of economic protest have, of course, been quite important in American political history. See, for example, John R. Hicks, *The Populist Revolt* (Lincoln:

political unrest. Protests, demonstrations, and other forms of disorderly political activity became commonplace. Though only a small number of individuals actually participated in such activities, unusually large numbers of citizens became sympathetic to nonelectoral modes of participation. For example, in 1972, 60 percent of the respondents in a survey conducted by researchers at the University of Michigan indicated at least conditional approval of protest marches. Similarly, 56 percent of all respondents indicated that they might under some circumstances approve of civil disobedience.

Against this backdrop of considerable public approval of the idea of protest, we can see a rather interesting pattern. Increased approval of protest and civil disobedience was by no means uniformly distributed throughout the American public. Increases in approval of demonstrations and the like appear to have been concentrated primarily in those segments of the public least fully integrated into the national electorate. First, approval of protest in 1972 was considerably more evident among younger segments of the public than among older citizens. The proportion approving civil disobedience, indicated by Table 2.10, was lowest among those over the age of 50 and highest among individuals between the ages of 21 and 35, who would presumably have had relatively little electoral experience.

Second—and this is what is particularly interesting—within each age group, approval of disruptive forms of participation was generally greatest among those who reported little or no past electoral activity. This pattern is particularly evident among both the youngest and oldest respondents. Respondents over the age of 50 who reported having voted in all past elections for which they were eligible were quite a bit less likely to indicate approval for civil disobedience than their age peers with spottier electoral records. Similarly, among individuals in the 21 to 35 age group, approval of civil disobedience increased sharply as frequency of past voting diminished. Indeed,

University of Nebraska Press, 1961); V.O. Key, *Politics, Parties and Pressure Groups* (New York: Crowell, 1964), pp. 255-262; Daniel Mazmanian, *Third Parties in Presidential Elections* (Washington, D.C.: Brookings Institution, 1974); Richard Hofstadter, *The Age of Reform* (New York: Knopf, 1955); and M.S. Stedman and S.W. Stedman, *Discontent at the Polls* (New York: Columbia University Press, 1950).

TABLE 2.10 *Popular attitudes toward civil disobedience in 1972, by age.*

Age	% expressing approval	% expressing disapproval	
21-35	20.7	33.3	(N = 863)
36-50	18.3	44.5	(N = 688)
51 and over	9.6	56.1	(N = 925)

TABLE 2.11 *Electoral participation and popular approval of civil disobedience in 1972, by age.*

	Frequency of Past Voting Participation		
Age	Voted in all elections for which eligible	Voted in most or some elections	Never voted
21-35	17.8%* (N = 321)	16.6% (N = 175)	24.7% (N = 174)
36-50	18.7% (N = 347)	19.2% (N = 291)	10.9% (N = 46)
51 and over	9.4% (N = 477)	9.2% (N = 404)	15.9% (N = 44)

* That is, 17.8 percent of those in the 21-35 age group who voted in all elections for which they were eligible indicated that they approved of breaking an unjust law.

viewing the data reported by Table 2.11 as a whole, approval of protest was highest among younger individuals who had never voted and lowest among older persons who had frequently voted in the past. In a sense, approval of civil disobedience would appear to be associated with lack of socialization into the electorate.

These results are hardly conclusive. It may, as always, be the case that other attitudinal or social factors underlie both frequency of past voting and approval of protest. Controlling for a number of reasonable possibilities, however, fails to alter substantially the pattern of the results. Among those taking a "dovish" position on the Vietnam war, for example, approval of civil disobedience continues to vary with past voting frequency. Similarly, even among those who claim never to "trust the government to do right," respondents who report a high frequency of past voting participation appear to be least willing to condone disruptive alternatives.[38]

Thus, at the attitudinal level, those most habituated to conventional electoral participation seemed least prepared to support protest, civil disobedience, and other unconventional forms of political activity. By contrast, those segments of the public less fully integrated into the electorate—younger citizens and older individuals who had seldom or never voted—appeared most supportive of political activity outside the formal electoral arena.

Favorable attitudes toward protest activities do not, of course, directly translate into participation in such forms of political action. Only a tiny fraction of those who came to approve of demonstrations ever took to the streets themselves. These attitudinal data are, however, consistent with behavioral findings reported by Sears and McConahay's study of participation in the Watts riot of 1965.[39] By comparing actual riot participants with those who lived in the police "curfew zone" but took no part in the riot, Sears and McConahay found, among other things, that rioters had a far weaker record of past political participation than others in the sample.

The implication of these findings is as follows: Citizens who have learned to use routine electoral channels to express their views and grievances will only with great reluctance condone or support, and indeed are very unlikely to participate in, more violent and disruptive forms of political activity. On the other hand, individuals who, for one reason or another, have not been integrated into the electorate and under normal circumstances simply do not participate, are much more likely to press their demands in a disruptive or even violent

---

[38] For example, among respondents who favored an immediate American withdrawal from Vietnam, approximately 40 percent of those who voted "all" or "most" of the time expressed disapproval of protest. Only 30 percent of those who had "never" voted did so. At the same time, among respondents favoring a complete American military victory, more than 60 percent of those who voted all or most of the time disapproved of protest. However, only 30 percent of the "hawks" who had never voted expressed disapproval of protest activities.

[39] David O. Sears and John B. McConahay, *The Politics of Violence* (Boston: Houghton Mifflin, 1973), ch. 6.

manner if some circumstance does induce them to seek to take part in political affairs. Given sufficient cause, of course, even the most faithful voters can presumably abandon the polls in favor of more direct mechanisms for the assertion of their grievances. But the greater danger of violence and disruption comes from those who find electoral channels unavailable or who have not been trained to use them. At the very least, such individuals offer a potential base of support for activists. Seen in conjunction with our analysis of the impact of economic downturns upon political activity, these findings suggest that the availability of electoral channels of mass political involvement and the habituation of citizens to their use tends to protect the regime from more violent and dangerous forms of political action.

MASS PUBLIC OR ELECTORATE?

Taken together, law, civic education, and party not only democratize political activity but also help to transform the mass public into an electorate. The distinction between a mass public and an electorate is crucial. A mass public interacts with the state in a variety of ways. Usually it is absolutely quiescent, passively allowing itself to be governed. On other occasions, however, segments of it are violent, governable, if at all, only through coercion. An electorate, by contrast, is orderly and predictable in its relationship with the state. An electorate only votes.

That elections socialize political activity and thereby inhibit disorder does not by itself indicate that what citizens decide in elections has no importance. Despite the constraints they impose upon mass political involvement, American elections are by no means shams. They permit citizens to select and depose leaders and perhaps to hold the individuals in office accountable for their actions. Indeed, by comparison with a number of other nations, the United States has not even begun to socialize participation fully. Twentieth-century dictatorships, for instance, use elections and other formal participatory mechanisms to thoroughly control the scope and frequency of citizen involvement and to channel participation almost completely in directions desired by the government. One notable group of examples are the mass demonstrations organized by totalitarian governments to induce citizens to demand some course of action already settled upon by the leadership. By contrast, the United States permits its citizens considerable choice about whether, how, and when to participate in politics.

Nevertheless, even in the United States, a particular avenue of participation is encouraged to the near exclusion of most others, and even in the United States, elections serve to control mass political involvement and to cushion its impact on the regime. As we shall now see, moreover, because an electorate only votes, the scope, frequency, and intensity of its involvement in government and politics is subject to formal constraint and delimitation. Electoral limits on mass political activity go beyond the simple inhibition of political violence and disorder.

ELECTIONS AND THE INSTITUTION-ALIZATION OF POPULAR INFLUENCE

3

The substitution of elections for spontaneous or privately organized modes of political action not only affects the form of mass political involvement, but also has important implications for its consequences. On the one hand, elections formalize and equalize popular influence in the governmental process, thus substantially altering the relationship between rulers and those they rule. But at the same time, even democratic elections can also formally delimit the effects of mass intervention into politics and, in several important respects, diminish the potential for mass influence in political life.

Elections are generally conceived to be the principle means through which citizens can influence their leaders. Certainly, democratic elections permit citizens to routinely select and depose public officials, and can potentially serve to facilitate popular influence over officials' conduct. But however effective this electoral sanction may be, it is hardly the only means through which citizens can reward or punish public officials for their actions. Spontaneous or privately organized forms of political activity, or even the threat of their occurrence, can also induce those in power to heed their subjects' wishes. The behavior of even the most rigid autocrats, for example, can be influenced by the possibility that their policies may provoke popular disobedience, clandestine movements, or riot and insurrection. To be sure, the likelihood that an autocrat will be removed from office may generally be less than the chance that an elected official will suffer defeat at the polls. At the same time, however, the potential cost of removal via mass insurrection can be significantly greater than the penalties associated with electoral defeat. Though American congressional representatives are occasionally retired to the private practice of law by their constituents, thus far at least, few have lost their heads as a result.

Elections do not create a possibility of popular influence where none existed before. Rather, they substitute an institutional mechanism for the informal sanctions, including riot and insurrection, that might otherwise by available to a mass public. Elections transform citizens' capacity to influence their rulers' behavior from a matter of purely private activities and resources to a result of mass participation in a routine public function. This transformation has at least four critical consequences.

First, elections formalize and thus fundamentally alter the character of popular influence over governments' actions. Citizens' preferences could influence public officials long before the advent of elections. But in the absence of formal mechanisms for its expression and enforcement, the potential for popular influence tends to be inversely related to rulers' power. Rulers are likely to be most concerned with their subjects' wishes when their military and administrative capacity to compel obedience or forcibly maintain their positions is weakest, and least concerned with citizens' views when their own power is most secure. Popular influence stemming from rulers' fear of disobedience, riot, or insurrection, for example, is likely to be greatest when the state's military and internal security forces are weakest or least reliable. The advent of the democratic election, however, meant that even when rulers had the capacity to compel obedience, popular influence was no longer necessarily reduced. Citizens' capacity to influence their rulers' conduct had become at least partially independent of rulers' military and administrative power. The effectiveness of the electoral sanction, unlike that of the threat of riot and insurrection, does not necessarily vary with the state's power. Even the most powerful elected official can be voted out of office. With the advent of the democratic election, popular influence and rulers' power were no longer necessarily inversely related but could instead potentially coexist.

Second, elections help to equalize citizens' capacities to influence rulers' conduct. Whatever the possibility of external influence upon public officials' behavior, in the absence of elections or other formal mechanisms this potential is almost inevitably unequally distributed. Without an institutional mechanism, popular influence can be derived only from private activities and personal resources. The capacity to influence officials' actions may, for example, vary with wealth, with social position, or even with the propensity to riot. But, whatever the relevant resources, so long as they are solely private and informal, their distribution in any population is certain to be unequal. By introducing a formal, public means of influencing official conduct, however, elections can compensate for private inequalities in political resources. While elections are not likely to fully offset the effects of private inequality, they provide those individuals who have few private resources with a compensatory public source of political influence. The more important the vote's role relative to that of private sources of influence, the more that elections are likely to diminish the political implications of economic, social, and other private inequalities.

At the same time, though, that they formalize and equalize the possibility of popular influence, elections have a third consequence. By institutionalizing citizens' capacity to influence rulers' conduct, elections delimit popular influence. Elections introduce a means of mass influence that is itself subject to formal governmental control and manipulation. In every nation, the electoral rules and procedures that both translate individual choices into collective decisions and determine the impact of those decisions upon the government's composition are used by those in power to regulate electoral outcomes and their likely consequences. Electoral rules can obviously be employed to diminish or even to preclude the possibility of electoral influence. Examples of authoritarian elections without choice are, of course, numerous. But even where competition and choice are routine possibilities, election law can play an important role in preserving an established distribution of power. The democracies characteristically do not attempt to prevent mass influence via the ballot box. Instead, electoral law in the democratic context is typically used to organize the expression of mass opinion in such a way that its force is channeled to the advantage of the regime. Rather than prevent mass electoral influence, the democracies attempt typically to "influence mass influence," so that the electorate's decisions themselves will accord with and thus reinforce the power and wishes of those who rule.

Finally, elections substitute participation in leadership selection for what might otherwise amount to direct mass intervention into, or resistance to, policymaking and administrative processes. While rioters may force a government to adopt one or another policy, or physically prevent the implementation of a governmental program, voters are limited to the occasional selection of some public officials. An electorate decides only who will govern. It is not directly involved with decisions about what the government will do. Although leadership selection and policy selection can obviously be linked with one another, the relationship is often tenuous. Popular selection of leaders does not translate directly into popular selection of policies.

Thus, while elections are generally thought to be synonymous with mass political influence, their consequences are not so simple. Elections formalize and equalize mass influence, but can at the same time constrain and delimit the effects of mass intervention into political life. It is undoubtedly true that popular influence through democratic electoral institutions is significantly greater than, say, that which is available to citizens ruled by a dictatorship sufficiently powerful to prevent dissent and disorder. But this comparison, often implicit when the importance of democratic elections is discussed, is not necessarily the most apt. In what is perhaps the more usual case, governments are not powerful enough to stamp out clandestine oppositions or prevent political violence and disorder. And where they are not, the influence that the masses can exert through these modes of political expression, or even their threat, can be substantial. It is hardly necessary to look further than the recent histories of Iran and Rhodesia for examples.

The alternative to democratic elections is not clearly and simply the absence of popular influence but can instead be unregulated and unconstrained mass intervention into governmental processes. It is, indeed, often precisely because spontaneous forms of mass political activity can have too great an impact upon governments' actions that elections are introduced. Walter Lippman once observed that "new numbers were enfranchised because they had power, and giving them the vote was the least disturbing way of letting them exercise their power."[1] The vote can provide the "least disturbing way" of allowing the masses to exercise power because elections formally delimit mass influence that rulers are unable to forcibly contain. If the masses had no power without them, elections would never have been introduced.

POPULAR INFLUENCE AND RULERS' POWER

In the absence of elections or other formal mechanisms, citizens' capacity to influence rulers' conduct tends to be an inverse function

---

[1] Walter Lippman, *The Essential Lippman.* ed. by Clinton Rossiter and James Lare (New York: Random House, Vintage Books, 1965), p. 12.

of rulers' power. So long as they command military forces and an administrative apparatus sufficiently powerful to compel popular obedience and prevent threats to their own rule, governments can afford a measure of indifference to popular pressure. If, however, the state's administrative and military forces are too weak, or their loyalty too uncertain to enforce rulers' injunctions or to suppress popular unrest, then those in power are likely to become more concerned with their subjects' needs and preferences. For example, European monarchs were generally most solicitous of their subjects' views when they lacked the military power and administrative means to collect needed taxes.[2] Thus the origins of representative government in Britain are closely linked with the crown's financial difficulties in the thirteenth and fourteenth centuries. Because it did not have the ability to forcibly acquire badly needed new revenues, the crown was compelled to summon representative knights and burgesses to obtain local consent for additional tax levies.[3] In exchange for this consent, the king often found himself obliged to grant a variety of concessions to local wishes. Or, to take a contemporary example, the Polish regime's inability to forcibly prevent riots in the 1950s, 1960s, and 1970s—riots that led to the fall of two governments—made it quite sensitive to popular demands. In 1976, price increases planned for meat, butter, vegetables, and other staples were quickly rescinded when workers in Warsaw staged a series of demonstrations and others set fire to Communist party headquarters in the city of Radom. Ultimately, fear of popular unrest led the government to establish a national Gallup-type poll on questions of public policy. Apparently

---

[2] For discussions, see, for example, Gabriel Ardant, "Financial Policy and Economic Infrastructure of Modern States and Nations," in Charles Tilly (ed.), *The Formation of National States in Western Europe* (Princeton, N.J.: Princeton University Press, 1975), p. 196; and Rudolf Brown, "Taxation, Sociopolitical Structure, and State-Building: Great Britain and Brandenburg-Prussia," *ibid.,* p. 253. See also Carl J. Friedrich, *Constitutional Government and Democracy* (Boston: Little, Brown, 1941), p. 259.

[3] George L. Haskins, *The Growth of English Representative Government* (New York: A.S. Barnes, 1960), ch. 3. The title of this chapter, "Compulsory Self-Government," tells the whole story.

the government concluded that its ability to satisfy popular opinion, and thus to avoid unrest, could be enhanced if it had a better notion of the character of popular preferences.[4] In 1980, the government of the People's Republic of China also discovered the value of the scientific study of public opinion. China's Institute of Psychology endorsed the use of such polls as "tools in the science of management."[5] Thus the scientific public opinion poll serves as the twentieth-century technocratic equivalent of the representative assembly of provincial notables—helping the government to avoid trouble by providing it with some conception of what its subjects will tolerate. At least in the Polish case, however, public opinion polls did not prove to be totally effective. In 1980, approximately 350,000 Polish workers left their jobs for almost a month to demand a number of economic and political reforms. Ultimately the spreading strikes forced the government to promise several concessions to the workers, including the creation of trade unions not controlled by the government or Communist party apparatus. Several days later, the Polish Communist party's First Secretary, Edward Gierek, was compelled to resign, becoming the third Polish leader in recent years to be forced from office partially because of popular dissatisfaction. The reason why the Polish government was willing to make concessions to its subjects is clear. In the words of Stanislaw Kania, who succeeded Gierek as Polish Communist party leader, "Everything must be done to solve the crisis with political means because no other means are available."[6] The government did not believe its military and internal security forces to be sufficiently reliable to permit their use against strikers. Only the specter of intervention by Soviet forces limited the trade union movement's capacity to compel the government to accede to its demands.

---

[4] Geoffrey Smith, "Can Marxism Stand Prosperity?" *Forbes,* July 1, 1977, pp. 41-46.

[5] James P. Sterba, "Peking Backs Use of Opinion Polls," *New York Times,* August 25, 1980.

[6] Drew Middleton, "Polish Army's Role Discounted in Study," *New York Times,* December 21, 1980.

So long as mass influence is informal, based simply upon rulers' fear of riots or inability to forcibly levy taxes, its continuity is uncertain. An increase in the state's power or a diminution of subjects' capacity to resist its application almost inevitably reduces rulers' incentive to respond to their subjects' wishes. For example, in Brandenburg-Prussia the capacity of the Estates to obtain concessions from the crown in exchange for fiscal support was effectively undermined during the seventeenth century. Beginning with the reign of Frederick William, the Great Elector, in 1640, the creation of a state bureaucracy capable of administering tax collection and a peacetime standing army capable of enforcing payment opened the way to centralized absolutist rule.[7] A similar illustration of this phenomenon is the failure of the French Estates-General to maintain the type of influence over the crown through control of taxation that developed in Britain. The growth of French rulers' military power, beginning in the fifteenth century, greatly diminished the possibility of taxpayer resistance. As this possibility decreased, so did the king's interest in bargaining with his subjects for their support.[8] In this context it would be no surprise if the contemporary Polish government's interest in public opinion surveys and independent trade unions lasted only so long as it lacked the capacity to forcibly prevent serious popular disruption.

The advent of the election had the consequence of at least partially separating popular influence from rulers' power. Elected officials may control sufficient military and administrative machinery to compel popular obedience and preclude their own forcible removal. Yet even the most powerful elected official can be voted out of office. The democratic election provides citizens with a sanction that, unlike the threat of insurrection or tax resistance, is not directly affected by the state's power. With the advent of the democratic election, popular influence and rulers' power were no longer neces-

---

[7] Samuel E. Finer, "State and Nation-Building in Europe: The Role of the Military," in Tilly, *Western Europe*, pp. 134-144.

[8] Ardant, "Financial Policy," p. 127. See also G.N. Clark, *The Seventeenth Century* (Oxford: Oxford University Press, 1929), ch. 6.

sarily inversely related. Increases in the state's power did not automatically occur at the expense of continued popular influence.

Some empirical indications of this consequence of elections can be obtained by comparing the relationship between social welfare expenditures and the size of internal security forces in nations that have and nations that do not have institutionalized democratic electoral practices. Social welfare expenditures, of course, cannot be said to measure popular influence per se. They do, however, offer one set of indicators of governments' attention to their citizens' needs. Similarly, the size of states' internal security forces is certainly not a precise measure of governments' "power." Ideally, we would wish to be able to take account of a variety of different aspects of governments' administrative, military, and policy capacities. Ideally, we would also wish to be able to take account of variations in the loyalty and efficiency of internal security forces, as well as cross-national variations in citizens' willingness and capacity to resist the application of force. The virtues of firearms regulation notwithstanding, a well-armed citizenry has, upon more than one occasion, served to discourage tyrannical behavior by those in power.[9] In addition, some governments with the military and police capacity to suppress dissent lack the political ability or will to fully take advantage of the force at their disposal. Nevertheless, the size of a state's internal security apparatus offers one rough indicator of the government's potential ability to compel popular obedience.

My argument suggests that in the absence of formal electoral sanctions, a government's attention to its citizens' welfare is likely to vary inversely with its capacity to compel popular obedience. The greater rulers' ability to deal with potential dissent and resistance, the less their incentive to attend to their citizens' needs. By contrast, where formal electoral sanctions are available to citizens, we would expect to find little or no relationship between the state's coercive capacity and its attention to public welfare.

---

[9] For example, see the discussion in *The Federalist*, no. 46. E.M. Earle (ed.), *The Federalist* (New York: Modern Library, 1937), pp. 304-312.

As a test of these possibilities, all 71 nations for which the requisite social welfare and internal security data were available were divided into three groups on the basis of the classification of their electoral processes found in the *World Handbook of Political and Social Indicators.* The first group consists of those nations whose electoral procedures were termed "rigged" by the *World Handbook.* In these nations, elections do not involve competition or permit the possibility of opposition to those in power. The second group consists of those nations whose electoral practices the *World Handbook* deemed to be marked by "substantial irregularity." That is, although a semblance of competition might be tolerated, electoral outcomes unfavorable to those in power are not likely to be permitted. The third category consists of those nations whose electoral practices the *World Handbook* labeled "competitive." In this group, which includes the Western democracies, electoral competition and the electoral defeat of those in power is a routine possibility.

Taking each of these three groups of nations separately, I have correlated national expenditures for health and education with a measure of the effective size of each state's internal security apparatus.[10] To take account of differences in national wealth, welfare expenditures are expressed as percentages of each nation's gross national product. Table 3.1 reports the results of these correlations.

---

[10] Obviously, a simple count of the number of troops available to a nation's rulers is not an adequate measure. Though the likely effectiveness of an internal security apparatus of any given size undoubtedly varies with a great many factors, at the very minimum, we should take account of cross-national variations in population and land area. Presumably an internal security apparatus large enough to quash any dissent that might emerge in a principality containing several hundred thousand inhabitants might not prove very formidable in a nation with tens of millions of citizens spread over a continent. At the same time, it is also important to take account of cross-national variations in vulnerability to violence and disruption. An internal military apparatus large enough to protect one nation's commerce and communications from disruption might not be adequate where communications, industry, and commerce were more complex or extensive. Modern industrial nations, in particular, depend upon extensive industrial, transport, food, power, communications, and fuel networks that can be both difficult to patrol and quite sensitive to damage or disruption. It is partially for this reason, as we observed earlier, that modern industrial nations depend upon relatively

TABLE 3.1 *The relationship between national social welfare expenditures and national internal security forces in dictatorships and democracies—Pearson correlation coefficients.*

	Expenditures for education	Expenditures for health
Size of internal security forces in nations whose electoral processes are rigged	−.12 (N = 21)	.01 (N = 21)
Size of internal security forces in nations whose electoral processes exhibit substantial irregularities	−.15 (N = 26)	−.10 (N = 24)
Size of internal security forces in nations with competitive elections	.00 (N = 31)	.10 (N = 30)

The pattern of findings that emerges from this analysis indicates rather striking differences between the first two groups of nations, on the one hand, and the third group, on the other.

In the first two groups, nations whose electoral practices were deemed to be rigged or marked by substantial irregularities, social welfare expenditures generally tend to be inversely related to the size of the state's internal security apparatus. This inverse association is clearly consistent with the argument that in the absence of formal

---

higher levels of popular acquiescence than is required by their more traditional counterparts. Thus the indicator used in this analysis attempts to take account of cross-national differences in population, land area, and vulnerability. Internal security forces per population and land area can be expressed in terms of density of coverage, which is given by $(I/\text{capita}) \times (I/\text{square mile})$, where I is the number of relevant troops. We use size of gross national product as a surrogate for the various economic and technological characteristics likely to be associated with vulnerability. The indicator takes the form $[(I/\text{pop.}) \times (I/\text{sq. mi.})] \div GNP$, which can be interpreted as the density of national internal security protection divided by the nation's vulnerability to disruption. Obviously, I have neither taken account of all possible sources of cross-national variation in effectiveness of internal security forces nor constructed the only plausible indicator using the factors I do take into account. Because the data were collected during a period when they would likely have been affected by the Indo-China war, Laos, Cambodia, and Vietnam were excluded from analysis.

electoral sanctions, governments' attention to citizens' needs is likely to diminish as their capacity to suppress potential dissent or resistance increases.

By contrast, in the third group of nations, those with competitive electoral practices, social welfare expenditures do not exhibit this inverse association with the size of the state's internal security forces. Expenditures for education in the 31 nations composing this group show no relationship whatsoever with size of internal security apparatus; health expenditures exhibit a positive association. In these nations, welfare expenditures do not appear to diminish as states' coercive capabilities increase. Governments' attention to citizens' needs does not appear to be inversely related to governments' power.

As is always the case, these results cannot be deemed conclusive. They depend, for example, on a rather indirect measure of popular influence, a measure of governments' power that is at best partial, and they are based upon data drawn from a relatively small number of nations. In addition, it is important to remember that the expenditure differences between electorally competitive nations and the other two groups *do not* necessarily represent differences in total welfare expenditures. Welfare expenditures in many nations in the rigged group are greater than or equal to expenditures in electorally competitive nations. The differences among the three groups of nations have to do with the *correlates,* not the *amounts,* of welfare expenditures. We shall return to this point later.

Even with these caveats, however, what emerges from this analysis is empirical support for the argument that democratic elections tend to eliminate or erode the inverse relationship between popular influence and governmental power. By providing citizens with a formal capacity to select and depose leaders, elections permit popular influence and the state's power to coexist. It is for this reason that the advent of the democratic election potentially marks an enormous turning point in the relationship between the citizen and the state. For, given a formal electoral means of influencing their rulers' actions, a means independent of rulers' military and administrative power, citizens potentially stand to benefit from rulers' power rather than from their weaknesses. It is the advent of the democratic election that opens the possibility of citizens using rulers' power for their own benefit rather than simply benefiting from rulers' inability to muster sufficient power to compel citizens to obey their commands. It is, indeed, largely because of this characteristic of democratic electoral processes that the enormous expansion of the state's power in the twentieth century has not seemed entirely to foreclose the possibility of popular influence over governmental conduct.

EQUALITY OF POPULAR INFLUENCE

Elections not only can substantially alter the relationship between popular influence and the state's power, but they can also transform the political relationships among citizens themselves. In particular, democratic elections can potentially equalize citizens' capacities to influence their rulers' conduct.

The creation of institutional, public mechanisms of popular consultation is virtually a necessary condition for political equality. In the absence of elections or other formal mechanisms, popular influence, like mass participation itself, is almost inherently undemocratic. So long as influence can be exerted only through informal channels, the existence of social, economic, or any of a host of other individual inequalities inevitably means that citizens will vary in the resources and skills that they can bring to bear in any effort to affect a government's behavior. For example, differences in wealth or economic status can obviously have considerable impact upon individuals' capacity to influence national policies. In most market-oriented societies, the business community is likely to exercise a good deal of influence simply as a function of the dependence of these societies upon adequate business performance. But beyond this, individuals who control considerable wealth can use it in a variety of ways—ranging from the outright bribery of public officials to the manipulation of information to even the employment of armed bands of adherents—that can provide them with a measure of influence out of all proportion to their numbers in the community.

Elections furnish citizens with a public resource, the ballot, that can at least partially compensate for the political effects of economic or social inequality. Elections, of course, cannot be expected to completely offset the consequences of unequally distributed wealth or other private resources. Obviously, private resources can be used to influence electoral processes. Inequalities of wealth, position, or organization are likely to mean that the capacity to affect governments' actions is unequally distributed even in the context of democratic elections.

Nevertheless, the vote offers those individuals who have few private political resources a public resource with which they may attempt to control officials' behavior. And, indeed, as voters all citizens have a formally equal potential to influence the actions of those in power. The more that governments are influenced by popular voting, the more equal citizens' capacities to affect national policies are likely to be. If the vote was the only relevant political resource, its equal distribution would mean that whatever influence citizens' possessed would also be distributed equally.

Some interesting empirical indications of the compensatory effect of elections can be obtained by looking once again at the patterns of national social welfare expenditures that we examined previously in Table 3.1. In this instance, we shall compare the relationship between social welfare expenditures and the distribution of an important political resource, wealth, in nations that do and nations that do not permit democratic elections. If elections can compensate for inequalities in private political resources, we would expect that individual differences in wealth would be less likely to result in unequal political influence in nations characterized by democratic electoral procedures than in those lacking elections or other formal means of popular control. In other words, we would expect elections to partially offset the political consequences of economic inequality.

To examine this possibility, I have again divided the nations for which data were available according to the *World Handbook's* classification of their electoral procedures. Because the necessary data could be obtained only for a small number of cases, the rigged and substantial irregularities classifications were combined. The electorally competitive category remained unchanged.

Taking each of the two categories separately, national expenditures for health, education, and social security were correlated with four standard indices of the concentration of wealth. These are the gini index, which measures the difference between an "ideal" equal distribution and the actual distribution of any given commodity; the Schutz coefficient, which measures how much more than average is possessed by those with a greater than average share of any commodity; the half-goods index, which measures the size of the smallest population receiving half of any given value; and the fair share point, which measures the size of the population receiving less than an average share of the commodity in question. Social welfare expenditures were again expressed as percentages of each nation's gross national product.

To the extent that wealth is an important political resource, we would generally expect the relative influence of wealthy individuals to increase as the concentration of wealth increased. That is, we would expect that the greater the share of a nation's wealth held by those persons with more than average wealth or, alternatively, the more that wealth was concentrated in a small number of hands, the greater the potential influence of the wealthy in national affairs. Any number of examples suggest that where wealth is heavily concentrated, so, too, is political power. To cite just one instance, in a number of Latin American nations the possibility of land reform was blocked for many years by small but immensely wealthy land-owning interests.[11] Moreover, we would generally also expect that across any group of nations, as the relative influence of wealthy individuals in a nation's affairs increased, national social welfare expenditures would tend to diminish. This assumption is obviously not always correct, but in general the rich would probably prefer not to see the redistributions of wealth often entailed by welfare programs.

If these assumptions are correct, we would expect that across any group of nations, in the absence of some restraining factor, welfare expenditures will be inversely related to the concentration of wealth at any given point in time. Assuming that the capacity of wealthy individuals to influence national affairs increases as the proportion of

---

[11] For a discussion of the problems surrounding land reform, see Samuel Huntington, *Political Order in Changing Societies* (New Haven, Conn.: Yale University Press, 1968), pp. 380-396.

national wealth in their possession increases, and assuming that such individuals are generally cool to welfare spending, we would expect that in the absence of some intervening factor, welfare spending would be lowest where the concentration of wealth is greatest. And, indeed, an inverse relationship between social welfare spending and the concentration of wealth is precisely what is obtained when we correlate the two in nations lacking democratic elections.

Table 3.2 reports the correlation between national welfare expenditures and the concentration of wealth for nations with electoral systems classified as rigged or irregular. All of the correlations were calculated to indicate the association between welfare expenditures and the extent of inequality in the distribution of wealth. Obviously, in the case of the half-goods index, this required inversion of the coefficient's sign.

Though the number of cases involved is so small that the sizes of the correlation coefficients cannot be taken too seriously, it is immediately evident that the concentration of wealth and social welfare expenditures are inversely related in this group of nations. As the concentration of wealth increases, welfare expenditures tend to diminish.

Of course, standing by themselves, these findings might simply mean that substantial welfare spending tended to reduce the concen-

TABLE 3.2 *The relationship between national social welfare expenditures and economic inequality in nations lacking democratic elections —Pearson correlation coefficients.*

	Expenditures for social security	Expenditures for education	Expenditures for health
Half-goods index	−.32*	−.36	−.04
Schutz coefficient	−.45	−.33	−.02
Fair share point	.07	−.50	−.09
Gini index	−.42	−.36	−.05
	(N = 6)	(N = 11)	(N = 11)

* Signs for correlations involving the half-goods index are reversed to make their interpretation consistent with that of the other coefficients.

tration of wealth. Yet these results not only seem consistent with our expectations concerning the policy impact of concentration of wealth, but also provide a striking backdrop for the substantially different relationship between welfare expenditures and unequally distributed wealth that obtains in electorally competitive nations.

If democratic elections can compensate for individual inequalities in political resources, then we would expect that in the electorally competitive group of nations, welfare expenditures do not necessarily diminish as the concentration of wealth increases. If elections have the compensatory effect that we have suggested, economic inequality should not necessarily mean political inequality in nations that have instituted democratic electoral procedures.

Table 3.3 reports the correlations between welfare expenditures and the concentration of wealth for those nations classified as electorally competitive by the *World Handbook*. Again, the small number of cases involved makes the sizes of the correlations somewhat suspect. But what seems nevertheless to be clearly indicated by these results is the absence of any negative association between welfare expenditures and the concentration of wealth in these nations. In the electorally competitive group, welfare spending does not appear to diminish as the concentration of wealth increases.

TABLE 3.3 *The relationship between national social welfare expenditures and economic inequality in electorally competitive nations— Pearson correlation coefficients.*

	Expenditures for social security	Expenditures for education	Expenditures for health
Half-goods index	.20*	.34	.36
Schutz coefficient	.23	.50	.44
Fair share point	−.18	.00	.01
Gini index	.17	.43	.38
	(N = 19)	(N = 22)	(N = 22)

* Signs for correlations involving the half-goods index are reversed to make their interpretation consistent with that of the other coefficients.

These findings cannot be considered conclusive evidence of the compensatory effects of elections. The number of cases I was able to examine is very small, and the analysis takes into account only one private political resource, wealth, when obviously there are many possible sources of political influence. In addition, it is important to point out that the results suggest neither that welfare spending is greater nor that inequality of wealth is smaller in electorally competitive nations than in those without democratic electoral practices. Indeed, taken as wholes, the two groups of nations overlap considerably both in welfare expenditures and in terms of the concentration of wealth. It is the *relationship* between social welfare spending and the distribution of wealth that differs in the two groups.

This difference, however, appears to provide some evidence of the compensatory effects of elections. In nations lacking democratic electoral practices, welfare spending appears to diminish as the concentration of wealth increases. In those nations that permit democratic elections, on the other hand, welfare spending is not negatively associated with the concentration of wealth. Assuming, again, that the potential political influence of wealth increases with its concentration, and that the wealthy would, if they could, reduce levels of welfare expenditures, these findings lend credence to the view that democratic elections can help to offset the potential political implications of economic inequality. In the electorally competitive group of nations, economic inequality does not appear to translate directly into inequality of political influence.

REGULATION OF MASS POLITICAL INFLUENCE

The substitution of elections for informal modes of mass political action makes popular influence independent of the state's power and enhances political equality. Yet, however important they may be, these changes should not be mistaken for increases in the extent of mass political influence. The correlates and extent of popular influence are two entirely different matters. For example, that popular influence ceases to vary with changes in the state's power may mean that it has become unvaryingly insignificant. Or, in the same vein, political equality can mean equality of political impotence.

By eroding the inverse relationship between popular influence and the state's power, elections may sometimes give citizens a greater capacity to influence their rulers than they would otherwise have had. But, at the same time, the introduction of elections can give the state an opportunity that it would not otherwise have had to formally delimit the extent of mass political influence. Elections are means of popular control of the state that are themselves controlled by the state. The substitution of elections for spontaneous modes of mass political action allows governments an opportunity, if not necessarily to reduce, at least to regulate the likely consequences of popular intervention into policymaking processes. Whether citizens or their rulers have the most to gain from this substitution no doubt varies from case to case. And of course, once established, electoral processes may not be as easily amenable to control as rulers might have intended. But from the perspective of those in power, the alternative to elections can be unregulated and unlimited mass influence over their actions. Even democratic elections, by contrast, can permit governments to formally control the effects of mass participation in political life.

Though each has many variants, three general forms of control have played especially important roles in the electoral history of the Western democracies. First, governments often attempt to regulate the composition of electorates in order to diminish the electoral weight of groups they deem to be undesirable. Second, governments almost invariably seek to manipulate the translation of voters' choices into electoral outcomes both through the organization of electorates and through organization of electorates' decisions. Third, virtually all ruling groups attempt at least to partially insulate policymaking processes from electoral intervention through regulation of the relationship between electoral decisions and the composition or organization of the government.

ELECTORAL COMPOSITION

Perhaps the oldest and most obvious device used to control electoral outcomes and their likely consequences is manipulation of the electorate's composition. At the time of the initial introduction of elections in Western Europe, for example, the suffrage was generally limited, through property or other restrictions, to groups that could be trusted to vote in a manner acceptable to those in power. To cite just one illustration, property qualifications in France prior to 1848 limited the electorate to 240,000 of some 7 million men over the age of 21.[12] During the same era, other nations manipulated the electorate's composition by assigning unequal electoral weights to different classes of voters. The 1831 Belgian constitution, for example, assigned individuals anywhere from one to three votes depending upon their property holdings, education, and position.[13] The well-known 1848 Prussian constitution divided voters into three classes on the basis of property, tax payments, and official or professional position. Though the size of each class was unequal—in some districts the uppermost class contained only a handful of persons—each class selected an equal number of electors, who in turn selected representatives to the lower house of the legislature.[14]

But even in the context of an ostensibly universal and equal suffrage, the composition of an electorate may still be amenable to manipulation. Examples range from the discriminatory use of poll taxes and literacy tests to such practices as manipulation of the placement of polls and scheduling of voting hours to depress participation by one or another group. Probably the most important example of the regulation of an electorate's composition despite universal suffrage is the personal registration requirement associated with voting in the United States.

Levels of voter participation in twentieth-century American elections are quite low by comparison to those of the other Western democracies.[15] Indeed, voter participation in off-year congressional

---

[12] Stein Rokkan, *Citizens, Elections, Parties* (New York: David McKay, 1970), p. 149.

[13] John A. Hawgood, *Modern Constitutions since 1787* (New York: D. Van Nostrand, 1939), p. 148.

[14] Charles Seymour and Donald P. Frary, *How the World Votes* (Springfield, Mass.: C.A. Nichols, 1918), pp. 20-23.

[15] For comparisons of voter turnout in the United States and Western Europe, see Walter Dean Burnham, "The Changing Shape of the American Political Universe," *American Political Science Review* 59 (1965): 7-28. See also Kevin Phillips and Paul H.

elections in the United States has barely averaged 50 percent in recent years. During the nineteenth century, by contrast, voter turnout in the United States was extremely high. Records, in fact, indicate that in some counties as many as 105 percent of those eligible voted in presidential elections.[16] Some proportion of this total obviously was artificial—a result of the widespread corruption that characterized American voting practices during that period. Nevertheless, it seems clear that a considerably larger proportion of those eligible actually went to the polls in nineteenth-century American elections than is the case at present.

As Fig. 3.1 indicates, the critical years during which voter turnout declined across the United States were between 1890 and 1910. These years coincide with the adoption of laws, across much of the nation, requiring eligible citizens to appear personally at a registrar's office to register to vote some time prior to the actual date of an election. Personal registration was one of several "Progressive" reforms of political practices initiated at the turn of the century. The ostensible purpose of registration was to discourage fraud and corruption. But to many Progressive reformers "corruption" was a code word, much as "crime" has been a code word in recent years. Progressives objected to the types of politics practiced in the large cities where political machines had organized immigrant and ethnic populations. Reformers not only objected to the corruption that surely was a facet of machine politics but also opposed the growing political power of these polyglot urban populations and their leaders.

Blackman, *Electoral Reform and Voter Participation* (Washington, D.C.: American Enterprise Institute, 1975), ch. 3.

[16] Several counties in the state of New York, for example, appear to have had very enthusiastic electorates in the nineteenth century. Data are presented by Allan E. Mayefsky, "Personal Registration Laws and Voting Participation in New York State," unpublished honors thesis, Cornell University, 1975. For discussions of nineteenth-century electoral corruption, see Joseph P. Harris, *Registration of Voters in the United States* (Washington, D.C.: Brookings Institution, 1929); and Philip E. Converse, "Change in the American Electorate," in Angus Campbell and Philip E. Converse (eds.), *The Human Meaning of Social Change* (New York: Russell Sage Foundation, 1972). See also Clinton R. Woodruff, "Election Methods and Reforms in Philadelphia," *The Annals* 27 (March 1901): 181-204.

FIG. 3.1 *U.S. voter turnout, 1860-1976.*

Source: U.S. Bureau of the Census, Historical Statistics of the United States.

From the point of view of middle-class reformers, the electoral system was corrupt, in part because it facilitated participation and influence on the part of the wrong types of persons.[17] Like some other Progressive reforms, voting reform may also have been congenial to the interests of the business elites that became dominant in American politics during the late nineteenth century. Personal registration created a more conservative electorate more amenable to the types of policies favored by business groups.

---

[17] Two excellent discussions of the political character of Progressive reform are Walter Dean Burnham, *Critical Elections and the Mainsprings of American Electoral Politics* (New York: Norton, 1970), ch. 4, and Samuel P. Hays, "Political Parties and the Community-Society Continuum," in William N. Chambers and Walter Dean Burnham (eds.), *The American Party System* (New York: Oxford University Press, 1975).

At any rate, personal registration imposed a new burden upon potential voters and altered the format of American elections. While registration existed in a number of states before 1890, these early laws had little consequence. It had not been uncommon in most areas for voters simply to walk into a polling place on the day of the election and cast ballots with little or no official interference. Those early registration laws that were enforced were similar in effect to present-day European requirements. The burden of registration was placed on election officials rather than on voters. It was the task of these officials to compose lists of qualified voters; no action on the part of the voter was necessary before the day of the election.

Under the new systems of personal registration adopted after 1890, it became the duty of individual voters to secure their own eligibility. This duty could prove to be a significant burden for potential voters. During a personal appearance before the registrar individuals seeking to vote were (and are) required to furnish proof of identity, residence, and citizenship. While the inconvenience of registration varied from state to state, it was usually the case, first, that voters could register only during business hours on weekdays. This, of course, meant that to many voters registration might entail the loss of some portion of a day's pay. Second, voters were usually required to register a long while, in some states up to several months, before the next election. This requirement forced potential voters to make an investment of time and effort just when their interest in electoral politics was likely to have ebbed. Third, to register once was generally not sufficient to permit a citizen to continue to vote in more than a handful of elections. Most personal registration laws required a periodic purge of the elections rolls, ostensibly to keep them up-to-date. In most instances voters had to reregister periodically to maintain their eligibility. Although personal registration requirements helped to diminish the widespread electoral corruption that accompanied a completely open voting process, they also made it much more difficult for citizens to participate in the electoral process.[18]

---

[18] See Converse, "American Electorate," p. 283; Walter Dean Burnham, "Theory and Voting Research," *American Political Science Review* 68 (September 1974): 1002-1023; and Converse, "Comment on Burnham's Theory and Voting Research," *ibid.*, pp.

As might be expected, registration requirements have their greatest impact upon the most poorly socialized segments of the electorate. Registration requirements, as Table 3.4 suggests, particularly depress participation on the part of those with little education and low incomes.[19] The explanation for this biased impact of registration is two-fold. First, the simple obstacle of registering on weekdays during business hours is most difficult for working-class persons to overcome. Registration imposes an additional cost to voting that is more easily borne by middle- and upper-class citizens. Second, and more important, registration requires a greater degree of political involvement and interest than does the act of voting itself. To vote, a person need only be concerned with the particular election campaign at hand. Yet as we noted, registration in many states is prohibited up to several months prior to the next election. This prohibition forces individuals to make the decision to register on the basis of an abstract interest in the electoral process rather than a simple concern with a specific campaign. As a number of studies have suggested, even if they become interested in specific campaigns, lower-class, poorly educated persons are less likely than middle- and upper-class individuals to have such an abstract or general interest in the electoral process. An abstract interest in electoral politics is largely a product of education. Those with relatively little education may become interested in political events once the stimuli of a particular campaign become salient, but by that time it is too late to register to vote.[20]

1024-1027, for discussions of the historical, political, and methodological issues raised by the sharp changes in American voting patterns that occurred at the turn of the century. For a discussion of contemporary nonvoting, see Arthur T. Hadley, *The Empty Polling Booth* (Englewood Cliffs, N.J.: Prentice-Hall, 1978).

[19] The relationship between education and registration is discussed in Raymond E. Wolfinger and Steven J. Rosenstone, *Who Votes?* (New Haven, Conn.: Yale University Press, 1980), especially chs. 2 and 4.

[20] The relationship between social class and interest in politics is examined in Fred I. Greenstein, *Children and Politics* (New Haven, Conn.: Yale University Press, 1969), ch. 5; and Robert Weissberg, *Political Learning, Political Choice and Democratic Citizenship* (Englewood Cliffs, N.J.: Prentice-Hall, 1974), pp. 100-103.

TABLE 3.4 *Socioeconomic differences between registered voters and individuals of voting age who were not registered in 1972 and 1976.*

	1972		
	% attended college	% employed	% with income over $10,000
Registered	33.4 (N = 1066)*	57.1 (N = 1068)	51.9 (N = 1024)
Not registered	14.1 (N = 277)	47.5 (N = 276)	27.8 (N = 263)

	1976		
	% attended college	% employed	% with income over $12,000
Registered	36.3 (N = 1737)	55.9 (N = 1743)	25.2 (N = 1621)
Not registered	17.4 (N = 489)	48.1 (N = 491)	14.8 (N = 466)

* Of the registered voters in the sample, 33.4 percent had attended college.

That they have a greater impact on the voting turnout of individuals from lower socioeconomic strata means that personal registration requirements not only diminish the size of the electorate but also have a systematic impact on the electorate's composition. Personal registration tends to create an electorate that is, in the aggregate, better educated, higher in income and social status, and composed of fewer blacks and other minorities than the citizenry as a whole. Moreover, those groups particularly affected by registration requirements differ from the remainder of the electorate, in the aggregate, in their attitudes toward important public issues.[21] In particular, support

---

[21] This interpretation differs from the one presented by Wolfinger and Rosenstone, who appear to conclude that registration requirements do not substantially affect the "demographic, partisan or ideological characteristics" of the electorate. However, Wolfinger and Rosenstone base their assessment upon a comparison of the actual electorate to the electorate likely to result if every state adopted the registration laws in effect in the most permissive state in 1972. My assessment, by contrast, is based on a comparison of the actual electorate with the electorate that might result if all unregistered but otherwise eligible individuals were registered. In a sense, Wolfinger

for a variety of redistributive social programs is somewhat greater among individuals who are not registered to vote than among registered voters.

The implications of the differences reported by Table 3.5 are relatively clear. Full electoral mobilization in the United States would create an electorate more receptive to a variety of broad social welfare initiatives than the present, relatively constricted, and as a result, more conservative electorate. Presumably this is why elimination of personal registration requirements is generally not viewed favorably by many conservatives.[22]

There is, of course, a major drawback to personal registration or any other mode of electoral regulation that inhibits voting participation. Should they seek to participate, groups barred from voting may instead select some other and perhaps less desirable form of political activity. Manipulation of the electorate's composition may work to the advantage of those in power during periods of political quiescence but can backfire when and if groups excluded from voting have some sudden incentive to participate in political life. In this respect, the implications of personal registration do differ somewhat from those of outright disenfranchisement. Given sufficient stimulus, excluded groups may register to vote. The voter registration drive has been an integral part of minority protest activity in contemporary American politics. And, indeed, a federally sponsored drive to register Southern blacks as voters was an integral part of the United States government's response to the problem of black political protest activities in the 1960s. Nevertheless, to attempt to control an electorate by discouraging some of its potential members from voting is also potentially to defeat a major purpose of elections. In the twentieth

---

and Rosenstone compare the existing electorate to an alternative *likely* electorate. I compare the existing electorate to the *possible* electorate—possible if registration laws were eliminated altogether or if the burden of registration was assumed by the government, as it is in most European nations. See Wolfinger and Rosenstone, *Who Votes?* ch. 4.

[22] See Phillips and Blackman, *Electoral Reform.* See also Wolfinger and Rosenstone, *Who Votes?* p. 81.

TABLE 3.5 *Support for social programs among individuals registered and not registered to vote in 1976.*

	Favor government aid to blacks and minorities	Favor government job guarantees	Favor continued private role in health insurance	Favor job safety regulation
Registered to vote	19.5%* (N = 1492)	18.3% (N = 1439)	53.2% (N = 1735)	70.5% (N = 1422)
Not registered to vote	25.5% (N = 353)	25.6% (N = 347)	43.3% (N = 485)	80.8% (N = 364)

* Of those registered to vote in 1976, 19.5 percent approved of government aid to blacks and other minorities.

century the United States has been among the few nations sufficiently politically quiescent to permit its leaders the luxury of excluding "undesirable" elements from the electorate. For the most part, control of electorates in the twentieth century has depended upon techniques compatible with full electoral mobilization.

ORGANIZATION OF ELECTORATES AND DECISIONS

With the major exception of American personal registration requirements, control of electorates through regulation of their composition has in the twentieth century given way to control through manipulation of the relationship between individual voters' choices and collective electoral decisions. Rather than regulate who will choose, governments in the twentieth century generally prefer to allow, in fact to encourage, everyone to choose and then simply to manipulate the likely outcomes.

The translation of individual choices into collective electoral decisions can be influenced in two ways. The first of these is manipulation of the criteria by which popular votes are translated into governmental representation. For example, the selection of a majority, plurality, or some form of proportional criterion for the translation of votes into legislative seats can obviously have important implications for electoral outcomes and their likely consequences. Second, the organization of electorates themselves offers considerable potential for the management of electoral outcomes. The number and arrangement of electoral districts, for example, can have important consequences for the relative electoral importance of different groups and forces. In combination, the organization of electorates and organization of electoral decisions offer governments a virtually endless array of possibilities for the manipulation of elections. Of course, not all of these possibilities are open to any given government at any point in time. Electoral arrangements conceived to be clearly "stacked," or illegitimate, may induce some segments of an electorate to refuse either to participate or to recognize the validity of the result. Some form of proportional representation, for example, may be a necessity in nations severely divided along religious or ethnic lines.[23] Nevertheless, a good deal of electoral engineering is possible even within the limits imposed by governments' desire to uphold the legitimacy of electoral processes.

An enormous literature has been devoted to the comparison of majority, plurality, and proportional electoral systems, as well as to the mathematical intricacies of various established and proposed modes of proportional representation.[24] This discussion can, therefore, be brief. In general, majority and plurality systems create higher thresholds for legislative representation; that is, they require more votes for the acquisition of a legislative seat and more severely over-represent the most successful party than do proportional systems. Under the terms of a majority system, for example, a party may in principle need to acquire more than 50 percent of the popular vote before winning any legislative representation. On the other hand, a party that receives, say, 35 percent of the vote in a three-party

---

[23] Rokkan, *Citizens, Elections, Parties,* p. 157.

[24] A useful survey can be found in Wolfgang Birke, *European Elections by Direct Suffrage* (Leyden, Netherlands: A.W. Sythoff, 1961). For an analysis of the effects of alternative electoral systems, see Douglas Rae, *The Political Consequences of Electoral Laws* (New Haven, Conn.: Yale University Press, 1971). An excellent bibliography on electoral systems is presented in Rokkan, *Citizens, Elections, Parties.*

plurality race may win 100 percent of the legislative seats. As a result, in nineteenth-century European political history majority and plurality systems initially served the interests of established conservative parties by reducing the representation of emerging working-class groups. However, as working-class parties gained in strength and threatened to win electoral majorities, conservative groups came to see proportional representation as a barrier against socialism. In Sweden, for example, conservative groups first fought the introduction of proportional representation but later made it a precondition for their acceptance of universal manhood suffrage.[25]

Among proportional systems themselves, there is a very wide range of variation in thresholds and in the degree of overrepresentation offered the largest parties. The "d'Hondt" system, which was among the first introduced in Western Europe, lowers the threshold of representation and degree of overrepresentation very little by comparison with majority and plurality systems. On the other extreme, what is called the method of the "greatest remainder" facilitates the representation of small splinter groups and under some circumstances actually tends to underrepresent the largest party. Though not directly related to the question of thresholds, modes of balloting can also be important. List systems, for example, probably tend to be more conducive to party formation and organization than preferential systems.

The precise consequences of any given proportional system, however, depend upon the composition of the electorate, the number of legislative seats decided in each district, the number of established parties, and the extent and geographic distribution of support for each party. As a result, any given proportional system can have different consequences in different areas at different times. Considerable fine tuning may be necessary to achieve a desired outcome. A well-known example is the electoral system devised for the French elections of 1951. The parties of the government coalition faced the Communists on the left and the Gaullist RPF on the right. Unfortunately, the distribution of electoral support for the government

---

[25] Rokkan, *Citizens, Elections, Parties,* pp. 157-158.

coalition meant that any single electoral arrangement would work to the advantage of either the Communists or the RPF or both. Therefore, the government coalition devised an electoral system with three different forms. First, in the rural areas of France, where the government coalition was strongest, the d'Hondt system of proportional representation was used in order to overrepresent the government's support. Second, in Paris and its surroundings, where the government coalition was weakest, it introduced the largest remainder sytem of proportional representation in order to underrepresent the Communists and Gaullists. Third, outside the Paris region, a system called *apparentement*, which awards all the seats in a district to any coalition of parties winning a majority of popular votes, was introduced to further maximize the government coalition's rural support. The consequence of this complex electoral engineering was that the government coalition was able to translate barely 50 percent of the popular vote into more than 60 percent of the seats in the legislature.[26]

Manipulation of the criteria by which votes are translated into representation has played some role in American electoral history. For example, the elimination of proportional representation in the selection of New York City council delegates was specifically designed to prevent the election of Communist party representatives.[27] On the other hand, the introduction of proportional representation for the selection of delegates to the Democratic party's 1972 national convention was designed in part to maximize the voting strength of minority groups and, not entirely coincidentally, to improve the electoral chances of the candidates they were most likely to favor.[28]

---

[26] Andrew Milnor, *Elections and Political Stability* (Boston: Little, Brown, 1969), ch. 3.

[27] Frank Sorauf, *Party Politics in America* (Boston: Little, Brown, 1976), p. 241. See also Belle Zeller and Hugh A. Bone, "The Repeal of Proportional Representation in New York City—Ten Years in Retrospect," *American Political Science Review* 42 (1948): 1122-1148.

[28] On Democratic party reforms, see Austin Ranney, *Curing the Mischiefs of Faction* (Berkeley and Los Angeles: University of California Press, 1975). See also William J. Crotty, *Political Reform and the American Experiment* (New York: Crowell, 1977), chs. 7 and 8; and Nelson Polsby and Aaron Wildavsky, *Presidential Elections* (New York: Scribners, 1980), especially chs. 6 and 7. A brief but excellent discussion critical

Despite these and other exceptions, however, the typical electoral arrangement in the United States is the single-member district plurality election. As a result, American electoral engineering has generally consisted of the manipulation of electoral districts to increase the likelihood of one or another desired outcome. The principle of the gerrymander hardly needs elaboration. Different distributions of voters among districts produce different electoral outcomes; those in a position to control the arrangements of districts are also in a position to manipulate the results. For example, Brooklyn's twelfth congressional district during the 1950s twisted and turned, almost fully bisecting the borough from northwest to southeast. The explanation of the district's peculiar shape was simple. "There are very few Republicans in Brooklyn and distributed in ordinarily shaped districts they would never make a majority anywhere. But the Republican legislature strung GOP areas into a district winding through the borough, and the result was Republican victories until this year."[29]

The Supreme Court's reapportionment decisions during the 1960s hardly put an end to the practice of gerrymandering. In fact, the Court's decisions appear to have prompted a wave of "incumbent gerrymanders" involving the redrawing of congressional district lines in such a way as to increase the safety of many legislative seats.[30]

---

of party reform is Everett C. Ladd, Jr., "Party Reform since 1968—A Case Study in Intellectual Failure," paper presented at the Project '87 Conference on the American Constitutional System under Strong and Weak Parties, Williamsburg, Virginia, April 27-28, 1979. See also Everett C. Ladd, Jr., *Where Have All the Voters Gone? The Fracturing of America's Political Parties* (New York: Norton, 1978).

[29] Anthony Lewis, *New York Times*, November 27, 1960, quoted in Sorauf, *Party Politics*, p. 247. The term "gerrymander" was, of course, coined to describe a district allegedly drawn in the shape of a salamander by Massachusetts Governor Elbridge Gerry in 1812. Interestingly enough, Governor Gerry was not responsible for this original gerrymander. The governor was apparently opposed to what he considered an inequitable redistricting plan but signed the legislature's districting bill into law because he believed that the governor could not properly oppose the state legislature on such matters. See Robert G. Dixon, *Democratic Representation* (New York: Oxford University Press, 1968), p. 459.

[30] David Mayhew, "Congressional Representation: Theory and Practice in Drawing the Districts," in Nelson Polsby (ed.), *Reapportionment in the 1970s* (Berkeley and Los Angeles: University of California Press, 1971), especially pp. 281-284.

Whether the means employed is organization of electorates or organization of their decisions, governments have the capacity to manipulate electoral outcomes. This capacity, again, is not absolute. Electoral arrangements conceived to be illegitimate may prompt some segments of the electorate to seek other ways of participating in political life. Moreover, no electoral system that provides universal and equal suffrage can, by itself, long prevent an outcome favored by large popular majorities. Yet faced with opposition short of an overwhelming majority, governments' ability to manipulate the translation of individual choices into collective decisions can be an important factor in preserving the established distribution of power.

INSULATION OF
DECISION-MAKING PROCESSES

Virtually all governments attempt at least to partially insulate decision-making processes from electoral intervention. The most obvious forms of insulation are the confinement of popular election to only some governmental agencies, various modes of indirect election, and lengthy tenure in office. In the United States, of course, the framers of the Constitution intended that only members of the House of Representatives be subject to direct popular selection. The president and senators were to be indirectly elected for rather long terms to allow them, as the *Federalist* put it, to avoid "an unqualified complaisance to every sudden breeze of passion; or to every transient impulse which the people may receive."[31]

Somewhat less obvious are the insulating effects of electoral arrangements that permit direct, and even frequent, popular election of public officials but tend to fragment or disaggregate the impact of elections upon the government's composition. In the United States, for example, the Constitutional provision of staggered terms of service in the Senate was designed to diminish the impact of shifts in electoral

---

[31] Earle, *The Federalist*, no. 71, p. 464.

sentiment upon the Senate as an institution. Since only one-third of its members were to be selected at any given point in time, the composition of the institution would be partially protected from changes in electoral preferences. This would avoid what the *Federalist* called "mutability in the public councils arising from a rapid succession of new members."[32]

The division of the nation into relatively small, geographically based constituencies for the purpose of selecting members of the House of Representatives was, in part, designed to have a similar effect. Representatives were to be chosen frequently. However, the fact that each was to be selected by a discrete constituency was thought by Madison and others to diminish the government's vulnerability to shifts in the national mood or, in particular, to any mass popular movements that might arise. In a sense, the House of Representatives was compartmentalized in the same way that a submarine is divided into watertight sections to confine the impact of any damage to the vessel. First, the geographic particularization of the national electorate would increase the salience of local issues by granting local opinion its own national representative. Second, the salience of local issues would mean that a representative's electoral fortunes would be more nearly tied to factors peculiar to his or her own district than to the public's response to national issues. Third, given a geographical principle of representation, the formation of national policy majorities was conceived to be less likely than the formation of local majorities that might or might not share common underlying dimensions. No matter how well-represented individual constituencies might be, the aggregate influence of constituents on national policy questions would be fragmented. In Madison's terms, the influence of "faction" would thus become "less likely to pervade the whole body than some particular portion of it."[33]

Another example of an American electoral arrangement that tends to fragment the impact of mass elections upon the government's

---

[32] *Ibid.*, no. 62, p. 405.

[33] *Ibid.*, no. 10, p. 62.

composition is the Australian ballot.[34] Prior to the introduction of the official ballot in the 1890s, voters cast ballots composed by the political parties. Each party printed its own ballots, listed only its own candidates for each office, and employed party workers to distribute its ballots at the polls. This ballot format had two important consequences. First, the party ballot precluded secrecy in voting. Because each party's ballot was distinctive in size and color it was not difficult for party workers to determine how individuals intended to vote. This, of course, facilitated the intimidation and bribery of voters. Second, the format of the ballot virtually prevented split-ticket voting. Because only one party's candidates appeared on any ballot, it was very difficult for a voter to cast anything other than a straight party vote, unless, of course, he happened to bring scissors and paste to the polls with him.

The official "Australian" ballot represented a significant change in electoral procedure. The new ballot was prepared and administered by the state rather than the parties. Each ballot was identical and included the names of all candidates for office. This reform, of course, increased the secrecy of voting and reduced the possibility for voter intimidation and bribery. Because all ballots were identical in appearance, even the voter who had been threatened or bribed might still vote as he wished, without the knowledge of party workers. But, perhaps even more important, the Australian ballot reform made it possible for voters to make their choices on the basis of the individual rather than the collective merits of the candidates. Because all candidates for the same office now appeared on the same ballot, voters were no longer forced to choose a straight party ticket. It was, indeed, the introduction of the Australian ballot that gave rise to the phenomenon of split-ticket voting in American elections.[35]

---

[34] For an analysis of the impact of the Australian ballot, see Jerrold G. Rusk, "The Effect of the Australian Ballot Reform on Split Ticket Voting: 1876-1908," *American Political Science Review* 64 (December 1970): 1220-1238. See also Converse, "American Electorate"; Burnham, "Voting Research"; and Converse, "Comment on Burnham."

[35] The Australian ballot reform should be seen as a "permissive" reform. It obviously

It is this second consequence of the Australian ballot reform that tends to fragment the impact of American elections upon the government's composition. Prior to the reform of the ballot it was not uncommon for an entire incumbent administration to be swept from office and replaced by an entirely new set of officials. In the absence of a real possibility of split-ticket voting, any desire on the part of the electorate for change could be expressed only as a vote against all candidates of the party in power. Because of this, there always existed the possibility, particularly at the state and local levels, that an insurgent slate committed to policy change could be swept into power. A single popular insurgent could carry an entire new administration into office with him. The party ballot thus increased the potential impact of elections upon the government's composition. In the absence of ticket splitting, popular voting was more likely to produce a new administration controlling enough public offices to be in a position to effect significant changes in public policy. Though this potential may not always have been realized, the party ballot at least increased the chance that electoral decisions could lead to policy changes.

Because it permitted choice on the basis of candidates' individual appeals, the Australian ballot lessened the likelihood that the electorate would sweep an entirely new administration into power. Ticket splitting meant that the outcome of elections came increasingly to be divided partisan control of government. In the state of New York, for example, until very recent years voters had the opportunity to individually elect seven executive officers: governor, lieutenant governor, secretary of state, attorney general, state treasurer, state comptroller, and state engineer-surveyor. Staggered terms meant that the electorate seldom was asked to fill more than five of these positions in any one electoral year. Nevertheless, prior to the introduction of the Australian ballot, all the officials elected during any single point in time were invariably affiliated with the same party. Shifts in partisan control affected all available offices simultaneously. In 1893,

---

did not cause split-ticket voting. Rather, the Australian ballot merely facilitated ticket splitting relative to voting a straight party ticket.

for example, all five executive positions at stake in the election shifted from Democratic to Republican hands. This state of affairs gradually began to change after the introduction of the Australian ballot in 1895. In 1902, a Democratic attorney general was elected alongside a Republican treasurer, secretary of state, and lieutenant governor. In 1907, a Republican governor was elected at the same time that all six of the other executive posts were won by Democrats. This pattern of divided executive control became commonplace during the next decade and is the norm in contemporary New York politics.

Taken together, regulation of the electorate's composition, regulation of the translation of voters' choices into electoral decisions, and regulation of the impact of those decisions upon the government's composition allow those in power a measure of control over the consequences of mass participation in political life. These techniques do not necessarily have the effect of diminishing citizens' capacity to influence their rulers' conduct. In the democracies, at least, these techniques are generally used to influence electoral influence. They permit governments a measure of control over what citizens will decide that governments should do. Perhaps the most clear-cut illustration is personal registration in the United States. Registration requirements do not diminish the impact of electoral decisions. Rather, they influence the types of decisions that the electorate is likely to make. Though those decisions may, in turn, affect the government's behavior, their shape and content have been subject to prior manipulation. Similarly, regulation of the translation of voters' choices into collective electoral decisions cannot clearly be said to limit electoral influence. This form of regulation, instead, acts to channel the force of electoral influence itself into directions favorable to those in power.

As we noted previously, governments are often not completely free to establish whatever electoral rules they might wish. Electoral procedures generally conceived to be illegitimate can threaten to induce citizens to seek alternative forms of political expression. Election law in the democracies, moreover, can seldom by itself prevent outcomes favored by overwhelming majorities. But within these limits, even rulers who must dutifully bow to the voice of the people can take a hand in determining what that voice will tell them.

THE LIMITS OF ELECTORAL INTERVENTION

Whatever the precise character of the legal constraints, however, the substitution of elections for spontaneous forms of political activity inherently delimits mass intervention into governmental and policy-making processes. Elections limit to occasional voting what might otherwise amount to direct mass intervention into or resistance to administrative and policymaking processes. There is no doubt that voting can have implications for a government's actions. Democratic elections may permit citizens to select officials who represent their own interests and viewpoints. A fear of electoral reprisal may at times induce those in power to take account of citizens' policy preferences. It might, indeed, appear peculiar to suggest that an institution that permits citizens to select representatives and to hold officials accountable limits mass political intervention.

Yet these very concepts of representation and accountability that are central to democratic electoral institutions exemplify precisely the limited scope of electoral intervention into the governmental process. These concepts denote an indirect relationship between popular participation and governmental decision making. Popular acceptance of the doctrines of electoral representation and accountability itself constitutes popular acceptance of constraints upon political participation. Indeed, it is chiefly in order to induce citizens to accept limited participation that even dictatorial governments are often so careful to link voting with representation.[36] There is more than a grain of truth to Rousseau's observation that the moment a people agrees to the substitution of representation for participation it surrenders its political freedom.[37]

---

[36] On this point, see the excellent discussion in Nelson Polsby, "Legislatures," in Fred Greenstein and Nelson Polsby (eds.), *Handbook of Political Science* (Reading, Mass.: Addison-Wesley, 1975), vol. 5, pp. 257-303, especially p. 266. See also William Gamson's discussion of representation as cooptation in *Power and Discontent* (Homewood, Ill.: Dorsey Press, 1968), ch. 6. Also very revealing is the statement by a Soviet legislator in Vikenty Narbutovich, "How I Became a Legislator," in Theodore J. Lowi and Randall B. Ripley (eds.), *Legislative Politics, USA* (Boston: Little, Brown, 1973), pp. 90-94.

[37] Jean Jacques Rousseau, *The Social Contract*, trans. and ed. by G.D.H. Cole (New York: E.P. Dutton, 1950), p. 94.

First, elections limit the scope of mass political intervention to leadership selection. Voters do not directly participate in policy-making. Only in occasional referenda at the state and local levels do Americans vote for policies. Of course, leadership selection can serve as an indirect form of policy selection. Voters may conceivably base their choices on candidates' stands on important national issues or attempt to reward and punish incumbents on the basis of their records on major questions of public policy. But even though the electorates' choice of leaders can have policy implications, this indirect relationship between popular voting and the governments' behavior is usually tenuous and ambiguous.

It is often quite difficult for voters to identify whatever policy differences may exist among opposing candidates for office. Even at the national presidential level, where candidate positions might be expected to be most visible, the electorate appears to have considerable difficulty distinguishing the candidates' stands on major issues.[38]

In 1972, for example, a year when the candidates exhibited unusually sharp differences on many public issues, voters' perceptions of the differences between Nixon and McGovern did not always accord with the candidates' actual positions. According to Page, Nixon and McGovern differed considerably more on womens' rights, taxes, and pollution—and less on marijuana and busing—than the public was aware.[39] In 1968, when the war in Vietnam was an issue of

---

[38] The question of "issue voting" has received a good deal of attention in recent years. See Richard W. Boyd, "Popular Control of Public Policy," *American Political Science Review* 66 (1972): 429-449; Benjamin Page and Richard A. Brody, "Policy Voting and the Electoral Process," *ibid.*, pp. 979-995; Arthur H. Miller, Warren E. Miller, Alden S. Raine, and Thad A. Brown, "A Majority Party in Disarray," *ibid.* 70 (1976): 753-778; Gerald M. Pomper, "From Confusion to Clarity: Issues and American Voters," *ibid.* 66 (1972): 415-428; David Repass, "Issue Salience and Party Choice," *ibid.* 65 (1971): 389-400; and John L. Sullivan and Robert E. O'Conner, "Electoral Choice and Popular Control of Public Policy," *ibid.* 66 (1972): 1256-1268. See also V.O. Key, *The Responsible Electorate* (Cambridge, Mass.: Harvard University Press, 1966); and Robert Erikson and Norman R. Luttbeg, *American Public Opinion* (New York: Wiley, 1973). For an interesting discussion of the different forms that a relationship between electoral preferences and public policy might take, see Robert Weissberg, *Public Opinion and Popular Government* (Englewood Cliffs, N.J.: Prentice-Hall, 1976), chs. 5 and 8.

[39] Benjamin I. Page, *Choices and Echoes in Presidential Elections* (Chicago: University of Chicago Press, 1978), p. 95.

overwhelming importance to most voters, the electorate was confused and divided over where the major candidates stood. Fifty-seven percent saw no difference between Nixon and Humphrey on Vietnam policy; 26 percent believed that Nixon was more "hawkish"; 17 percent saw Humphrey as the more hawkish of the two candidates.[40]

Part of the explanation of voters' inability to perceive policy differences between the candidates may simply be that candidates generally take similar positions. Some theories of electoral competition, of course, suggest that the strategies of both candidates in a two-candidate race usually lead them to adopt roughly equivalent issue positions.[41]

Another and perhaps more obvious explanation is that whatever the number of candidates in a race, contenders for office normally have strong incentives to make their issue positions as vague, ambiguous, and uncontroversial as possible.[42] Much of the subject matter of political debate consists of what Stokes has called "valence issues." That is, candidates often attempt to define their positions in such a way as to support courses of action that all voters very likely favor or, alternatively, to express their disapproval of matters clearly opposed by everyone.[43] In recent years, for example, all presidential aspirants have condemned inflation, unemployment, and poverty. Some candidates have espoused such notions as "peace with honor" or "law and order with justice." And every political hopeful has taken a firm stand against "corruption," just as, in earlier eras, candidates advocated "a chicken in every pot" or opposed the spread of "Communist totalitarianism." Presumably, few voters oppose the elimination of inflation, unemployment, or poverty. Only the most perverse members of the electorate, it might be assumed, would oppose a candidate for his or her firm stand against corruption. From the perspective of candidates for office, such positions are potentially attractive to all

---

[40] *Ibid.,* p. 181.

[41] See Anthony Downs, *An Economic Theory of Democracy* (New York: Harper and Row, 1957), especially Part II.

[42] Page, *Choices and Echoes,* ch. 6.

[43] Donald E. Stokes, "Spatial Models of Party Competition," in Angus Campbell *et al., Elections and the Political Order* (New York: Wiley, 1966), p. 170.

voters and at the same time are unlikely to alienate any potential source of support. Yet what is perfectly rational behavior on the part of candidates makes it virtually impossible for voters to use their ballots to affect the course of national policy. Where no alternatives are available, no choices can be made.

Second, elections limit the frequency of mass political intervention. Voters are involved in the political process, only occasionally leaving public officials free to govern without fear of popular intervention most of the time. In the United States, except under the most extraordinary circumstances, public officials have fixed and secure tenure in office for a set period of time. The purpose of a fixed term in office was very clearly stated by Alexander Hamilton in the *Federalist:*

> *The republican principle demands that the deliberate sense of the community should govern the conduct of those to whom they trust the management of their affairs; but it does not require an unqualified complaisance to every sudden breeze of passion; or to every transient impulse which the people may receive. . . . When occasions present themselves in which the interests of the people are at variance with their inclinations, it is the duty of the persons whom they have appointed to be the guardians of those interests to withstand the temporary delusion in order to give them time and opportunity for more cool and sedate reflection.*[44]

A fixed term allows public officials the opportunity to withstand the vicissitudes of public opinion and thereby the opportunity to make unpopular decisions. During officials' tenure in office they govern. The popularity of elected officials and public approval of their behavior ebb and flow between elections, but without directly affecting them.

It is, of course, true that the prospect of ultimate electoral recall may induce those in office to obey their constituents' wishes. But, given low levels of public awareness of the actual records of public officials and given the variety of other resources available to incum-

---

[44] Earle, *The Federalist,* no. 71, p. 464.

bents, even the threat of electoral defeat may not be enough to prompt them to work for programs desired by their constituents. For example, recent studies have suggested that the legislative records of incumbent congresspersons in the United States have only a slight effect upon their subsequent electoral fortunes.[45] Not only do voters appear to be little more than vaguely aware of representatives' legislative records, but also congresspersons themselves often engage in a number of activities designed to increase their electoral chances while obscuring their actual records in office. Mayhew's discussion of "advertising," "credit claiming," and "position taking" as congressional strategies is instructive in this context.[46]

Finally, by very virtue of the fact that elections make participation democratic, they diminish the intensity of mass political intervention. As I noted in Chapter 2, public facilitation of political activity can compensate for low levels of political interest, motivation, and knowledge. Given sufficient public facilitation, even individuals with little interest in the result will take part in political affairs. By the same token, public facilitation compensates for lack of intensity of preference. In the absence of public facilitation of political activity, "spontaneous" participants tend to exhibit clear and intense issue and policy preferences. For the most part, only those with relatively strong preferences will be sufficiently motivated to engage in political activity that they must initiate themselves.

If we examine, in Table 3.6, the attitudes of individuals who engage in political activities other than or in addition to voting, we see first that individuals who exhibit more intense preferences on public issues are more likely to participate in forms of political action that are not publicly facilitated.

Second, those who engage in forms of political action that are not publicly facilitated tend to cluster at the extremes of opinion on many

---

[45] On this point, see David R. Mayhew, *Congress: The Electoral Connection* (New Haven, Conn.: Yale University Press, 1974), ch. 1, especially pp. 28-49. See also Donald E. Stokes and Warren E. Miller, "Party Government and the Saliency of Congress," in Campbell *et al., Elections,* p. 199.

[46] Mayhew, *Congress,* ch. 1.

TABLE 3.6   *The relationship between intensity of preference and non-electoral participation.*

	Intensity		
	0	1-3	4-9
Participated in two or more non-electoral forms of political action	15.5%* (N = 45)	16.5% (N = 200)	28.2% (N = 936)

*That is, 15.5 percent of the least intense group engaged in two or more nonelectoral forms of political action. Intensity is defined in terms of the number of *strong* agreements or *strong* disagreements indicated by respondents in the 1960 Institute for Social Research survey to nine attitudinal questions. 1960 data were used because "strongly agree" and "strongly disagree" were dropped as response categories in subsequent Institute for Social Research election surveys.

public issues. The question of American policy in Vietnam in 1972 is an example. As Fig. 3.2 indicates, larger percentages of those favoring the more extreme Vietnam policy alternatives engaged in nonelectoral forms of political action than was true among those at the center of the opinion scale.[47]

In the absence of public facilitation, participation tends to be an expression of strongly held preferences. With public facilitation, even those individuals who are relatively indifferent or unmotivated often participate. By very virtue of the fact that they greatly expand mass political involvement, elections create more permissive constituencies, and help governments to claim popular acquiescence without necessarily imposing any particular constraints upon their actions. Indeed, political leaders have often exhibited some awareness of this potential. Both Bismarck and Disraeli, for example, were convinced that suffrage expansion would create more conservative electorates.[48] In an electorate, those with strong preferences are usually submerged by the

[47] For a similar line of argument, comparing the distribution of attitudes among voters with the attitudes of individuals who wrote letters to newspapers, see Aage R. Clausen, Philip E. Converse, and Warren E. Miller, "Electoral Myth and Reality: The 1964 Election," *American Political Science Review* 59 (June 1965): 321-332.

[48] Rokkan, *Citizens, Elections, Parties,* p. 31.

FIG. 3.2 *Percentage of respondents engaging in two or more nonelectoral forms of political action in 1972.*

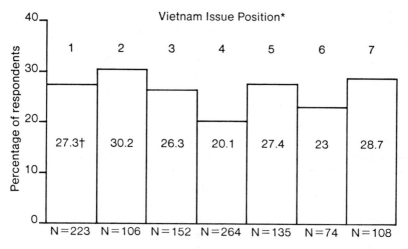

Vietnam Issue Position*

	1	2	3	4	5	6	7
	27.3†	30.2	26.3	20.1	27.4	23	28.7
	N=223	N=106	N=152	N=264	N=135	N=74	N=108

Percentage of respondents

* Scale position 1 indicates a preference for "immediate withdrawal" of American troops from Vietnam. Position 7 indicates a preference for a "complete military victory."

† That is, 27.3 percent of those favoring "immediate withdrawal" engaged in two or more nonelectoral forms of political action.

more apathetic majority. If balloting had occurred in 1776, for example, the American colonies would no doubt have remained part of the British Empire.

VOTING AND MASS POLITICAL INFLUENCE

Thus, while elections formalize and equalize, they can also delimit the potential for mass influence in political life. The character and effect of formal governmental control and manipulation of electoral processes varies from nation to nation and within any nation over time. As a number of observers have suggested, for example, the potential for mass influence associated with nineteenth-century American electoral arrangements was, in several respects, greater than may be true in the twentieth century. The introduction of personal registration, the Australian ballot, and as we shall see, the direct primary at the turn of the century enhanced the state's capacity at least to influence, if not to diminish, the impact of mass participation.[49] Yet whatever the precise character of prevailing electoral arrangements, by comparison with spontaneous or privately organized modes of political action, voting is *inherently* limited in scope, frequency, and intensity. The assumption often implicit in discussions of popular influence through elections is that democratic electoral processes create a possibility of mass influence where none would otherwise exist. But it is against the backdrop of electoral limits on mass political intervention that the potential for popular influence through elections must be assessed.

Whether the influence that citizens can exert through electoral means is greater or less than the possibilities associated with more informal modes of political action very likely depends upon the state's military and administrative power. As we noted earlier, it is undoubtedly true that the potential for popular influence through democratic electoral institutions is greater than the influence available to citizens ruled by a dictatorship sufficiently powerful to stifle dissent and suppress opposition. In this type of situation informal modes of political action would presumably be foreclosed or ineffective.

But because elections themselves formally delimit mass political action, where the state lacks the capacity to forcibly eliminate dissent and disobedience the potential for popular influence through informal means might well be greater than the possibilities stemming from voting. In this type of case, elections may formally delimit popular influence that the state could not otherwise forcibly contain.

Some empirical support for this view can be obtained if we re-examine the patterns of national welfare expenditures that we analyzed earlier. We saw then that welfare spending in electorally rigged and

---

[49] The theme of electoral demobilization runs through Burnham's most provocative essays. See Burnham, "The Changing Shape," "Party Systems and the Political Process," in Chambers and Burnham, *The American Party System,* and *Critical Elections,* especially chs. 5, 6, and 7. For criticisms, see Converse, "American Electorate."

irregular nations appeared to vary inversely with the size of national internal security forces, while those in the electorally competitive nations did not. As I noted, however, despite these differences in the correlates of welfare spending, the actual proportions of gross national product spent on welfare in the three groups of nations overlapped. As a number of other studies have also suggested, dictatorships and democracies do not necessarily differ in their average expenditures on social welfare programs.[50]

Against this backdrop, however, if we compare the three classes of nations while taking account of the propensity of welfare spending in the electorally rigged and irregular groups to vary with the size of national internal security establishments, a striking pattern begins to emerge. Table 3.7 indicates that, on the average, the proportion of gross national product spent on health and education by the electorally competitive nations is greater than that spent by the authoritarian regimes with relatively large internal security forces. But at the same time, average social welfare expenditures by the democracies are generally smaller than those of the electorally rigged and irregular regimes whose internal security establishments rank in the smallest 20 percent.

Welfare spending certainly cannot be taken to be a fully satis-factory measure of popular influence. Nevertheless, to the extent that welfare spending offers at least some indication of governments' responsiveness to their citizens' needs, these findings provide a measure of empirical support for my argument. Welfare spending by the democracies is, on the average, greater than spending by the authoritarian regimes that rank relatively high in their capacity to forcibly suppress dissent and opposition. Yet those authoritarian governments with a more limited capacity to forcibly compel obedience appear to exhibit, on the basis of one indicator at least, a responsive-ness to their citizens' needs that is greater than or equal to that of the electorally competitive nations. It would, of course, be inappropriate

---

[50] See Frederick L. Pryor, *Public Expenditures in Communist and Capitalist Nations* (Homewood, Ill.: Irwin, 1968). See also Harold L. Wilensky, *The Welfare State and Equality* (Berkeley and Los Angeles: University of California Press, 1975), especially ch. 2.

TABLE 3.7 *Average social welfare expenditures in dictatorships and democracies.*

	Mean % of National GNP Spent On	
	Education	Health
Electorally rigged nations with relatively large internal military forces (N = 18)	3.5	2.2
Electorally irregular nations with relatively large internal military forces (N = 21)	3.1	1.7
Electorally competitive nations (N = 27)	3.8	2.1
Electorally rigged nations with relatively small internal military forces (N = 5)	3.7	3.2
Electorally irregular nations with relatively small internal military forces (N = 5)	4.5	2.2

to conclude solely on the basis of this evidence that popular influence in electorally competitive nations is definitely less than that exhibited by the weaker authoritarian states. Yet the pattern of findings is quite consistent with the argument that elections can delimit mass influence in political life. Where the state, for one reason or another, lacks the ability to compel obedience and suppress opposition, the potential for mass influence through informal mechanisms may be greater than that which would result from voting.

A concrete illustration of the limited potential of elections compared with more spontaneous modes of mass political action can be drawn even from recent American history. The expansion of black voting opportunities during the 1960s is sometimes thought to have helped bring about important improvements in the lives of black Americans. It is true that the economic and material well-being of blacks in the United States improved somewhat during the 1960s. It is certainly the case that a variety of pieces of federal legislation such as the Economic Opportunity Act of 1964 and the equal employment opportunity provisions of the 1964 Civil Rights Act seemed to promise significant economic benefits to blacks. Nevertheless, it is probably the case that such federal programs and whatever benefits they produced should be seen primarily as responses to violent or disorderly modes of political action on the part of blacks—sit-ins, demonstrations, and riots—rather than as effects of black participation at the polls.

Figure 3.3 reports, over time, black voter registration in the southern states, the number of black elected officials in the United States, the number of instances per year of black protest activity, black family income, and the number of federal statutes enacted for the benefit of blacks between 1955 and 1977.[51] During the 1960s, black voter registration—primarily in the South—increased dramatically; at the same time, the incidence of more disruptive and violent forms of political action by blacks also increased sharply. Coincident with these increases in both formal and informal modes of political activity, blacks scored substantial economic gains and legislative successes. After the 1960s, however, black involvement in riots, demonstrations, and the like abated. Although blacks continued to vote in relatively large numbers and, indeed, began to elect a fairly large number of public officials, black legislative success dwindled. As voting came to supplant more violent and disorderly modes of political action on the part of blacks, federal policy began to shift in the direction of "benign neglect." Albeit less markedly, the relative economic position of blacks also began to deteriorate.

Though the American government may have possessed the military and police capacity to suppress black protest during the

---

[51] The black to white median family income ratio is reported by U.S. Department of Commerce, Bureau of the Census, "The Social and Economical Status of the Black Population" (Washington, D.C.: U.S. Government Printing Office, 1978), p. 31 and 1979 supplement. Data on the annual incidence of riots and demonstrations by blacks between 1955 and 1972 are compiled in the New York City Public Library's Schomburg Collection under the heading "The Civil Rights Movement (National Media)." Black voter registration figures from 1955 to 1968 are drawn from Converse, "American Electorate." Data for 1972 and 1976 are reported by U.S. Department of Commerce, Bureau of the Census, "Black Population," p. 145. The number of black elected officials in the United States is reported in *ibid.*, p. 143. The graphic depiction of the number of major pieces of federal legislation designed to benefit blacks is based on a count of all newly enacted federal statutes pertaining to civil rights or economic opportunity cited by the *Congressional Quarterly Almanac* during each year between 1957 and 1976 (Washington, D.C.: Congressional Quarterly Service).

FIG. 3.3 *Voting, protest, and mass influence in politics: the case of civil rights.*

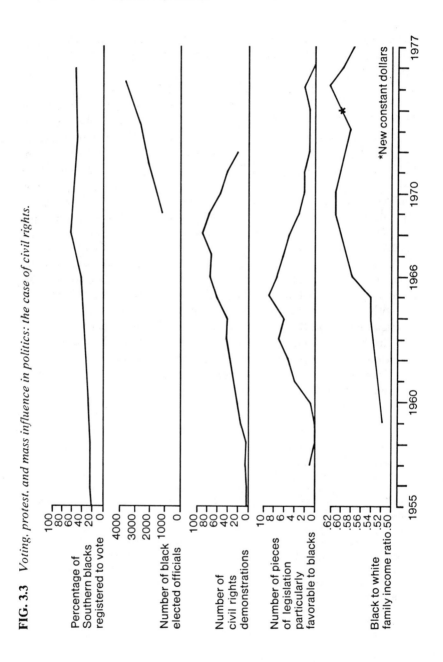

1960s, the costs would certainly have been enormous. And fortunately, the government had neither the ability nor the will to fully employ the force ostensibly at its disposal. But the right to vote may, in effect, have helped to delimit what the state could not forcibly contain.

Neither the experience of blacks over the past two decades of American history nor the contrast between welfare expenditures in democracies and weak dictatorships means that citizens can exert no influence through democratic electoral processes. Surely they can. Moreover, it may well be that influence through informal modes of political action cannot be maintained for long. Eventually, perhaps, spontaneous and privately organized forms of action and opposition give way to a political passivity that permits those in power to rule without interference. Yet spontaneous forms of political activity can, under some circumstances, be more effective than voting, And it is the introduction or expansion of the suffrage itself that often has the effect of reducing the threat of mass disruption and paving the way for political quiescence.

ELECTIONS AND THE ACQUISITION OF POLITICAL POWER

★★★

Closely related to elections' consequences for popular influence over those in power are their implications for the acquisition of power itself. Democratic elections provide a formal means through which insurgents may challenge and perhaps displace established rulers. Moreover, elections permit ordinary citizens to play formal roles in the process of leadership succession. Nevertheless, precisely because they do institutionalize access to power and citizens' influence over leadership selection, elections can constrain and delimit both.

In the democracies elections are taken to be the principle means through which insurgents can challenge and depose existing rulers. But, of course, the possibility of such challenges, as well as popular influence over their outcomes, long antedate the emergence of democratic electoral practices. All ruling groups eventually give way to new ones. Not only do age and death continually take their toll of any ruling elite, but social, political, and economic transformations inevitably lead to the decline of established ruling groups and the emergence of successors. In what has become a famous passage, Mosca once noted: "As soon as there is a shift in the balance of political forces . . . then the manner in which the ruling elite is constituted changes also. If a new source of wealth develops in a society, if the practical importance of knowledge grows, if an old religion declines or a new one is born, if a new current of ideas spreads, then, simultaneously, far-reaching dislocations occur in the ruling class."[1] And not infrequently, the masses have played a part in at least hastening these "dislocations." From the urban plebs and the peasants who dismantled the *ancien regime* in France to the rioters who ousted the Shah and installed Khomeini in Iran, the attitudes and behavior of the masses have often been decisive factors in the transformation of ruling elites.

Once again, elections do not bring into being processes that would otherwise never occur. Elections provide neither the sole opportunity for new groups to challenge those in power nor the only possibility that the wishes and actions of the masses will influence the outcome. Instead, elections socialize and institutionalize what might

---

[1] Gaetano Mosca, *The Ruling Class* (New York: McGraw-Hill, 1939), p. 65.

otherwise occur informally and perhaps violently as insurrection, rebellion, or revolution.

The availability of formal channels does not ensure their use by groups competing for power. Electoral mechanisms often fail to gain full acceptance from all of a government's opponents. And, of course, those who hold power are occasionally loath to part with it merely because of a setback at the polls. When elections are first introduced into a nation's politics the probability that insurgents will use them, like the chance that incumbents will permit them to be fairly used, often depends upon the existence of some rough balance of force between government and opposition. As I noted earlier, those in power are generally more tolerant of electoral opposition if they are not certain of their own capacity to suppress their enemies by force. At the same time, insurgents are more likely to at least experiment with the electoral route if they are uncertain of their own ability to forcibly achieve their aims. For example, the decision of some nineteenth-century European socialist parties to embrace parliamentary tactics, as well as their conservative adversaries' inclination to permit them to do so, was related to mutual uncertainty of the consequences of more violent forms of political struggle. So long as insurgents cannot be sure of their capacity to seize power by force, the formal opportunity to acquire at least a measure of power through elections, coupled with severe sanctions against the alternatives, can be quite persuasive. Indeed, this carrot and stick are generally joined even in contemporary politics. In the United States, for example, the authorities are seldom amused by even the most far-fetched plot to forcibly overthrow the government, yet candidates of the electoral opposition can receive subsidies from the public treasury.

Over time, the availability of elections and the habituation of citizens to their use inhibits mass support for the forms of political action often required for nonelectoral bids for power. It is the availability of elections that, at least in part, explains why revolutionary movements normally attract so little popular enthusiasm in the democracies. Moreover, the same socialization processes that teach the masses the virtues of voting can have an even greater impact upon the beliefs of elites. Political elites, after all, generally have had the benefit of considerably more civic education than the masses, both in school and during the course of their adult lives. Within the American political elite, for example, attachment to the electoral rules of the game is generally much stronger than in the public at large.[2] In a nation like the United States, with an electoral tradition of long standing, the possibility of bidding for power through forcible means probably does not occur to most politicians. Even over the long term, the existence of democratic electoral processes does not absolutely guarantee that all groups will limit themselves to campaigning for votes. Revolutionary movements that abjure the electoral path are not unknown in the Western democracies. And even when competitors for office have learned to use elections, differences of principle or interest may become so compelling that the electoral losers will not accept the verdict of the ballot box. It was Lincoln's electoral victory in 1860, after all, that sparked the American Civil War. Yet, where formal electoral procedures are open, competitors for power normally have strong incentives to take advantage of them. And as a result, elections can transform leadership succession from a spontaneous or privately organized and often violent process to a formal and routine public function.

This transformation has at least four important consequences that to some extent parallel those we observed in the previous chapter. First, the creation of a formal route to political office means that the state's power can be acquired without having to be overcome. In the absence of elections or other formal mechanisms, the possibility that groups outside the ruling circle can displace established leaders is inversely related to the state's power. In general, the larger and better organized the state's military and administrative apparatus, the less the likelihood that those who command it can be removed from office. Certainly, autocrats who command a powerful and loyal military machine are more difficult to dislodge than their militarily impotent colleagues. Elections separate the state's power from rulers'

---

[2] For example, see Samuel Stouffer, *Communism, Conformity and Civil Liberties* (New York: Wiley, 1966). See also Robert Weissberg, *Political Learning, Political Choice and Democratic Citizenship* (Englewood Cliffs, N.J.: Prentice-Hall, 1974), pp. 132-133.

capacity to retain it. The capabilities of the armed forces commanded by rulers subject to democratic election normally have little bearing upon leaders' chances for remaining in office. Elections permit new groups to displace those holding power even when the power in question could itself not be successfully opposed. And by the same token, where democratic elections are available, those who aspire to rule need not seek to weaken or destroy the power of the very government they hope to lead.

Second, democratic elections permit ordinary citizens to play a routine and peaceful role in the process of leadership selection. Of course, even in the absence of elections or other formal mechanisms, the outcomes of struggles over office and power can be influenced by the public's actions. But for reasons we have already discussed, only in the electoral context is "mass participation" likely to fully reflect mass opinion. Even the most popular of popular uprisings, for example, typically involves only a small and unrepresentative fraction of a nation's population. The ballot allows all citizens a formal opportunity to select, from among those competing for office, the individuals or groups whose perspectives they believe to be most compatible with their own. It may often prove difficult for voters to accurately assess the views of the various contenders. Nevertheless, the opportunity to choose among alternative candidates and perhaps to replace those in office with a more congenial crowd can be a significant source of mass influence in the governmental process. During the course of American political history, at least, the mass electorate's ability to effect large-scale changes in the composition of the ruling political elite has had upon occasion enormous consequences for government and policy.

The opportunity for routine mass involvement, taken together with the possibility allowed insurgents to acquire power without having to overcome it, distinguish democratic elections from virtually all other forms of leadership selection. By no means the least important implication of the difference between elections and other forms of succession is that democratic elections permit insurgents to challenge even the most powerful rulers and allow the masses to influence the outcome, without the violence and disorder that might otherwise characterize political competition. Indeed, it is especially against the backdrop of the suffering and misery that so often result from struggles for political power that the possibility of peaceful electoral leadership transitions is so significant.

At the same time, however, this possibility of nonviolent leadership change is not without its price. We saw in the preceding chapter that by socializing and institutionalizing the role of the masses, elections can constrain popular influence in politics. In a very similar manner, the creation of an institutional mechanism for the acquisition of power may permit rulers to establish regulations and conditions limiting access by new groups. Often, access to public office via elections is confined to membership in a representative body that, at best, shares power with other units of government not subject to popular election. Typically, formal but limited access is introduced by governments severely threatened by insurgent challenges, first as a way of formally delimiting what rulers find themselves unable to forcibly contain and second to help protect the power structure by coopting potentially dangerous opponents. But even where electoral access to most significant governmental agencies is possible, a variety of formal rules and conditions may still have an impact upon the character of contests for public office and the capacity of the masses to influence their outcomes. In twentieth-century American politics the most important such rules are those affecting party organization. The full potential for mass electoral influence over the acquisition of power can seldom be realized without organization. In a politics without parties, as V. O. Key pointed out some years ago, there exists little basis for "effectuation of the popular will."[3] Organization is an essential ingredient for effective electoral competition by groups lacking substantial economic or institutional resources. Party building has typically been a strategy pursued by groups that must organize the collective energies and resources of large numbers of individuals to counter their opponents' superior material means or institutional standing. The declining role of parties in twentieth-century American politics has undoubtedly not only served to diminish the capacity of

---

[3] V.O. Key, *Southern Politics* (New York: Random House, Vintage Books, 1949), ch. 14.

mass electorates to determine by whom they will be ruled, but also lessened the opportunity for subordinate groups to acquire political power. What is significant in the present context is that, at least in some measure, this decline of party can be traced back to a number of institutional changes in the American electoral process, especially including the direct primary and civil service reform, aimed specifically at regulating access to power and reducing mass intervention into political life. Again, precisely because they do institutionalize the means through which insurgents may challenge established rulers, elections can help to formally delimit both access to power and mass influence over the succession process.

Even beyond the question of legal and institutional limits on access to power, however, elections are in some respects inherently conservative institutions. The decline of party may serve to exacerbate the conservative consequences of elections. But elections, fundamentally, tend more to reflect than affect the distribution of power in society. Though votes may be equally distributed, the resources needed to acquire them seldom are. Effective electoral competition requires substantial economic, institutional, or organizational means that only a small number of individuals and groups can muster. At the same time, the substitution of voting for more spontaneous forms of mass political action inhibits the often violent forms of political activity that may unfortunately play an important compensatory role for groups lacking economic or institutional resources. Rather than create a mechanism through which those without power can acquire it, formal electoral processes instead generally allow those who possess social or economic power to maintain or acquire political authority.

ACCESS AND THE STATE'S POWER

In the absence of elections or other formal mechanisms, the likelihood that established rulers can be successfully opposed by new groups is generally a matter of insurgents' ability to forcibly overcome the state's power. Where rulers command powerful and loyal military or internal security forces and an efficient administrative apparatus, they have little to fear from external challenges, though perhaps a shift in power within the ruling circle may remain a possibility. Where, on the other hand, the military forces at the disposal of the established government are weak, or their loyalty and morale uncertain, whatever insurgent challenges may arise are more likely to pose a threat to the regime.

Traditional autocratic governments are often surprisingly vulnerable to violent overthrow. Armed insurrection in the streets of the capital by insurgents with sufficient resolve and organization may be all that is required to depose a regime with a relatively narrow base of support.[4] Indeed, the morale and loyalty of the troops commanded by such governments is often so weak that relatively little violence is needed to persuade them to abandon the struggle. The classic illustration is, of course, Trotsky's account of the manner in which revolutionary mobs in the streets of St. Petersburg were able to win the support of at least some of the troops sent to disperse them.[5] Or, to take a more recent example, the military force commanded by the government of Iran's Shah managed only token resistance before giving up the struggle and in some cases joining the fight against their former ruler.

It is often when they are most severely threatened by insurgent challenges that governments are most willing to open formal channels of access to power in an attempt to coopt the support of at least some of the regime's opponents. Typically, the government's moderate adversaries are offered a measure of power in the hope that this will help to avert a full seizure of control by more radical insurgents.[6] Thus the Shah of Iran belatedly handed partial control of the government to Shaipur Baktiar, a long-standing but relatively moderate foe

---

[4] Samuel Huntington, *Political Order in Changing Societies* (New Haven, Conn.: Yale University Press, 1968), chs. 1 through 7, offers many examples.

[5] Leon Trotsky, *The History of the Russian Revolution*, edited by F.W. Duppe (Garden City, N.Y.: Doubleday, 1959), especially chs. 7 and 8.

[6] See William Gamson, *Power and Discontent* (Homewood, Ill.: Dorsey Press, 1968), ch. 6. The examples are endless. In 1980, even the Union of South Africa announced a plan for black representation in the national legislature—a plan that, of course, did not envisage much real sharing of power. See John F. Burns, "South Africa's Whites Are Debating Plan to Share Power," *New York Times*, June 15, 1970.

of the regime, as part of an ultimately unsuccessful effort to avert the seizure of power by forces supporting Khomeini. A similar example is offered by the decision of Ian Smith's Rhodesian government to hold national elections designed to result in a regime at least nominally led by blacks. Under the terms of Smith's agreement with the election's eventual winner, Bishop Abel Muzorewa, and the other black participants, blacks were guaranteed 72 of the 100 legislative seats to be filled, though control of the army, police, judiciary, and civil service would remain in the hands of the white minority. The principal purpose of permitting black moderates at least some share in government was obviously to forestall a forcible seizure of full governmental power by the more radical black nationalists who had been engaged in guerilla warfare against the regime for a number of years. "The hope in Salisbury," as the *New York Times* put it, "is that the combination of a black-led government and sustained military pressure ultimately will persuade the insurgents to give up and accept the government's amnesty offer."[7] And had it not been for external factors, this hope might not have been disappointed.[8]

Of course, in some instances the state's power is sufficient to permit rulers to forcibly withstand challenges for very long periods of time. Protracted guerilla warfare, gradually weakening the state's military and administrative control, may persist for years before insurgents are able to decisively confront the forces loyal to the established regime and bring about a change of rule. The Chinese Communists, for example, fought Nationalist forces for almost 22 years before they were able to seize power. And obviously, in other cases attempts to acquire power by force ultimately prove futile. The world's prisons—and graveyards—contain their share of unsuccessful revolutionaries.

Democratic elections permit the state's power to be acquired by groups outside the existing ruling circle without the use of force.

---

[7] John F. Burns, "Ian Smith's Old Enemies Have Become Muzorewa's," *New York Times,* June 3, 1979.

[8] External factors of course included interested economic sanctions, political pressure, and a withdrawal of South African support.

Elections separate the state's power from rulers' capacity to retain it. And as a result, even rulers whose power could not successfully be forcibly opposed may be formally removed from office. A simple empirical illustration of this vitally important characteristic of democratic elections can be obtained by comparing the relationship between the incidence of leadership turnover and the size of national internal security forces in nations that do and nations that do not permit democratic electoral procedures. With the help, once again, of the *World Handbook of Political and Social Indicators,* all the nations for which data were available were divided into two groups— the first group consisting of those nations whose electoral practices the *World Handbook* deemed rigged or irregular and the second group consisting of nations that permit competitive elections.

In the first group of nations, the incidence of leadership turnover is inversely correlated with the size of national internal security forces. The relationship between the two variables is -0.12 (N $= 44$). This negative association suggests that as the state's power increases, at least as measured by its internal security apparatus, the likelihood that national leaders will be removed from office is diminished. In those nations, on the other hand, which the *World Handbook* classifies as possessing competitive elections, no correlation exists between the size of national internal security forces and the incidence of leadership turnover. Leadership transitions in these nations occur according to a prescribed formula, generally at set intervals. In nations lacking democratic electoral mechanisms, presumably national internal security forces can become sufficiently powerful to virtually rule out any possibility that groups outside the ruling elite can acquire power. Few leadership transitions can be expected to occur in Albania or Bulgaria or East Germany, for example. In the democracies, by contrast, governments can be toppled at the polls even if they command the most formidible internal military formations.

At the same time, in nations lacking democratic elections, the frequency with which leadership transitions do occur is positively correlated with the incidence of riots, demonstrations, and strikes. This association, reported by Table 4.1, is certainly suggestive of the means necessary to depose established rulers in the absence of democratic electoral procedures. In the democracies, again by con-

TABLE 4.1 *Leadership transitions and violent forms of political action in dictatorships and democracies—Pearson correlation coefficients.*

	Incidence of riots	Incidence of demonstrations	Incidence of strikes
Leadership transitions in nations lacking democratic elections (N = 44)	.33	.18	.36
Leadership transitions in nations with competitive electoral processes (N = 38)	−.02	−.06	−.05

trast, there would appear to be no relationship whatsoever between the frequency of leadership transitions and the incidence of violent forms of action. In the democracies, power can be acquired without having to be overcome.

POPULAR SELECTION OF LEADERS

Elections not only create a formal channel for the acquisition of political power, they also permit citizens a formal—and democratic—role in determining who will rule them. Of course, the results of contests for office and power are not determined solely by the actions of the electorate. The mass electorate becomes involved in the process of leadership selection only near its conclusion, when most of the hypothetical alternatives have already been eliminated. Nevertheless, the electorate's choices may still have important consequences for the composition and character of the ruling elite. In the United States, for example, "critical elections" have been associated with major changes in the social and demographic backgrounds of the groups in power.[9] Similarly, so-called ruralizing elections in new

[9] On the significance of critical elections for elite transformation, see David Brady, "Critical Elections, Congressional Parties, and Clusters of Policy Changes," paper presented at the Annual Meeting of the American Political Science Association, San

African and Asian nations replaced Westernized elites with leaders drawn from more parochial strata.[10]

The mass electorate's capacity to influence the composition of the ruling elite, however, is not important simply for its own sake. Instead, the public's capacity to help decide by whom it will be ruled is significant primarily for its potential impact upon administration and policy. It is sometimes thought that whatever influence citizens' views have in the policymaking process is mainly a function of officials' fear of reprisal at the polls. And, of course, elected officials must take some account of their constituents' wishes if they hope to remain in office. But the threat of reprisal is only one of the potential sources of electoral influence in public life. Obviously, the simple choice among alternative contenders for office can also have policy implications. Faced with a choice between one group of candidates favoring "balanced budgets" and another group espousing heavy spending on social programs, voters' decisions can be important. Or the electoral defeat of one set of officials by another group with different views, interests, and orientations might result in policy changes. The electorate's capacity to affect the composition of the ruling elite is potentially at least as important a source of influence over public affairs as officials' fear of reprisal at the polls. A variety of factors often combine to limit the impact of voters' choices. We discussed some of these in Chapter 3 and will examine some of the others later in this chapter. Yet in the course of American political history, the mass electorate's capacity to decide who would rule has, upon occasion, significantly affected political institutions and national policies. Voters' simple choices among alternative contenders for office can at times have profound consequences.

Francisco, California, September 1975. See also Michael R. King and Lester G. Seligman, "Critical Elections, Congressional Recruitment and Public Policy," in Heinze Eulau and Moshe Czudnowski (eds.), *Elite Recruitment in Democratic Politics* (New York: Halstead Press, 1976); and Barbara Deckard Sinclair, "Party Realignment and the Transformation of the Political Agenda," *American Political Science Review* 71 (September 1977): 940-953.

[10] On the concept of ruralizing elections, see Robert D. Putnam, *The Comparative Study of Political Elites* (Englewood Cliffs, N.J.: Prentice-Hall, 1976), p. 151.

The relationships between popular choices and public policy are obviously among the central questions of democratic politics. With the advent of survey research, these relationships have been the objects of intensive scrutiny. Though the techniques of survey analysis are essential for dealing with many important questions about the linkages between voting and policy, it is not true that all major problems in this area require survey data for an adequate solution. We shall first establish criteria for citizen policy choice that permit us to draw meaningful conclusions without interview data. Then, using data from party platforms, United States statutes, and aggregate voting statistics, we shall determine to what extent electoral choices in the United States have been translated into policy decisions over time.

VOTING AND PUBLIC POLICY

The absence of historical survey data precludes inferences about the reasons behind individuals' choices at the polls for all but the most recent periods. Our lack of information, however, does not make this decision any less of a choice. Whatever the preferences of voters, votes are, in effect, choices among alternatives. In the same sense that the behavior of consumers vitally affects the national economy whether or not consumers are completely aware of the differences among products, the decisions made by voters can have major policy consequences whether or not voters are fully aware of the implications of their actions.

If we concentrate on the consequences of voting behavior, two factors become particularly important. First, the potential consequences of popular voting are conditioned by the alternative policy positions represented by opposing candidates and parties. Given the presence of alternatives, the electorate makes at least implicit choices. If insurgent candidates offer policy alternatives substantially different from those defended by incumbents, electoral choices have the capacity to change national policy. In European political history, for example, the presence of radical alternatives offered the potential for change even when voters did not take advantage of these possibilities.

Second, voting behavior can directly affect public policy to the extent that winning candidates and parties are able to acquire sufficient control over the levers of government to implement policies based on their preelection positions. If sets of winning candidates are, in fact, able to implement policies consistent with their preelection positions, the electorate's implicit choices are translated into national policy.

Our principal clues about the historical relationships between voting behavior and public policy in the United States are suggested by the theory of critical elections. Seminal studies of American voting behavior conducted by V. O. Key and others suggest that during critical periods in American political history, major reorientations have occurred in the partisan attachments of large portions of the electorate.[11] The voter alignments established during these critical periods, 1798-1800, 1826-36, 1852-60, 1874-80, 1892-96, and 1928-36, support, over relatively long periods of time, the dominance in government of the victorious party.

Schattschneider, Burnham, and others have suggested that voter realignments involved choices about national policy.[12] During these critical eras, new groups penetrated or replaced one or the other of the two major parties, altered the terms of political conflict, and substantially increased the magnitude of choice available to voters.

---

[11] V.O. Key, "A Theory of Critical Elections," *Journal of Politics* 17 (February 1955): 3-18; Walter Dean Burnham, *Critical Elections and the Mainsprings of American Electoral Politics* (New York: Norton, 1970); Walter Dean Burnham, "Party Systems and the Political Process," in William N. Chambers and Walter Dean Burnham (eds.), *The American Party System* (New York: Oxford University Press, 1975). See also James Sundquist, *Dynamics of the Party System* (Washington, D.C.: Brookings Institution, 1973); Michael P. Rogin and John L. Shover, *Political Change in California* (Westport, Conn.: Greenwood, 1969); Paul Kleppner, *The Cross of Culture* (New York: Free Press, 1970); Michael Holt, *Forging a Majority* (New Haven, Conn.: Yale University Press, 1969); Samuel McSeveney, *The Politics of Depression* (New York: Oxford, 1972); Gerald Pomper, *Elections in America* (New York: Dodd, Mead, 1968), ch. 5; and Angus Campbell, "A Classification of Presidential Elections," in Angus Campbell *et al., Elections and the Political Order* (New York: Wiley, 1966).

[12] E.E. Schattschneider, *The Semi-Sovereign People* (New York: Holt, Rinehart and Winston, 1960).

In effect, insurgents offered the electorate policy alternatives substantially different from those favored by incumbents and thus allowed the electorate an opportunity to alter national policy. Changes in the substance of political alternatives, "redefinition of conflict," in Schattschneider's terms, forced voters to make new decisions and thus served as the proximate cause of voter realignment. The emergence of the Republican party in the 1850s, for example, resulted in redefinitions of partisan conflict to emphasize competing sectional rights. Populist control of the Democratic party in the 1890s presented the electorate with the opportunity to vote in favor of redistributions of economic rights in favor of small-scale agrarian enterprises.

To analyze the character of the alternatives available to voters over time, I have examined the content of American national party platforms.[13] The platform is, of course, a frequently maligned document. It is often said that platforms are never read by voters, are quickly forgotten by elected officials, and contain little besides vacuous generalizations. Oddly enough, however, platforms are frequently the objects of intense intraparty controversy and are, from time to time, taken seriously enough to be repudiated by candidates. Platform writing represents an occasion for party leaders and factions to attempt to come to terms with one another on the conditions for cooperation in the coming campaign. The completed platform is a symbolic contract among the party's major factions—a contract in which each important faction has stated the terms on which it has agreed to cooperate with the national party's campaign efforts. In 1980, for example, Kennedy agreed to support Carter's reelection bid only after Carter forces had agreed to Kennedy's platform demands. The platform is thus a serious statement of the actual preelection positions of the major factions that make up each party and, taken as

---

[13] I am aware that few voters read platforms. Platforms are employed as indicators of the general preelection positions of the two parties. Although some historical problems are raised, Democratic and Whig platforms were compared in 1844, 1848, and 1852. The source of party platforms was Kirk H. Porter and Donald B. Johnson (eds.), *National Party Platforms* (Urbana: University of Illinois Press, 1966), and 1968 supplement. See also Pomper, *Elections in America,* chs. 7 and 8, for a different form of analysis of party platforms.

a whole, can be read as a summary of the party's position on broad sets of issues. Moreover, though the platform is not especially intended to be read by voters, it is a public campaign statement. Platforms offer a general indication of the types of issues, alternatives, and promises that characterize each party's appeals to voters.

I have analyzed all (1844-1968) Democratic and Republican national party platforms, employing seven broad categories of issues.[14] Platforms were analyzed in terms of the following categories:

1. *Capitalism:* the aggregation of wealth and control over the distribution of wealth by business, financial, and mercantile elites.

2. *Internal sovereignty:* the exercise of power and increase of the sphere of action of the central government *vis-a-vis* states, localities, and individuals.

3. *Redistribution:* the reallocation of wealth in favor of the economically disadvantaged.

4. *International cooperation:* cooperation with and friendship toward other nations.

5. *Universalism:* the equality of rights and privileges for domestic minorities.

6. *Labor:* labor and labor organizations.

7. *Ruralism:* farms, farmers, and the rural way of life.

These categories were selected, in part, because of their inclusion of policy areas that have been important throughout American history. The categories were defined in such a manner as to permit the scoring of positive and negative advocacy statements. The unit of measure is the paragraph. A score indicates that within a given paragraph there occurred a statement or symbol of positive or

---

[14] For details see Benjamin Ginsberg, "Critical Elections and the Substance of Party Conflict: 1844 to 1968," *Midwest Journal of Political Science* 16 (November 1972): 603-625. See also Benjamin Ginsberg, "Elections and Public Policy," *American Political Science Review* 70 (March 1976): 41-49. Please note that the policy change coefficients reported in the present analysis differ slightly from those reported in "Elections and Public Policy." The present coefficients are correct. The corrections do not materially affect the conclusions presented in the earlier paper.

negative advocacy of the category as defined above. Thus the statement "We oppose federal interference in local affairs" would be considered a negative advocacy of internal sovereignty, that is, opposition to "the exercise of power and increase of the sphere of action of the central government" and scored as a negative mention of the category for the appropriate party and year.

Any given paragraph may receive a maximum of 14 scores—1 positive and 1 negative for each of the seven categories. In practice, because the platforms tend to be divided into relatively short, thematic paragraphs, the range tends to be 0 to 3 scores per paragraph. To compare platforms, absolute scores were converted into percentages based on N, the number of paragraphs. The rescoring of a sample of one-third of the platforms by a second coder resulted in a 0.94 overall level of agreement as determined by a standard intercoder reliability equation. The scores reported by the first coder were employed throughout.

To determine whether the scope of choice available to voters increases during critical eras, let us examine the scope of the alternatives presented to voters by the Democratic and Republican parties over time.

The degree of difference between the two parties on any issue involves at least two elements. The first element is the relative polarity of the parties' positions on the issue of dimension in question. Liberalism and conservatism, for example, define differential polarities of position along some issue dimensions. The second element defining the degree of difference between the two parties is the relative weight or importance assigned by the parties to the policy area in question. In those instances, for example, when the parties present differential polarities of position on some particular policy, given the expectation of relatively fixed budgets of money and time, they may also differ on the issue's salience or priority on the agenda of public policy. The total degree of difference between the two parties on any issue is a function of the interaction between differences of polarity and salience. The issue alternatives presented by opposing parties are conventionally said to be radically different, for example, when differences of polarity on issues are exacerbated by differences on the salience or priority of the issues.

In a hypothetical case, the Democratic and Republican parties might offer voters a choice both of differential issue polarities and of the importance to be assigned social welfare policy. The distance between the positions of the two parties, and thus the degree of choice available to voters on the issue, is a function of both the differential polarities and weights assigned the issue by the two parties. This total distance between the positions of the parties can be defined as the product of the two differences, or $P_D S_D$, where P_D equals the difference in polarity and S_D is equal to the difference in salience assigned the issue by the two parties.[15]

In any given year, the two parties may differ on a number of individual issues. The total degree of difference between the "bundles" of issue polarities and weights presented by the two parties defines the overall degree of choice available to voters. This total difference is defined as the sum of the products of the differing polarities and weights of the parties on each individual issue, or

$$\sum_{i=1}^{N} P_D S_D$$

The larger this overall difference, the greater the total distance between the bundles of issue positions presented voters by the two parties.

For any issue, the difference in polarity between the two parties is given by the percentage difference between the positive percentages of references to that issue by each party weighed by the total salience of the issue.[16]

---

[15] Every unit of difference in polarity is acted upon by a unit of difference in salience. We are, therefore, interested in the product of the two differences. Intensity and polarity cannot be summed in either a scalar or vector sense. The vector sum or Euclidean solution might be appropriate if the two independent variables were comparably measured and addable. Not only is this not the case, but my assumption is that the effects on the dependent variable are the results of a multiplicative interaction. Whether this assumption is correct depends upon whether my results are consistent with the hypothetical results.

[16] I assume that the magnitude of differences in polarity are, in part, related to the total importance of the issue.

Let:

$A =$ the proportion of positive references in the Democratic platform

$B =$ the proportion of negative references in the Democratic platform

$C =$ the proportion of positive references in the Republican platform

$D =$ the proportion of negative references in the Republican platform

Then, for any issue the difference in polarity, P_D, is equal to

$$\frac{AD - BC}{(A + B)(C + D)} \, [A + B + C + D]$$

The differential salience between the two parties on any issue, S_D, is given by

$$(A + B) - (C + D)$$

Then, the total distance between the positions of the two parties on any individual issue is given by $P_D S_D$. The overall distance between the positions of the two parties across issues is

$$\sum_{i=1}^{N} P_D S_D$$

Table 4.2 reports the overall distance between the issue positions of the two parties during each national election year from 1844 to 1968. Differences on each individual issue are reported by Table 4.3. For convenience, signs appearing on Table 4.3 always indicate the relative direction of Democratic polarity.[17]

---

[17] Signs indicate the polarity of the Democrats relative to the Republicans, not the absolute polarity of the Democratic position.

The data reported by Table 4.2 indicate that the overall degree of difference between the issue positions of the two parties has varied considerably over time. The greatest degrees of difference, though, are found during periods of voter realignment.

TABLE 4.2 *Overall differences of issue position between the national parties over time.*

Year	Degree of difference
1844	.016
1848	.177
1852	.292*
1856	.228*
1860	.111
1864	.118
1868	.132
1872	.029
1876	.017
1880	.075*
1884	.008
1888	.016
1892	.063
1896	.094*
1900	.080
1904	.063
1908	.018
1912	.054
1916	.028
1920	.009
1924	.031
1928	.007
1932	.069*
1936	.017
1940	.026
1944	.014
1948	.008
1952	.019
1956	.009
1960	.007
1964	.041
1968	.013

* Years of relatively large issue differences between the Republican and Democratic party platforms.

Extremely large issue differences occur throughout the Civil War and pre-Civil War periods, centering particularly around 1852 and 1856. Individual issue differences, reported by Table 4.3, indicate

TABLE 4.3 *Degrees of difference between the national parties over time.*

Year	Capital-ism	Internal sover-eignty	Redistri-bution	Interna-tional Coopera-tion	Univer-salism	Labor	Ruralism
1844	−.009	0	0	+.007	0	0	
1848	−.046	−.100	0	−.031	0	0	0
1852	−.050	−.239	0	−.001	−.002	0	0
1856	−.030	−.144	0	+.054	0	0	0
1860	0	−.023	0	−.059	−.029	0	0
1864	0	−.118	0	0	0	0	0
1868	−.018	−.084	0	−.027	−.003	0	0
1872	0	−.011	0	+.018	0	0	0
1876	+.012	−.005	0	0	0	0	0
1880	−.021	−.023	0	0	−.031	0	0
1884	0	−.005	0	−.003	0	0	0
1888	−.011	0	0	+.005	0	0	0
1892	−.051	−.008	0	+.004	0	0	0
1896	−.086	0	0	+.008	0	0	0
1900	−.045	0	0	+.035	0	0	0
1904	−.006	−.005	0	+.052	0	0	0
1908	−.015	0	0	+.003	0	0	0
1912	−.049	−.003	0	−.002	0	0	0
1916	−.015	0	0	+.013	0	0	0
1920	+.001	0	−.001	+.007	0	0	0
1924	−.029	0	0	+.001	0	+.001	0
1928	−.004	0	0	+.003	0	0	0
1932	−.064	0	0	−.005	0	0	0
1936	−.007	+.005	+.005	0	0	0	0
1940	−.015	+.004	+.004	+.003	0	0	0
1944	+.002	0	0	−.010	0	+.002	0
1948	−.006	0	0	+.002	0	0	0
1952	−.005	+.004	+.004	−.005	0	+.001	0
1956	−.005	0	0	+.004	0	0	0
1960	−.001	+.002	−.002	+.002	0	0	0
1964	−.002	+.002	+.009	+.020	+.001	0	0
1968	0	+.006	+.006	+.001	0	0	0

that differences on Internal Sovereignty issues account for the bulk of the differences between the two parties during this period.[18]

Issue differences between the parties during the Populist period, centering at 1896, rank second in order of magnitude. These differences occur primarily in the Capitalism category.

Relatively large issue differences are exhibited in 1880, at the close of Reconstruction, primarily in the Capitalism, Internal Sovereignty, and Universalism categories.

The 1932 platforms rank fourth in terms of degree of issue difference between the two parties. The bulk of this difference occurs in the Capitalism category.

These findings indicate that during each realigning period, the overall degree of difference between the two parties and thus the relative degree of choice available to voters was considerably greater than usual.[19]

While we cannot obtain data in the attitudes of voters during these periods, we have determined that electoral realignment was, in fact, associated with increases in the scope of choice available to voters. During these critical periods, the insurgent party exhibited considerably more than usual policy disagreement with the incumbent party. Whatever the attitudes of voters, these increases in the scope of voter alternatives meant that votes in favor of the insurgent party during each of these periods were also implicit choices favoring policy changes. During two realigning eras, 1826-36 and 1892-96, voters defeated insurgent parties, while during the four remaining periods, 1789-1800, 1852-60, 1874-80, and 1928-36, voter realignment

---

[18] This finding is very much in accord with Stokes's assertion that the period just prior to the Civil War was *the* era in American political history when political conflict was most nearly focused on a single issue dimension. Donald E. Stokes, "Spatial Models of Party Competition," in Campbell *et al.*, *Elections* (New York: Wiley, 1966), p. 177.

[19] It is interesting to note that 1912 and 1964, years often associated with substantial amounts of partisan conflict and changes in voting behavior, rank fifth and sixth, respectively, in terms of the magnitude of the differences between the two parties. It is also interesting that the level of conflict between the two parties appears to have diminished considerably over time. Analysis of the causes and consequences of this diminution of conflict is unfortunately beyond the scope of this chapter.

resulted in victory for insurgents and changes in party control of the government. The data suggest that during these four periods the behavior of the electorate represented, in effect, a majority choice in favor of policy changes.[20] Let us now see whether the electorate's implicit choices were translated into national policy.

CHANGES IN PUBLIC POLICY OVER TIME

To determine whether major changes in public policy occurred in 1801, 1861, 1881, and 1933, the dates immediately following insurgent victory during critical eras, I analyzed all United States statutes between 1789 and 1968.[21] The purpose of this analysis was to determine the extent to which policymakers attempted to implement policies consistent with the implicit choices made by voters. Each statute was scored as nominally favoring or opposing policy objectives within the same several broad categories used in my analysis of national party platforms. For example, a statute that granted privileges or property to a railroad corporation received a "+ Capitalism" score as nominally promoting "the aggregation of wealth by business, financial, and mercantile elites." Because a single statute might be aimed at more than one object, multiple scores were permitted. Each statute could, therefore, receive a maximum of seven scores, one

---

[20] Because of the temporal limitations of the data one can, of course, make only inferences about the 1798-1800 period. The 1874-80 period, in many respects, represents an anomalous case. Voter realignment during this period primarily, but not exclusively, involved the return of the Southern Democratic vote. Party competition during this period included the conservative Republican and Southern Democratic alliance that led to Hayes's disputed election in 1876. Changes in radical Republican policy, though of different types, were espoused by both parties during this period. In some respects, the election of 1880 represented the electorate's implicit ratification of the results of the elite compromise reached in 1876, that is, to proceed with rapid industrial expansion while permitting the formal return of the South to national political participation. This compromise meant that the South would be an economically and, for a time, politically subordinate region but would be autonomous in the area of race relations.

[21] *United States Statutes at Large* (Washington, D.C.: U.S. Government Printing Office, 1789-1968), vols. 1 to 82.

positive or negative in each category. My interest, in the case of each statute, was the nominal intention of policymakers rather than the laws' impacts or effects. I asked only whether policymakers nominally attempted to implement policies consistent with their preelection positions. Obviously, policies often fail to achieve their objectives, but the reasons for failure are numerous and not necessarily related to the aims of policymakers.

These procedures required the analysis of each of the more than 60,000 public laws issued in the United States over a 180-year period. Fortunately, American public laws, in the eighteenth and nineteenth centuries at least, tended to be short and to the point. The precise intent of most statutes is obviously subject to varying interpretations. With the aid of historical materials and congressional hearings and records, however, it proved not to be difficult to determine the place of a statute in the broad domains defined by my policy categories. The rescoring of samples of statutes by additional coders resulted in an overall level of intercoder agreement of 0.86.

In spite of the many months of labor required, analysis of statutes rather than some other form of policy output (government expenditures, for example) appeared to represent the method best suited to my purposes. Since the aim was to determine whether the preelection positions of policymakers were implemented in public policies, it appeared to be necessary to look directly at the substance of the relevant public policies. Governmental expenditures offer another reasonable type of indicator, and are extremely useful for some purposes. However, expenditures are based, at least in part, on the actual cost of effecting policy aims. Differential costs of implementing various aims make comparisons across types of policy difficult.

It is, of course, true that some statutes are more important than others and that statutes vary considerably in the magnitude of the policy objectives they attempt to achieve. This analysis, which weighs each statute equally, ignores important qualitative differences among statutes. However, it is difficult to conceive of a systematic way to make qualitative evaluations of the importance of laws. The aims of policymakers in any policy area can best be characterized in terms of their overall behavior. The behavior of policymakers in the case of a relatively minor piece of legislation is not necessarily a less important indicator of their general aims than their behavior in the case of a major piece of legislation. This assumption is also implicit in most studies of roll call voting, for example. In addition, during the course of the analysis I was impressed with the general consistency, during each year, of the nominal aims of minor and major pieces of legislation in each individual policy area. It is very likely the case that many statutes that are generally considered qualitatively important are so considéred precisely because, and only if, they set the tone for other pieces of legislation, that is, if they are trend breaking or trend setting. For these reasons, to determine the extent to which policymakers attempted to effect policies consistent, on the aggregate, with the implicit choices made by voters, each U.S. statute was analyzed and each weighted equally.

To search for changes in public policy over time, I employed a variant of a procedure suggested by Ezekiel and Fox[22] and used by Burnham in his analysis of electoral data.[23] The time series provided by each category of policy was separately regressed on time, the linear trend removed, and a residual series obtained for each category. A T-test for difference of means was then applied to successive sets of five residuals within each category—years 1 through 5 compared with years 7 through 11, and so on. It should be noted that *T* is not used here as a conventional statistical test. We are dealing with a population rather than a sample, so there is no question of statistical significance. *T* is simply a convenient aggregative device: the numerator compares true population means; the pooled deviation in the denominator provides a smoothing effect to minimize the effects of isolated deviant years.

This search procedure permits comparison of the magnitudes of the differences between all successive sets of five years in each policy category. These magnitudes are reported in Table 4.4.

The data reported in Table 4.4 do not directly permit us to determine whether insurgent victory during realigning periods was

---

[22] Mordecai Ezekiel and Karl A. Fox, *Methods of Correlation and Regression Analysis* (New York: Wiley, 1959), p. 343.

[23] Burnham, *Critical Elections*, p. 13.

TABLE 4.4 Changes in public policy over time. (A positive score indicates a decrease; a negative score indicates an increase.

Year	Congress	Capitalism	Internal sovereignty	Redistribution	International cooperation	Universalism	Labor	Ruralism
1799	1	+2.400	+0.400	+2.050	-0.600	-1.260		-2.130
1801	2	+3.230	-0.670	+1.460	+0.350	+0.340		-3.120
1803	3	+2.410	-0.140	+1.820	+0.960	+1.540		-5.080
1805	4	+2.750	+0.900	+3.420	+2.000	+1.040		-5.380
1807	5	+2.730	-0.130	+1.610	+0.610	+2.550		-3.770
1809	6	+0.650	-0.770	-0.070	+0.350	+1.370		-3.300
1811	7	+0.130	-1.200	+0.110	+0.310	+0.020		-1.370
1813	8	+0.610	-1.230	-0.740	-1.010	-0.570		-1.000
1815	9	-0.370	-2.110	-1.560	-3.510	-0.570		-1.130
1817	10	+0.050	-0.740	-1.350	-1.610	-1.380		-0.470
1819	11	+1.250	+0.600	-0.640	-1.140	-0.220		-0.860
1821	12	+1.250	+2.630	-1.820	-1.350	+0.790		-2.310
1823	13	+0.830	+2.160	-1.750	-0.820	+0.790		-1.790
1825	14	+1.930	+1.370	-2.150	-0.670	+0.790		-1.060
1827	15	+0.950	+0.300	-1.840	-0.490	+0.790		-0.430
1829	16	+1.640	-0.400	-1.500	-0.610	+1.480		+0.080
1831	17	+1.550	-1.940	-2.010	+0.190	+0.050		+1.550
1833	18	+0.600	-1.080	-1.910	+0.150	+0.450		+2.980
1835	19	+0.220	-0.280	-1.810	+0.990	+0.450		+2.790
1837	20	+0.140	+0.800	-0.040	+1.510	+0.450		+1.400
1839	21	-0.050	+1.430	-0.600	+1.700	+0.460		+1.020
1841	22	-1.080	+1.550	+1.110	+0.470	+2.320		+1.130
1843	23	-0.030	+0.650	+1.260	+0.270	+0.980		+0.080
1845	24	-0.680	+0.080	+1.860	-0.040	+0.980		-1.210
1847	25	-1.000	-0.900	+1.400	-2.070	+0.980		-0.830
1849	26	-1.010	-1.680	+3.180	-2.390	+0.520		-1.970

Year	No.							
1851	27	+0.060	-1.260	+2.810	-2.440	-0.960		-2.560
1853	28	-0.460	-1.840	+4.070	-1.650	-1.060		-0.950
1855	29	-0.550	-1.580	+2.620	-1.770	-1.520		+0.230
1857	30	+0.440	-1.630	+0.880	-2.180	-2.100		+0.940
1859	31	-0.470	-2.130	+0.420	-1.210	-3.780		+3.940
1861	32	-1.690	-1.840	+0.230	-0.600	-5.410		+4.200
1863	33	-2.180	+0.380	-1.340	-1.970	-1.570		+2.020
1865	34	-1.720	+0.420	-0.480	-0.680	-0.580		+1.210
1867	35	-1.440	+0.730	+1.080	-0.350	+0.690		+0.030
1869	36	-0.370	+1.610	-0.080	+0.000	+2.060		-2.060
1871	37	+1.460	+1.950	-0.210	+0.170	+3.920		-3.230
1873	38	+1.860	+3.810	+0.560	+1.670	+2.440		-0.750
1875	39	+1.300	+3.820	-0.300	+2.060	+1.900		+0.530
1877	40	-0.500	+2.760	-0.520	+2.600	+1.960		+2.070
1879	41	-1.840	+3.710	+1.610	+1.800	+3.180		+2.140
1881	42	-3.260	+2.720	+1.830	+1.380	+6.090		+4.000
1883	43	-4.160	+0.940	+0.860	+1.840	+2.890	-3.590	+2.340
1885	44	-6.490	+0.870	+1.750	+1.130	+1.840	-2.740	+0.910
1887	45	-3.240	+0.340	+0.990	-0.440	+0.580	-0.320	+0.390
1889	46	-1.270	-0.450	+0.520	-0.870	+0.060	+1.080	+0.870
1891	47	-1.070	-0.140	+0.890	-0.360	-1.250	+1.340	+1.520
1893	48	-0.700	+0.840	+1.220	-0.600	+0.060	+2.520	+0.700
1895	49	-0.460	+0.370	+0.740	-0.380	+0.270	+3.400	+0.350
1897	50	-0.200	+0.440	+1.300	-0.020	+0.480	+1.840	+0.330
1899	51	-1.310	+0.020	+0.240	+1.500	+0.050	+1.390	-1.300
1901	52	-0.330	-0.180	-0.190	+0.590	+1.190	+0.290	-4.700
1903	53	+0.810	-1.120	+0.080	+0.810	+0.180	-0.150	-3.290
1905	54	+1.530	-2.650	+0.450	+0.420	-0.300	-1.760	-1.940
1907	55	+1.990	-2.490	-0.530	+0.520	+0.440	-2.280	-2.220
1909	56	+2.050	-3.840	+0.510	+1.010	-0.150	-1.600	-1.890
1911	57	+2.110	-3.940	+0.050	+1.220	-1.170	-0.030	-2.390

TABLE 4.4 (continued)

Year	Congress	Capitalism	Internal sovereignty	Redistribution	International cooperation	Universalism	Labor	Ruralism
1913	58	+1.970	-2.990	-0.410	+1.140	-1.280	+0.720	-2.950
1915	59	+1.510	-2.610	-0.490	+1.180	-1.280	+2.100	-2.270
1917	60	+2.110	-1.200	+0.580	+0.940	-2.510	+3.420	-0.110
1919	61	+1.810	+0.540	-0.050	-1.120	-0.020	+6.060	+0.180
1921	62	+3.880	+1.510	+0.920	-1.420	+0.630	+3.130	+1.830
1923	63	+3.570	+1.340	+0.970	-1.310	+1.250	+1.480	+3.000
1925	64	+2.460	+1.360	-0.250	-1.300	+1.310	-0.170	+1.010
1927	65	+2.230	+0.640	-1.090	-1.090	+1.570	-1.090	-0.490
1929	66	+3.740	-0.460	-1.970	-0.380	+1.200	-2.490	-1.470
1931	67	+3.880	-0.530	-3.150	+1.670	+1.560	-2.970	-3.110
1933	68	+3.780	+0.070	-3.490	+1.280	+0.600	-5.270	-4.420
1935	69	+4.870	+0.440	-2.310	+1.860	+1.940	-4.960	-2.110
1937	70	+2.890	+0.400	-0.750	+2.160	+1.950	-5.820	-0.470
1939	71	+3.380	+0.340	-0.520	+2.320	-0.190	-2.900	+1.060
1941	72	+2.350	-0.310	-0.380	+1.770	-0.190	-1.270	+1.880
1943	73	+0.820	-1.080	-0.990	-0.040	-0.450	-0.010	+2.430
1945	74	-0.560	-3.440	-0.580	-1.070	-2.000	+1.530	+2.090
1947	75	+0.070	-3.820	-1.030	-1.330	-2.620	+3.130	+0.670
1949	76	+0.380	-3.500	-0.040	-1.380	-1.410	+2.230	-0.520
1951	77	+0.630	-2.300	+0.080	-1.180	-2.240	+3.960	-0.500
1953	78	+1.380	-1.090	+1.920	-0.940	-2.800	+1.910	-1.200
1955	79	+1.970	+0.320	+0.310	+0.410	-1.240	+0.950	-0.510
1957	80	+0.470	+0.900	-0.640	+0.360	-1.000	+0.180	+1.080
1959	81	+0.300	+2.030	-1.920	+0.750	-1.360	+0.880	+1.660

associated with major policy changes. Discrete changes in national policy may result from any number of factors unrelated to realignment: international events, economic changes, and so on. To determine whether the policy changes occurring in 1801, 1861, 1881, and 1933 were of a greater magnitude than changes occuring during other years, I obtained the means of the absolute values of the T scores in each policy category for each year. The resulting summary scores, reported in Table 4.5, indicate the overall magnitude of the difference between public policies before and after each year. Inspection of Table 4.5 indicates that these values are, in fact, consistent with my proposition. The highest summary value occurs in 1881, followed in order of magnitude by 1933, 1805, and 1861. Each peak value summarizes a set of policy changes occurring around that year. The years 1805, 1861, 1881, and 1933 appear indeed to mark center points of transition for national policy.[24]

Reexamination of Table 4.4 to determine the elements that account for each summary value indicates that the 1805 peak is composed primarily of negative changes in the Capitalism, Redistribution, and International Cooperation categories and positive changes in the Ruralism category, all occurring in the period from 1801 to 1805 following the Jeffersonian victory. The primary components of the 1861 peak are positive changes in the Internal Sovereignty and Universalism categories and negative changes in the Ruralism category, from 1860 to 1863. The 1881 peak is accounted for primarily by positive changes in the Capitalism category and negative changes in the Internal Sovereignty, Universalism, and Ruralism categories from 1875 to 1885. The major components of the 1933 peak appear to be negative changes in the Capitalism category and positive changes in

---

[24] I should note that minority party victory is, on the average, associated with greater than usual degrees of policy change:

Mean change following critical years: 2.52 (.124).
Mean change following other minority victories: 1.66 (.064).
Mean change, all other years: 1.32.

The mean degree of choice available to voters prior to both critical changes and other minority party victories is given in parentheses. The year 1848 is included as a minority victory although the Whigs captured only the presidency.

TABLE 4.5 *Total change in policy over time.*

Year	Total change	Year	Total change	Year	Total change
1799	1.473	1853	1.672	1907	1.496
1801	1.528	1855	1.378	1909	1.579
1803	1.992	1857	1.362	1911	1.559
1805	2.582*	1859	1.992	1913	1.637
1807	1.900	1861	2.217*	1915	1.634
1809	1.085	1863	1.636	1917	1.553
1811	0.523	1865	0.974	1919	1.397
1813	0.860	1867	0.839	1921	1.903
1815	1.542	1869	1.077	1923	1.846
1817	0.933	1871	1.829	1925	1.123
1819	0.785	1873	1.969	1927	1.171
1821	1.692	1875	1.491	1929	1.673
1823	1.357	1877	1.601	1931	2.410
1825	1.328	1879	2.331	1933	2.701*
1827	0.800	1881	3.034*	1935	2.641
1829	0.952	1883	2.374	1937	2.063
1831	1.215	1885	2.247	1939	1.530
1833	1.195	1887	0.900	1941	1.164
1835	1.090	1889	0.731	1943	0.831
1837	0.723	1891	0.939	1945	1.610
1839	0.877	1893	0.949	1947	1.810
1841	1.277	1895	0.853	1949	1.351
1843	0.545	1897	0.659	1951	1.556
1845	0.808	1899	0.830	1953	1.606
1847	1.197	1901	1.067	1955	0.816
1849	1.792	1903	0.920	1957	0.661
1851	1.682	1905	1.293	1959	1.271

* Years of peak policy change.

the Redistribution, Labor, and Universalism categories from 1933 to 1935.

In each case, while the issue categories suggested by my analysis of platform content are among the principal elements of policy change, large changes also occur in other categories. Although random association cannot be excluded, historical analyses of party ideologies in many instances suggest relationships between these additional changes in policy and the set of issues on which we expected to find policy change. While issues related to the Capitalism category were emphasized by the two parties during the 1928-36 period, for example, belief systems during this period associated negative positions on Capitalism with positive positions on Labor and Redistribution, so that the coincidence of changes in these three categories is not surprising.[25]

Given such historical associations, the clusters of policy change we have identified seem to be consistent with the Schattschneider-Burnham thesis and my analysis of platform content data. Thus the policy changes associated with Jefferson's victory in the election of 1800 are consistent with an electoral choice in opposition to a pro-British foreign policy and neo-mercantilist economic policy.[26] Republican victory in 1860 was associated with changes in national policy consistent with an electoral choice in favor of national sovereignty and opposing the expansion of slavery.[27] The policy changes centering around 1881 are consistent with an implicit electoral choice favoring the termination of Reconstruction and the expansion of industrial and commercial activity.[28] Changes in policy after 1933 are in keeping

---

[25] William E. Leuchtenburg, *The Perils of Prosperity* (Chicago: University of Chicago Press, 1958); Samuel Lubell, *The Future of American Politics* (Garden City, N.Y.: Doubleday, 1955); and Arthur M. Schlesinger, Jr., *The Age of Roosevelt* (Boston: Houghton Mifflin, 1967), remain excellent sources.

[26] Two excellent sources are William N. Chambers, *Political Parties in a New Nation* (New York: Oxford University Press, 1963), and Noble E. Cunningham, *The Jeffersonian Republicans* (Chapel Hill: University of North Carolina Press, 1957).

[27] Among the best historical accounts are William W. Freehling, *Prelude to Civil War* (New York: Harper, 1965), and Eric Foner, *Free Soil, Free Labor, Free Men: The Ideology of the Republican Party before the Civil War* (New York: Oxford University Press, 1970).

[28] Stanley Cobben, "Northeastern Business and Radical Reconstruction: A Reexamination," in Ralph Andreano (ed.), *The Economic Impact of the American Civil War* (Cambridge, Mass.: Schenkman, 1962), pp. 144-164. See also Louis Hartz, "Government-Business Relations," in David T. Gilchrist and W. Donald Lewis (eds.), *Economic Change in the Civil War Era, Proceedings of a Conference on American Economic Institutional Change, 1850-1873* (Greenville, Del.: Eleutherian Mills-Hagley Foundation, 1965).

with voter choices favoring alterations in the economic system and redistributions of opportunities in favor of urban working-class elements.

It appears to be the case that the choices made by the electorate during these critical periods were translated into major changes in national policy. Voters' simple capacity to choose, it would appear, can have important policy consequences.

REGULATION OF ACCESS

The substitution of elections for more spontaneous or privately organized modes of political action creates a formal channel through which new groups may acquire political power. Indeed, democratic elections may permit new groups to acquire power that they might not have been able to overcome. At the same time, elections permit ordinary citizens to play formal and democratic roles in the process of leadership selection and thereby to make choices that may have considerable significance for government and policy.

Nevertheless, it would not be correct to presume that democratic elections are necessarily more effective than the alternative means through which insurgents might challenge those in power. Formal electoral channels permit power to be acquired without having to be overcome. But the very existence of a formal channel of access to power permits those who govern an opportunity that might not otherwise have been available to them: to formally limit access by new groups.

Because they permit the state's power to be acquired without having to be overcome, elections allow those holding power to set formal conditions for its acquisition and encourage those seeking power to attempt to fulfill those conditions. It is, indeed, often the case that elections are initially introduced into a nation's politics because, from the perspective of those who rule, the alternative appears to be the forcible and total seizure of power by their opponents. Elections offer those in power at least some chance to formally contain and regulate what they might otherwise lack the ability to prevent.

Formal restrictions on access to power through elections can be sufficiently severe that power may be more readily overcome than acquired through formal electoral means. Moreover, the influence that voters can bring to bear upon the process of leadership selection is not necessarily greater than the potential for mass influence through alternative forms of political action. Mass participation in the form of violence, revolution, or insurrection, though not democratic, can also have considerable influence upon the results of contests for power. And as we saw, the potential policy implications of electoral choices depend heavily upon the character of the available alternatives. To the extent that formal rules and conditions delimit access to power, the potential influence of the mass electorate is also reduced.

Typically, when elections or other institutional means of acquiring power are initially introduced into a nation's politics, access is formally limited to only a portion of the governmental structure. Most often access is confined to some form of representative body that, at best, shares governmental powers with other agencies. To take an obvious example, the framers of the American Constitution intended that access through direct popular election be limited to membership in the House of Representatives. Appointment to the executive and judicial branches of government as well as to the Senate was, by constitutional design, at least partially insulated from the electoral process. In some instances, those in power are perfectly content, even anxious, to permit their opponents full and free access to one or another relatively powerless governmental agency. In recent years several nations, including Mexico and the United Arab Republic, in which virtually all governmental power rests with the executive and bureaucracy, have taken steps to promote relatively free parliamentary elections. For example, in 1979 the Mexican government spent several million dollars urging its citizens to participate in the elections of members of the mainly ornamental Chamber of Deputies. In addition, the government legalized three formerly illicit opposition parties, including the Mexican Communist party, and introduced a system of proportional representation designed to ensure strong opposition representation in the Chamber. Indeed, according to some observers, the government made every effort to ensure a measure of success at the polls for its opponents. By permitting the opposition a strong voice in the all-but-powerless Chamber of Deputies, the Mexican government clearly hoped to channel dissent along harmless institutional lines and thereby to diminish the potential threat posed by insurgent forces.[29]

Obviously, in many nations at least some of the formal limitations that initially accompanied the introduction of electoral processes have disappeared or been seriously compromised over time. In the United States, for example, adoption by the states of direct popular selection of pledged presidential electors in the early nineteenth century, as well as amendment of the federal constitution to require direct electoral access to the Senate, certainly eroded the limitations on the scope of electoral access to power envisaged by the nation's founders.

But even when access to all or most significant governmental agencies is possible, a variety of other formal rules and conditions are often used to delimit insurgents' opportunities to acquire power through elections. In Chapter 3 we examined the three types of rules most commonly used by those in power to manipulate electoral outcomes—regulation of the electorate's composition, the translation of voters' choices into electoral decisions, and the impact of electoral decisions upon the government's composition. In addition to these forms of regulation, most of the Western democracies have at one time or another employed restrictions on candidacy and office holding to diminish the chance that individuals deemed to be undesirable might win election to public office. During the nineteenth century, prospective candidates in most nations had to meet property tests aimed at making certain that no individual who was not "independent and respectable" could be elected to public office. It was for this reason that several delegates to the American Constitutional Convention favored substantial property requirements for national officials. In the twentieth century, at least in the Western democracies, electoral

---

[29] Alan Riding, "Mexico Liberalizes Rules for Campaign," *New York Times,* May 6, 1979. Other recent examples include Egypt and Syria. See James F. Clarity, "Egyptians, in Relatively Free Voting, Elect Assembly," *New York Times,* October 29, 1976; and Elizabeth Picard, "Syria Returns to Democracy: The May 1973 Legislative Elections," in Guy Hermet, Richard Rose, and Alain Rouquié (eds.), *Elections Without Choice* (New York: Wiley, 1978), pp. 129-144.

rules are seldom used to completely preclude electoral access by new groups. To preclude electoral access would obviously increase the possibility that groups seeking political power would engage in non-electoral, possibly violent, forms of political action. Typically, election law is used only to stack the deck a bit in favor of those in power or to selectively inhibit insurgencies deemed to be particularly inappropriate. An example of the selective use of election law is the practice of most American states of formally discouraging independent candidates and, in the not so distant past, refusing a place on the ballot to individuals unwilling to affirm their loyalty to the American system of government.

REGULATION OF PARTY ORGANIZATION

Perhaps more important than any of the other formal conditions for the acquisition of power through elections, particularly in the twentieth-century American context, are those affecting party organization. The full potential for mass electoral influence over the acquisition of power can seldom be realized without organization. Parties facilitate mass electoral choice. As V. O. Key pointed out long ago, the persistence over time of competition between groups possessing a measure of identity and continuity is virtually a necessary condition for electoral control.[30] Party identity increases the electorate's capacity to recognize its options. Continuity of party division facilitates organization of the electorate on the long-term basis necessary to sustain any popular influence in the governmental process. In the absence of such identity and continuity of party division the voter is, in Key's words, confronted constantly by "new faces, new choices," and little basis exists for "effectuation of the popular will."[31]

Even more significant, however, is the fact that party organization is generally an essential ingredient for effective electoral competition by groups lacking substantial economic or institutional resources.

---

[30] Key, *Southern Politics*, ch. 14.
[31] *Ibid.*

Party building has typically been the strategy pursued by groups that must organize the collective energies of large numbers of individuals to counter their opponents' superior material means or institutional standing. In the course of European political history, for example, disciplined and coherent party organizations were generally developed first by groups representing the political aspirations of the working classes. Parties, Duverger notes, "are always more developed on the Left than on the Right because they are always more necessary on the Left than on the Right."[32] In the United States, the first mass party was built by the Jeffersonians as a counterweight to the superior social, institutional, and economic resources that could be deployed by the incumbent Federalists. In a subsequent period of American history, the efforts of the Jacksonians to construct a coherent mass-party organization were impelled by a similar set of circumstances. Only by organizing the power of numbers could the Jacksonian coalition hope to compete successfully against the superior resources that could be mobilized by its adversaries. Precisely these efforts at party building, it may be recalled, led to the Jacksonian era's famous controversies over the use of a "spoils system" for staffing federal administrative posts and Jackson's practice of depositing federal funds in "pet" state banks. The spoils system obviously meant the appointment of loyal party workers to the national bureaucracy. The pet banks were controlled by individuals with close ties to the party.[33]

In both the United States and Europe, the political success of party organizations forced their opponents to copy them in order to meet the challenge. It was, as Duverger points out, "contagion from the Left" that led politicians of the center and right to attempt to build strong party organizations.[34] But at the same time, groups with the means to acquire and hold power without much in the way of party organization often sought to discourage the development of an organized partisan politics. Conservatives, Huntington has observed, opposed parties because they properly saw them as threats to the

---

[32] Maurice Duverger, *Political Parties* (New York: Wiley, 1963), p. 426.

[33] Martin Shefter, *The Business of Politics* (New York: Basic Books, in press).

[34] Duverger, *Political Parties*, ch. 1.

established social and political order. Washington's warning against "the baneful effects of the spirit of party" came to be echoed by representatives of many social, economic, and military elites who saw their right to rule challenged by groups able to organize the collective energies and resources of the masses.

This type of opposition to party was the basis for a number of the institutional reforms of the American political process promulgated during the Progressive era. Many Progressive reformers were un- doubtedly motivated by a sincere desire to rid politics of corruption and to improve the quality and efficiency of government in the United States. But, simultaneously, from the perspective of middle- and upper-class Progressives and the financial, commercial, and industrial elites with whom they were often associated, the weakening or elimination of party organization would also have a number of other important political functions. The enervation of party would mean that power could more readily be acquired and retained by the "best men," that is, those with wealth, position, and education. The elimination of party organization, moreover, would have the effect of denying access to power to reformers' political opponents, who indeed relied on party organization. Not coincidentally, Progressive reform was aimed particularly at the destruction of the powerful urban political machines built by the representatives of lower-class ethnic voters.[35]

The list of antiparty reforms of the Progressive era is a familiar one. The Australian ballot, which we discussed in a different context, took away the parties' privilege of printing and distributing ballots. The introduction of nonpartisan local elections eroded the parties' control at the local level. The extension of "merit systems" for administrative appointments stripped party organizations of their critically important access to patronage. And, of course, the intro- duction of the direct primary substantially reduced party leaders' capacity to control candidate nominations.

Of all these reforms, the direct primary is in many respects the most interesting. The primary can be seen as an antiparty reform on

---

[35] Burnham, *Critical Elections*, ch. 4.

three separate counts. First, by weakening party leaders' capacity to control nominating processes, primary elections undermine the organizational coherence of established parties. Second, primaries tend to direct the attention of voters and political activists toward the nominating contests of the party most likely to win the general election and away from the interparty race. Over time, primary elections probably helped to erode two-party competition in at least some states.[36]

Third, and most interesting, primary elections have the effect of inhibiting the formation of new parties.[37] The primary allows dissident groups and ambitious individuals an opportunity to contend for office within, rather than in opposition to, the established parties and, as a result, permits the major parties to internalize forces that might otherwise have resulted in third-party races. In most American states, the introduction of the direct primary was followed by a marked diminution of third-party and independent efforts in the general election. Typically, the third parties that continued to appear after the advent of the primary tended to be either of the extremely doctrinaire or relatively exotic varieties and attracted little popular interest or support. The state of Ohio provides one of the most clear-cut examples. A mandatory primary for all congressional races was introduced in Ohio in 1911. Within three elections following the advent of the primary, as Fig. 4.1 suggests, third-party activity had ceased and never again came to be a significant factor in Ohio politics. With the exception of Progressive campaigns in the races immediately following the primary's introduction, only occasional Communist and Socialist-Labor candidates challenged major party nominees in Ohio congressional elections after 1911. Figure 4.2 indicates that these third parties seldom presented any particular threat to the Republicans and Democrats. After the advent of the primary, Ohio voters were not again offered an even remotely attractive third-party alternative.

---

[36] V.O. Key, *American State Politics* (New York: Knopf, 1956), chs. 4 through 6.

[37] Benjamin Ginsberg and Peter Galderisi, "Irresponsible Parties, Responsible Party Systems," paper presented at the Annual Meeting of the American Political Science Association, Washington, D.C., September 1978. For a fascinating discussion of the relationship between primary elections and party systems, see Peter Galderisi, "Primaries and the Party Establishments," doctoral thesis in preparation, Cornell University.

FIG. 4.1 *Average number of general election candidates per Ohio congressional district, 1870-1974.*

FIG. 4.2 *Proportion of the popular congressional vote received by Ohio third parties, 1870-1974.*

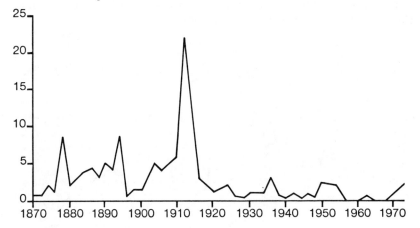

A similar pattern is evident in other states. In Indiana, for example, the introduction of a mandatory primary for congressional elections in 1915 was, as is shown by Fig. 4.3, followed by a decline in the number of general election candidates, though not so marked or persistent a decline as in Ohio. Yet, as was the case in Ohio, only the most politically or socially exotic groups entered Indiana general elections after the introduction of the primary. Figure 4.4 suggests that few even remotely attractive third parties or independents presented themselves in Indiana congressional races after 1915.

It is very likely that expansion of the role of primary elections at the national presidential level in recent years also has worked to discourage the formation of new parties. The availability of presidential primaries, even when coupled with federal campaign finance laws, state ballot access laws, and party rules that make third-party bids much less attractive than primary races, certainly does not totally prohibit or preclude the emergence of independent candidacies or new parties—witness John Anderson's candidacy in 1980. The availability of the primary does, however, increase the likelihood that groups that might have undertaken the organization of new parties will instead devote their energies and attentions to factional politics within one of the major party groupings.

FIG. 4.3 *Average number of general election candidates per Indiana congressional district, 1870-1974.*

FIG. 4.4 *Proportion of the popular congressional vote received by Indiana third parties, 1870-1974.*

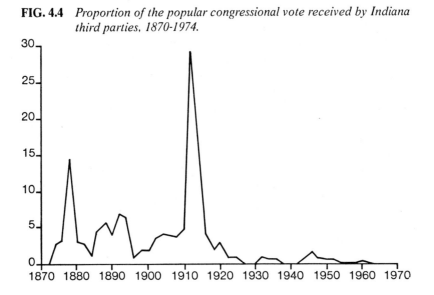

The vast majority of new parties in the United States, of course, have been politically inconsequential. But American political history suggests nonetheless that, even when short-lived, third-party challenges can have considerable impact. First, though their own electoral support may be limited, new parties can alter the balance of power between the more established partisan forces. More important, the formation of a new party can sharply redefine the focus of political debate and electoral choice. In a number of conspicuous instances third parties have precipitated conflicts that theretofore had been partially suppressed by the established party system. The formation of the Republicans and later of the Populists are, of course, cases in point. Factional activity within established party coalitions is generally far less disruptive to the agenda of issues and alternatives than independent or third-party activity. Factions campaigning in a primary, as Key pointed out long ago, have little visibility, little identity, and make little permanent impression on the electorate.[38]

---

[38] Key, *Southern Politics,* ch. 14.

All in all, the direct primary must be considered the single electoral institution most antithetical to the maintenance of a partisan politics. The primary simultaneously inhibits the emergence of new parties and diminishes the organizational coherence and competitiveness of existing parties. The extensive use of primary elections in the contemporary United States probably helps to preserve the general outlines of the established two-party system by discouraging the formation of parties to challenge the Democrats and Republicans. But the Democratic and Republican parties as organizations have hardly been helped by this result. The two-party system preserved by the primary might be characterized as a party system without parties—the term "two-party system" having come to refer more to the process whereby the number of candidates per office is typically reduced to only two, than to a politics characterized by competition between two organized entities.

THE DECLINE OF PARTIES

Though they were not the only factors at work, the direct primary and other antiparty reforms of the Progressive era at least laid the basis for the precipitous decline of party as a force in twentieth-century American politics. The details of this decline, involving the atrophy of party organizations across much of the United States and a diminution of the importance of partisanship as a factor in the behavior of voters and public officials, is too well-known to need elaboration here. Suffice it to say that in most areas of the United States party organizations are little more than skeletal remains, without much capacity to influence electoral outcomes and, as a result, with little influence over the behavior of public officials. Though candidates may still bear vestigal party labels, for the most part political campaigns have come to be essentially nonpartisan affairs, sometimes centered on issues, sometimes on personalities, but seldom on partisan differences. And in an interactive process, voters' partisan affinities increasingly have little more than a residual effect upon their behavior at the polls.[39]

Party is certainly no panacea. At the same time that they facilitate choice, parties can also suppress options. The history of every national party system may begin with intense controversy over government and policy. But as they mature, national party systems often tend to limit issues, controversies, and alternatives. Indeed, mature party systems can even develop oligopolistic tendencies as nominally competitive political elites, like their corporate counterparts, discover that a bit of cooperation can be more profitable than all-out competition. The case of the written agreement between the Colombian parties cited earlier is unique only for its blatancy. American political history furnishes any number of examples of collusive arrangements between ostensibly competitive parties on matters ranging from the apportionment of legislative seats to the division of electoral spoils.[40]

But while party is no panacea, in its absence the opportunity for mass electoral choice is certainly diminished. In the absence of party organization, voters may sometimes have the capacity and opportunity to make meaningful choices among candidates presenting competing policy alternatives. But—and this is of course among V. O. Key's most important contributions—in the absence of competing parties mass voting is more likely to be influenced by personality, geographic proximity, and incumbency as voters search for decision cues amidst a welter of "new faces" and "new choices" and candidates search for

---

[39] On the decline of partisanship as a factor in voting, see Norman H. Nie, Sidney Verba, and John R. Petrocik, *The Changing American Voter* (Cambridge, Mass.: Harvard University Press, 1976).

[40] Collusion has been so common that it is surprising that it receives so little attention in the literature. Some of the exceptions are David Mayhew, "Congressional Representation: Theory and Practice in Drawing the Districts," in Nelson Polsby (ed.), *Reapportionment in the 1970s* (Berkeley and Los Angeles: University of California Press, 1971), pp. 277-281; Donald Wittman, "Parties as Utility Maximizers," *American Political Science Review* 67 (June 1973): 490-498; and Walter Karp, *Indispensable Enemies* (Baltimore: Penguin Books, 1973).

safe and salable appeals.[41] While a diminution of partisan voting in presidential and congressional elections is sometimes conceived to mean increased "issue voting," more typically a weakening of partisan infuence gives even more of a boost to personality and incumbency effects.

Even more important, in the absence of party organization, the likelihood that groups lacking substantial economic or institutional resources can acquire some measure of power is considerably diminished. In contemporary American politics, for example, the institutional resources commanded by incumbent legislators make them extremely difficult to defeat. Barring scandal or the sort of massive, nationwide surge to the opposition that appears to have produced major Republican gains in 1980, incumbents can seldom be dislodged from office. The chief exceptions, of course, to the rule of the unassailability of incumbents are those races in which challengers are able to muster very substantial financial resources.[42]

In the absence of party organization, electoral politics essentially becomes a contest in which only those who command very substantial private resources or have access to governmental resources can hope to successfully compete. This type of politics holds out little hope for the acquisition of even a measure of power by subordinate social and economic groups. And this result is, of course, fully consistent with the spirit of Progressive reform. The capacity of the "best men" to enter politics is no longer hampered by the organized power of the masses.

VOTING AND THE LIMITS OF ACCESS

Even beyond the question of legal and institutional limits on access to public office through electoral processes, democratic elections by no means permit all groups an equal opportunity to acquire power.

---

[41] The "friends and neighbors" effect is described in Key, *Southern Politics,* p. 302.

[42] See Gary C. Jacobson, "The Effects of Campaign Spending in Congressional Elections," *American Political Science Review* 72 (June 1978): 469-491.

Indeed, elections are fundamentally conservative institutions. Electoral rules may sometimes mitigate, sometimes exacerbate the conservative character of electoral mechanisms. But, fundamentally, elections reflect more than affect the distribution of power in society. Effective electoral competition requires substantial resources—financial, institutional, educational—whose distribution tends to be related to social and economic position. Particularly in the absence of strong party organizations, groups at the upper ends of the social and economic spectrum have a distinct competitive advantage over those nearer the bottom—perhaps not a guarantee of victory in each and every instance, but a distinct advantage nonetheless. And, of course, even party can by no means fully compensate for social and economic inequalities. Even where parties are relatively strong, economically and socially inferior groups do not have an equal opportunity to attain access to the levers of political power. Democratic elections permit various elites to compete with one another and occasionally permit the masses to acquire some influence over them as a result. But when groups that lack financial means or access to important social institutions seek to compete with groups in possession of such resources, the outcome, as the critics of pluralist theories like to point out, is seldom in doubt.

Of course, elections offer subordinate groups a greater chance of access to political power than do some of the hypothetical alternatives. Relative to, say, inheritance as a mode of leadership selection, elections might appear to open the door to all comers. But generally the alternative to elections is not inheritance or some other closed process of succession. The more usual alternative is violence and disorder. Elections, indeed, are usually introduced precisely in order to discourage violent efforts to seize power. Relative to the more violent alternatives, elections must unfortunately be seen as delimiting access. Disorder and violence, even more than party organization, can have compensatory functions—offsetting or neutralizing superior economic and institutional resources. Riots, terrorism, and so on, have typically, if regrettably, been the chief means through which subordinate groups have been able to compensate for their opponents' social or economic advantages. Though the misery and suffering that can result may seldom be justified, it is unfortunately violence more often than voting that allows economically and socially subordinate groups to acquire political power. To be sure, elections by no means preclude social or economic transformations that may alter the balance of power among various forces. But elections are less likely to contribute to such processes of elite transformation than they are simply to reflect the new distribution of social or economic strength that results.

An interesting illustration of this conservative character of electoral institutions can be obtained by comparing the makeup of the elected American political elite over time with that of elites that have attained power through more violent means. In a series of studies completed approximately 30 years ago, Harold Lasswell and his associates examined the revolutionary elites—Soviet, Nazi, Italian Fascist and Chinese Communist—that changed the face of the world, albeit perhaps for the worse, in the twentieth century.[43] Most of the founders and early leaders of all four movements, including the Nazi party, were, not surprisingly, intellectual ideologues with middle- or upper-middle-class social origins and generally a good deal of formal education. These were the individuals with the background and training necessary to organize political movements and articulate political ideologies.

But more important, all four movements allowed members of previously subordinate social groups to make their way to the

---

[43] Harold Lasswell and Daniel Lerner (eds.), *World Revolutionary Elites* (Cambridge, Mass.: MIT Press, 1966). To some extent, of course, the Nazi seizure of power resulted from the party's success at the polls. Though the Nazis never received a majority of the votes cast in any free election, they did obtain over 11 million votes in 1932 and more than 17 million in 1933. In part, Nazi electoral success was made possible by the collapse of German social and economic institutions that offered unprecedented political opportunities to normally subordinate groups. At the same time, electoral success was only one factor contributing to Hitler's accession to office and electioneering only one of the techniques used by the Nazis in their bid for power. Indeed, Nazi electoral success, especially in 1933, was in part due to violence and intimidation of voters. For a fascinating account of the character of political action by the Nazi party prior to its acquisition of power, see Peter Merkl, *Political Violence under the Swastika* (Princeton, N.J.: Princeton University Press, 1975).

pinnacles of national power. The chief Nazi administrators, for example, were generally recruited from the lower strata of pre-Nazi German society. Italian Fascism brought to the fore men from the lower middle classes. In Russia and China the revolutionary seizure of power by Communist movements ultimately allowed individuals from the lower classes, including the peasantry, to achieve considerable governmental power. In general, leaving aside the intellectuals who founded the four movements, power in the regimes that resulted from the success of these movements was inversely related to status and position in the preexisting society.[44] In all four cases, violent political action served as a vehicle for a social revolution through which socially and economically subordinate groups were able to displace established elites and seize power.[45]

This portrait of social revolution through political action serves as a striking backdrop to the composition of the American political elite over time. Through virtually all of its history, the elected American political elite has had an upper-middle-class or upper-class background. Putnam notes, after examining all of the available data, that "two centuries of economic, social, demographic and geographic expansion have produced remarkably little change in the aggregate socioeconomic characteristics of the American elite." American political leadership at the national level, Putnam goes on to observe, "has remained largely the province of men from the middle and upper classes throughout the last two centuries."[46] Data reported by

---

[44] In Fascist Italy, social mobility was most pronounced in what Lasswell and Sereno call "rising agencies"—governmental agencies either established by, or whose powers were enlarged by, the Fascist regime. Harold D. Lasswell and Renzo Sereno, "The Fascists: The Changing Italian Elite," in Lasswell and Lerner, *World Revolutionary Elites.* The question of the extent of social transformation in Nazi Germany is discussed in detail by David Schoenbaum, *Hitler's Social Revolution* (New York: Norton, 1980), especially ch. 8. See also Ralf Dahrendorf, *Society and Democracy in Germany* (Garden City, N.Y.: Doubleday, 1967), ch. 25.

[45] The historical significance of violence is discussed in Barrington Moore, *The Social Origins of Dictatorship and Democracy* (Boston: Beacon Press, 1966).

[46] Putnam, *Political Elites,* p. 185.

Putnam indicate that only a small fraction of elected American political leaders have ever been drawn from lower social strata.[47]

This consistency of upper- and upper-middle-class rule by no means implies that there have been no elite transformations during the course of American political history. Elite transformations certainly have occurred. As we saw, particularly during periods of critical elections, groups reflecting different origins, interests, and viewpoints from those in power sought and won control of the government. But the consistently upper-class character of the American political elite does suggest that groups that have acquired political power through electoral mechanisms in the United States have previously attained a measure of social and economic standing.[48]

Electoral outcomes have tended to reflect rather than affect the distribution of power in American society.[49] Rather than provide those without power a means for its acquisition, elections have more often allowed those with power in society to acquire political authority.

---

[47] *Ibid.*, pp. 186-188. The one era in American history during which political action perhaps did bring about some measure of social transformation was, of course, the revolutionary period. See J. Franklin Jameson, *The American Revolution Considered as a Social Movement* (Boston: Beacon Press, 1956).

[48] Politics is sometimes thought to have served as the key route of social mobility, especially for immigrant groups in American cities. In fact, most immigrant groups made economic and social progress long before and, indeed, as a prerequisite to political advancement. See the discussion in Theodore J. Lowi, *At the Pleasure of the Mayor* (New York: Free Press, 1964), ch. 2, especially pp. 39-52. Interestingly enough, crime has probably been a more important ladder of social mobility than politics in American cities. See, for example, Daniel Bell, *The End of Ideology* (New York: Free Press, 1960), ch. 7.

[49] For a very interesting analysis that reaches a similar conclusion, see Kenneth Prewitt and Alan Stone, *The Ruling Elites* (New York: Harper and Row, 1973), ch. 7.

MASS PARTICIPATION AS A SOURCE OF NATIONAL AUTHORITY

5

Not only do elections contain and delimit the impact of mass political activity, but they also transform the otherwise sporadic and potentially dangerous political involvement of the masses into a principal source of national power and authority. First, elections bolster popular support for political leaders and for the regime itself. In particular, the formal opportunity to participate can help to convince citizens that the government is responsive to their needs and wishes. Second, elections help to persuade citizens to obey. Electoral participation encourages popular cooperation with the government's programs and policies, particularly popular acquiescence to the taxation and military service upon which the state's existence depends. Electoral participation, especially in the democratic context, has the effect of substituting consent for coercion as the foundation of the state's power.

Discussions of the possibility of influence through electoral institutions tend to assume that the effects of elections are unidirectional. Elections are presumed to serve solely, albeit imperfectly, as instruments of popular control of officials' conduct. Yet the possibility of influence through elections has more than one dimension. Whatever effect electoral participation has upon the activities of those in power, elections simultaneously afford governments an opportunity to influence their citizens' attitudes and behavior. At least since the nineteenth century, as we noted earlier, governments have attempted to use popular voting to enhance their own authority and legitimacy. Rulers have typically conceived routine mass participation to be a form of cooptation that could potentially increase popular responsiveness to the government's policy initiatives and diminish popular opposition to national authority.[1] The acquisition of popular consent

---

[1] See, for example, Edward Shils, *Political Development in the New States* (Gravenhage: Mouton, 1962); Aristide Zolberg, *Creating Political Order* (Chicago: Rand McNally, 1966); and Richard Rose and Harve Mossawin, "Voting and Elections: A Functional Analysis," *Political Studies* 15 (1967): 173-201. See also Murray Edelman, *The Symbolic Uses of Politics* (Urbana: University of Illionis Press, 1964), and Murray Edelman, *Politics as Symbolic Action* (Chicago: Markham, 1971). See also Easton's concept of "diffuse support" for a regime and political leaders. David Easton, *A Systems Analysis of Political Life* (New York: Wiley, 1965), especially ch. 18. This theme of the use of elections to build popular support runs through all the essays in

through participation is a basic underpinning of national power and has been a key factor in the growth and development of the modern state.

The emergence and expansion of modern states can, of course, be explained in a variety of different ways. Yet whatever the precise nature of the underlying causes, the fundamental requirement for the construction of nation-states was the extraction of revenues and services from their citizens. Money, labor, and military service were all essential for the creation and maintenance of the armies and bureaucracies that formed the backbone of the state. Without these resources, rulers could neither defend their territorial claims against external foes nor hope to subordinate such internal rivals as the church and the aristocracy.

To put the matter simply, there are two ways in which rulers can acquire revenues and services from their subjects—coercion and persuasion. A populace may be forcibly compelled to provide its rulers with revenues and services or may be persuaded to do so of its own free will. All governments, of course, employ elements of both persuasion and coercion. Generations of American men, for example, were offered a choice between voluntary military enlistment and involuntary conscription. Behind the warm handshake of the genial recruiting sergeant lurked the cold tentacles of the remorseless Selective Service System.

Though coercion and persuasion often complement one another in this way, it was clearly coercion that was the more important factor during the early history of state building. In what Finer characterizes as the extraction-coercion cycle, rulers used force to collect taxes and compel service in the military.[2] The growth of armies and bureaucracies increased rulers' capacity to extract revenues and service,

---

Guy Hermet, Richard Rose, and Alain Rouquié (eds.), *Elections Without Choice* (New York: Wiley, 1978). Contrary to the implication of this excellent volume's title, however, elections "without choice" are not the only sorts of voting processes that can be used to increase popular acquiescence.

[2] Samuel Finer, "State and Nation Building," in Charles Tilly (ed.), *The Formation of National States in Western Europe* (Princeton, N.J.: Princeton University Press, 1975), p. 84.

which in turn made possible the construction of larger armies and bureaucracies, and so on. This cycle of extraction and coercion was at the heart of state building in Western Europe. When, for example, Frederick William succeeded as Elector of Brandenburg-Prussia in 1640, he commanded a military force consisting of a mere 1300 mercenary troops, had virtually no central administrative machinery, and was at the mercy of the Estates for revenues. In stages over the next 40 years, Frederick used his troops to acquire more funds, with which he retained more troops, with which he in turn enforced the collection of more taxes. By the conclusion of Frederick William's reign in 1688, Brandenburg-Prussia boasted a standing army of 30,000 men and an elaborate administrative machinery. This cycle was continued by Frederick William I, who was able to construct what on a per capita basis was the largest standing army in Europe. This permanent force of 80,000 troops both supported and was supported by an extensive bureaucracy and tax collection apparatus.[3]

Though it was certainly crucial to the construction of nation-states, ultimately coercion alone is a shaky foundation for governmental power. Coercion tends to engender resistance. And, indeed, resistance was one of the major problems of state-building. Popular resistance to military service, to the expropriation of food and supplies for armies, and above all, to taxation were central themes in European history from the fifteenth century onward. In France, for example, several hundred antitax riots occurred during Richelieu's ministry alone.[4] In Spain, tax increases led to widespread urban rebellion in Castille in 1520.[5] In England, resistance to taxation and other royal demands led to serious rebellions in 1489, 1497, 1536, 1547, 1549, and 1553.[6] Between the fifteenth and eighteenth centuries the question of

---

[3] *Ibid.*, pp. 134-144. See also Gordon A. Craig, *The Politics of the Prussian Army* (New York: Oxford University Press, 1955), ch. 1.

[4] Charles Tilly, "Reflections on the History of European State-Making," in Tilly, *Western Europe,* especially pp. 22 and 71.

[5] *Ibid.*, p. 22.

[6] *Ibid.*

how to deal with popular resistance to taxation and service was among the chief preoccupations of European rulers. Even if popular resistance is not sufficient to topple a government or prevent the collection of taxes, opposition can make the costs of extraction very high. The expenditure of resources necessary to extract resources from a recalcitrant population may leave little net gain.

Ultimately, states that relied solely upon coercion were unable to compete successfully with those that managed to induce popular cooperation. It was the unprecedented size, ardor, and military success of the citizen armies of postrevolutionary France that provided the first concrete demonstration of the power that could be tapped by enlisting the active cooperation of a populace. The gradual expansion of participation during the remainder of the nineteenth century represented, in large measure, an attempt by other nations to copy the French example and to increase governmental power by harnessing the collective energy of the masses.[7] Again, the slogan coined during the nineteenth-century Swedish suffrage debates, "One man, one vote, one gun," is an excellent illustration of the relationship that was believed to exist between mass participation and the state's power.

The use of elections to enhance governments' power and authority is, of course, most dramatic in the totalitarian context. The "elections without choice" staged by authoritarian regimes are, indeed, pure cases of the use of mass participation to mobilize popular support, intensify mass identification with the state and its goals, and isolate the regime's opponents. Both European Communist and Fascist elections have typically included a good deal of ceremony and festivity. Though the vote may not include a choice, it is, upon occasion, treated as a quasi-religious confession of faith in the regime. For example, the 1933 German ballot asked, "Do you approve German man, and you German woman, the policy of your Reich's government and are you ready to declare it as the expression of your

---

[7] The Prussians, in particular, sought to learn from the French example. See Reinhard Bendix, *Kings or People* (Berkeley and Los Angeles: University of California Press, 1978), p. 416; Finer, "Nation Building," p. 163; and Craig, *Prussian Army*, ch. 2.

own conception of your own will and to confess yourself solemnly for it?"[8] Presumably there could be but one appropriate response.

But even though the overt efforts of authoritarian regimes to obtain mass consent through participation are more heroic and dramatic, over time it is the democratic election that is the more effective source of popular support. Particularly in the context of sophisticated advanced industrial societies, elections without choice tend ultimately to breed cynicism more than they generate support. In the Communist nations of Eastern Europe, for example, few citizens appear to believe that voting is an effective means of participating in political affairs. As a result, several of these regimes have begun to introduce a limited degree of choice in elections at the local level in an attempt to increase popular interest and involvement with the voting process.[9]

It is the election with choice, the election that allows at least the appearance of effective mass influence, that at the same time most effectively builds popular support for the regime. It is the democratic election that most readily convinces citizens that the government is responsive to their needs and wishes. And as a result, it is the democratic election that can induce citizens to contribute with a minimum of compulsion what the state might not have been able to take by force alone.

ELECTIONS AND POPULAR BELIEFS
ABOUT THE REGIME

Every election of leaders represents a test of and potentially a threat to popular support for the political regime. Electoral conflicts may

---

[8] Juan J. Linz, "Non-Competitive Elections in Europe," in Hermet, Rose, and Rouquié, *Elections Without Choice*, pp. 36-65.

[9] Alex Pravda, "Elections in Communist Party States," in Hermet, Rose, and Rouquié, *Elections Without Choice*, pp. 169-195. The People's Republic of China also began to introduce a measure of choice in local elections in 1979. According to the Communist party's theoretical journal, *Hunychi*, "the more democratic rights the workers enjoy, the stronger their sense of responsibility becomes." Fox Butterfield, "China Tests Voting for Minor Leaders," *New York Times*, December 10, 1979.

strain public acceptance of legal and institutional processes. Groups dissatisfied with the election's outcome may come to question or renounce the procedures by which that outcome was achieved. The results of an election may contribute to public doubt about the accountability of national authorities and the responsiveness of governmental institutions. It is not difficult to find cases of elections that exacerbated the estrangement of large segments of society from a regime. The election of Salvador Allende in Chile, for example, appeared to leave many middle-class Chileans ready to support insurrection. In the United States, fear of the destabilizing consequences of elections was often expressed at the time of the nation's founding. Alexander Hamilton, for example, was concerned that, "at the period which terminates the duration of the Executive, there will always be an awful crisis in the national situation."[10]

The impact of elections upon popular beliefs about the regime can be clearly seen by examining national opinion survey data drawn from two recent American presidential elections.[11] Both before and after the 1968 and 1972 national elections, the Survey Research Center of the University of Michigan asked a national sample several questions relating to trust in government and confidence in the government's responsiveness. By comparing pre- and postelection responses to the same questions, we can assess the effects of the two elections upon citizens' attitudes toward the regime.[12] While the impact of the 1968 and 1972 elections differ somewhat, both seem far removed from the "awful crisis" feared by Hamilton. Both elections, in fact, appeared to encourage even those citizens who voted for the

---

[10] Max Farrand (ed.), *The Records of the Federal Convention of 1787* (New Haven, Conn.: Yale University Press, 1966), vol. 1, p. 49.

[11] For a more detailed discussion, see Benjamin Ginsberg and Robert Weissberg, "Elections and the Mobilization of Popular Support," *American Journal of Political Science* 22 (February 1978): 31-55. See also Benjamin Ginsberg and Robert Weissberg, "Elections as Legitimizing Institutions," in Jeff Fishel (ed.), *Parties and Elections in an Anti-Party Age* (Bloomington: Indiana University Press, 1978), pp. 179-185.

[12] Because responsiveness is an important norm of all democratic regimes, citizens' perceptions of governmental responsiveness are an important component of popular attitudes about the regime. A very similar argument is made in David Easton and Jack Dennis, *Children in the Political System* (New York: McGraw-Hill, 1969).

losing candidate to believe that the government was responsive to their views.

THE IMPACT OF THE 1968 ELECTION

Table 5.1 reports the patterns of changes among respondents asked both before and after the 1968 presidential election whether people like themselves have "much say" about what the government does.[13] It is apparent, first, that a large proportion of those respondents who indicated prior to the election that people like themselves had no influence upon the government had come to believe that they did have quite a lot of "say" following the election. A much smaller percentage of those who thought initially that they did have considerable influence upon the government changed their views after the election. Second, it is evident that positive changes were concentrated primarily among those who actually voted in the election. Among individuals who indicated before the election that they had little say

---

[13] In 1968 the pre- and postelection forms of this question differed. Prior to the election respondents were asked, "Would you say that people like you have quite a lot of say about what the government does, or that you don't have much say at all?" After the election respondents were asked whether they agreed or disagreed with the statement, "People like me don't have any say about what the government does." Similar pre- and postelection differences in wording affect the "do public officials care?" item. Prior to the election respondents were asked, "Would you say that most public officials care quite a lot what people like you think or that they don't care much at all?" After the election respondents were asked to agree or disagree with the statement, "I don't think public officials care much what people like me think." Because of these changes in wording, it is conceivable that pre- and postelection differences in responses to the questions are merely artifacts of changes in the questions themselves rather than actual changes in respondents' attitudes. This possibility, however, seems remote. First, the 1968 results are quite similar to the results obtained in 1972 when the wording of the questions was not altered between waves of the survey. Second, the striking differences between the patterns of postelection change exhibited by voters and nonvoters, both responding to the same questions, cannot be explained in terms of changes in wording. It should also be mentioned that too few respondents answered "no opinion" or "don't know" to these questions to be taken into account in the analysis.

about what the government does, 55 percent of those who actually voted came to believe after the election that people like themselves did have quite a lot of say about the government's actions. Among nonvoters, by contrast, positive changes barely outstripped negative shifts.

A very similar pattern of postelection changes appears to occur in response to the question of whether or not public officials care what people like the respondent think. Indeed, on this question, the difference between voters and nonvoters is even more marked. Among voters, a sizable proportion of those who believed prior to the election that officials did not care offered a more positive appraisal after the election. Among those who did not vote, however, the proportion shifting to a negative view surpassed the percentage of respondents who came to believe after the election that public officials did care.

TABLE 5.1 *Changes in popular perceptions of "say" in government following the 1968 presidential election.* *

	Voters	Nonvoters	Total
Percentage of respondents with negative preelection perceptions who became positive following the election	55.0 (N = 700)†	34.6 (N = 263)	49.4 (N = 963)
Percentage of respondents with positive preelection perceptions who became negative following the election	15.5 (N = 278)	21.2 (N = 52)	16.6 (N = 330)

* The question asked prior to the election was, "Would you say that people like you have quite a lot of say about what the government does, or that you don't have much say at all?" The postelection form of the question asked respondents to agree or disagree with the assertion, "People like me don't have any say about what the government does."

† The number in parentheses is the base on which the proportion of changes was calculated. For example, 700 voters had negative perceptions prior to the election. Fifty-five percent of them became positive after the election; the other 45 percent remained negative.

Even more interesting, however, these patterns of attitudinal change do not appear to be related to the defeat or victory of the particular candidate favored by the respondent. If elections were sufficiently divisive that supporters of the losing candidate began to doubt the government's responsiveness to their needs, electoral contests might, in fact, precipitate "awful crises." Table 5.2 indicates, though, that among both Nixon and Humphrey voters the direction of attitude change following the election was overwhelmingly positive. Thus individuals who voted for the losing candidate tended to be as likely as those voting for the winner to develop a more favorable view of the government's responsiveness after the election. In the case of nonvoters, by contrast, the pattern of attitudinal changes is quite negative among the supporters of both candidates. It would appear that electoral participation, rather than candidate preference, is the key to understanding the attitude changes that occurred during the 1968 election.[14]

ATTITUDINAL CHANGES IN 1972

The 1972 presidential election generated considerably more conflict and controversy than any electoral contest in recent American history. Throughout the campaign unusually sharp policy divisions were manifested between the two candidates as well as between their supporters. We might have expected that in this climate of electoral division, McGovern's defeat could easily have had repercussions for his supporters' beliefs about the political regime itself.

However, to a considerable degree, attitude changes in 1972, as reported in Table 5.3, followed the same patterns that we observed in 1968. Despite the bitterness of the contest, belief in the government's responsiveness increased among voters for both candidates. It is apparent, though, that positive changes in citizens' attitudes in 1972, particularly among voters for the losing candidate, did not occur with

---

[14] Among those who participated in campaign activities in addition to voting, positive changes were even more marked.

TABLE 5.2 Changes in popular perceptions of whether or not public officials care following the 1968 presidential election.*

	Voters			Nonvoters			
	Humphrey	Nixon	All voters	Preferred Humphrey	Preferred Nixon	All nonvoters	Total
Percentage of respondents with negative preelection perceptions who became positive following the election	45.4 (N = 130)	45.5 (N = 132)	41.1 (N = 331)	24.6 (N = 57)	22.4 (N = 49)	24.2 (N = 153)	35.7 (N = 485)
Percentage of respondents with positive preelection perceptions who became negative following the election	24.5 (N = 261)	21.8 (N = 316)	25.1 (N = 630)	62.3 (N = 53)	45.6 (N = 57)	53.2 (N = 74)	30.3 (N = 770)

* The question asked prior to the election was, "Would you say that most public officials care quite a lot about what people like you think, or that they don't care at all?" The postelection form of the question asked respondents to agree or disagree with the assertion, "I don't think public officials care much what people like me think."

TABLE 5.3 *Changes in popular perceptions of "say" in government following the 1972 presidential election.* *

	Voted for Nixon	Voted for McGovern	Total voters	Total nonvoters
Percentage of respondents with negative preelection perceptions who became positive following the election	48.3 (N = 145)	26.5 (N = 98)	39.6 (N = 255)	27.4 (N = 175)
Percentage of respondents with positive preelection perceptions who became negative following the election	10.9 (N = 329)	17.1 (N = 152)	13.1 (N = 504)	28.7 (N = 129)

* Both pre- and postelection respondents were asked to agree or disagree with the statement, "People like me don't have any say about what the government does."

the same frequency as in 1968. On the question, "Do public officials care?" as Table 5.4 indicates, positive postelection changes among Nixon voters only slightly outstripped negative shifts, while among McGovern voters just the opposite was true. The difference between voters and nonvoters generally, however, remained quite marked.

A sharp difference begins to emerge between the patterns of change exhibited by Nixon and McGovern voters on several questions designed to measure popular confidence in government before and after the 1972 election. On these questions, Nixon voters tended to become positive after the election in much greater proportion than McGovern voters. Of course, these results are not directly comparable to any questions asked in 1968. When placed alongside our previous 1972 findings, however, they begin to suggest that the outcome of the election had a somewhat different impact on citizens' beliefs about the regime in 1972 than in 1968, with supporters of the losing candidate somewhat less likely to manifest positive postelection attitude changes in 1972 than supporters of the winning candidate.

Despite the potentially important differences between the two elections, though, the crucial fact remains that, like their 1968 counterparts, voters in 1972 tended in significant proportions to exhibit a

TABLE 5.4 *Changes in popular perceptions of whether or not public officials care following the 1972 presidential election.**

	Voted for Nixon	Voted for McGoverr	Total voters	Total nonvoters
Percentage of respondents with negative preelection perceptions who became positive following the election	28.7 (N = 171)	23.6 (N = 123)	26.2 (N = 309)	16.8 (N = 190)
Percentage of respondents with positive preelection perceptions who became negative following the election	21.7 (N = 290)	24.0 (N = 121)	22.2 (N = 427)	39.4 (N = 109)

* Both pre- and postelection respondents were asked to agree or disagree with the statement, "I don't think public officials care much about what people like me think."

stronger belief in the government's responsiveness following the election than they held prior to its occurrence (see Table 5.5).

PARTICIPATION AND SUPPORT FOR PUBLIC OFFICIALS IN 1972

Victorious presidential candidates often appear to benefit from at least temporary surges of popular support after their election. Studies of several presidential races have found evidence of increased popular confidence in a newly elected president.[15] Thompson, for example, in

---

[15] See Lynn Anderson and Alan R. Boss, "Some Effects of Victory or Defeat upon Perceptions of Political Candidates," *Journal of Social Psychology* 73 (1967): 227-240; J.H. Paul, "Impressions of Personality, Authoritarianism and the *Fait Accompli* Effect," *Journal of Abnormal and Social Psychology* 53 (1956): 338-344; Bertram Raven and Philip S. Gallo, "The Effects of Nominating Conventions, Elections and Reference Group Identification upon Perceptions of Political Figures," *Human Relations* 18 (1965): 217-230; and George Stricker, "The Operation of Cognitive Dissonance on Pre- and Post-Election Attitudes," *Journal of Social Psychology* 63 (1964): 111-119.

TABLE 5.5 *Changes in popular trust and confidence in government follow-ing the 1972 presidential election.*

	Trust govt. to do what is right*	Is govt. run for benefit of all†	Are govt. people capable‡	Honesty in govt.**
NIXON VOTERS				
Percentage of respondents with negative reelection perceptions who became positive following the election	49.0 (N = 159)	27.0 (N = 193)	41.0 (N = 179)	41.1 (N = 136)
Percentage of respondents with positive preelection perceptions who became negative following the election	20.6 (N = 320)	20.9 (N = 225)	19.1 (N = 274)	16.6 (N = 332)
McGOVERN VOTERS				
Percentage of respondents with negative preelection perceptions who became positive following the election	21.3 (N = 145)	14.8 (N = 156)	32.1 (N = 112)	30.3 (N = 102)
Percentage of respondents with positive preelection perceptions who became negative following the election	34.4 (N = 116)	42.7 (N = 81)	29.6 (N = 141)	26.8 (N = 153)

* "How much of the time do you think you can trust the government in Washington to do what is right—just about always, most of the time, or only some of the time?"

† "Would you say the government is pretty much run by a few big interests looking out for themselves or that it is run for the benefit of all the people?"

‡ "Do you feel that almost all of the people running the government are smart people who usually know what they are doing, or do you think that quite a few of them don't seem to know what they are doing?"

** "Do you think that quite a few of the people running the government are a little crooked, not very many are, or do you think hardly any of them are crooked at all?"

an analysis of the 1936 election, found evidence of a pro-Roosevelt surge one day after the election.[16] To test for changes in citizen attitudes in 1972, we can examine individual ratings of Nixon and McGovern on pre- and postelection "feeling thermometers." In both instances, respondents were asked to rate candidates on a 0 to 100 scale in terms of their "warmness" or "coolness" of feeling toward the candidate. Table 5.6 reports the aggregate patterns of changes in feeling thermometer ratings of the two candidates before and after the election.

While sizable numbers of citizens became more positive toward both, each candidate appears to have suffered net losses in popular support after the election. The only evidence of a net increase in support occurs among Nixon voters' pre- and postelection ratings of Nixon. Support for McGovern declined after the election even among a large number of McGovern voters.

Masked by these aggregate patterns of change, however, is a far more complex picture of the impact of the 1972 election on popular support for leaders. When we examine in Table 5.7 attitude shifts among respondents classified according to their postelection positions, there emerges an intriguing view of the mobilization of citizen support in democratic politics. First, in the case of citizen attitudes toward Nixon, marked positive postelection changes occurred among those respondents who began with very positive or negative evaluations of Nixon. Increases in support for Nixon were most substantial among Nixon voters, though previously negative nonvoters and McGovern voters also became more positive. Among those respondents who reported very positive preelection feelings toward Nixon, on the other hand, support declined somewhat after the election. Even among Nixon voters with very positive initial evaluations of Nixon, there occurred a slight ($\bar{x} = 3.5$ points) negative shift.[17] The small

---

[16] Arnold Thompson, "What Voters Think of Candidates Before and After Elections," *Public Opinion Quarterly* 2 (1938): 269-274.

[17] This pattern of moderation of extremes may initially appear to be a regression toward the mean effect rather than an election-related change. Given the nature of the data, it is probably impossible to measure precisely how much of this shift is due to a

TABLE 5.6 *Changes in ratings of McGovern and Nixon, by voting preference, 1972.*

	Feelings toward McGovern				Feelings toward Nixon			
		How Voted				How Voted		
	Nixon	Mc-Govern	No vote	Total	Nixon	Mc-Govern	No vote	Total
Became more positive	27.2	30.3	27.0	28.0	28.8	28.9	30.1	29.4
No change	32.3	31.0	27.3	30.9	45.1	26.6	32.5	36.7
Became more negative	40.5	38.7	45.8	41.0	26.1	44.5	37.4	33.9
Net change—% of respondents	−13.3 [−11.6]	−8.4	−18.8	−12.9	2.7 [−3.7]	−15.6	−7.3	−4.5
Net change— x̄ shift in ratings	−3.7* [−2.5]	−0.7	−4.4*	−3.0*	0.8 [−0.7]	−3.6	−0.8	−0.7
N =	951	513	531	971	518	563		

* P = .001 two-tailed T-test of significance

Analysis of variance:

Attitude toward McGovern	F-ratio	Sig.	Attitude toward Nixon	F-ratio	Sig.
Voting vs. nonvoting	2.811	.09	Voting vs. nonvoting	.010	.57
Nixon vs. McGovern vote	6.545	.01	Nixon vs. McGovern vote	20.170	.00

TABLE 5.7 *Mean pre- and postelection changes, by initial feeling and vote, 1972.*

	Change toward McGovern (mean) Initial Feelings toward McGovern*					Change toward Nixon (mean) Initial Feelings toward Nixon*				
	Very negative	Negative	Neutral	Positive	Very positive	Very negative	Negative	Neutral	Positive	Very positive
Voted for McGovern	48.4 (16)	16.2 (13)	10.3 (45)	3.2 (178)	−9.1 (261)	12.2 (130)	0.5 (109)	−2.7 (80)	−13.1 (156)	−29.0 (43)
Voted for Nixon	9.5 (338)	−3.8 (257)	−12.3 (158)	−16.9 (166)	−31.7 (32)	44.4 (9)	29.8 (21)	12.5 (39)	4.9 (293)	−3.5 (609)
Nonvoter	18.2 (97)	−0.3 (86)	−2.4 (121)	−12.2 (123)	−21.9 (104)	24.3 (46)	10.6 (58)	1.7 (74)	−1.8 (167)	−9.2 (218)
Total	13.0	−2.0	−5.2	−8.2	−14.3	16.8	7.1	2.0	−1.6	−6.3
N =	467	372	342	479	401	194	200	205	639	880

* Categorization of initial feelings were defined as follows: 0-25, "very negative"; 26-49, "negative"; 50, "neutral"; 51-57, "positive"; and 76-100, "very positive."

number of McGovern voters who began with highly positive images of Nixon became on the whole less positive, though still not negative, toward him.

Interestingly enough, a similar set of findings emerges from changes in McGovern ratings. Among respondents who initially had highly positive opinions of McGovern, there was a pronounced decline in support after the election. This decline occurred even among those who voted for McGovern. Among respondents with initially very negative opinions of McGovern, however, postelection ratings were an average of 13 points higher than before the election. Even Nixon voters who initially had very negative opinions of McGovern became more positive after the election.

Thus the 1972 election did have an effect upon popular support for public leaders. This effect, however, did not take the simple form of increases in support by most citizens. Overall, negative shifts outnumbered positive postelection changes. What is significant, however, is that those segments of the electorate initially most opposed to both candidates became markedly more positive after the election. The bulk of negative change amounted to positive evaluations becoming slightly less positive.

Unfortunately, no directly comparable data are available for other elections. Given, however, the unusual divisiveness of the 1972 contest, it is not unreasonable to assume that electoral contests generally have an even more important pronounced effect upon popular support for elected officials. Some credence is given this view by a *Newsweek* poll conducted after the 1976 presidential election. A large proportion of both Carter and Ford supporters

---

purely statistical artifact. Nevertheless, further analysis suggests that these patterns are *not* a result of simple regression to the mean. Specifically, if regression to the mean were occurring, we would predict that (1) variances would remain unchanged regardless of changes in the mean and (2) opinion changes would be equally distributed about the mean. Tests of these hypotheses suggest that a regression toward the mean explanation is not very plausible. Postelection attitude variances for Nixon voters, McGovern voters, and nonvoters were consistently (and statistically) significantly smaller, and the change patterns were highly asymmetrical. No doubt some regression toward the mean occurs, but this phenomenon cannot account for all the attitude changes observed.

reported more favorable opinions about the newly elected president than they held before the election.[18]

PARTICIPATION OR DEMOCRATIC CORONATION?

Participation would appear to have an effect upon citizens' beliefs about leaders and the political regime. The act of voting apparently helps to convince citizens that the regime and its leaders merit their support or at least do not deserve their animosity. But as important as the act of voting can be, it is interesting to note that many citizens appear to respond positively to the occurrence of an election even when they do not actually vote in it. For example, in 1968, 24 percent of those who believed before the election that public officials "did not care" and who did not vote adopted a more positive view after the election. For a sizable segment of the public, the simple event of an election appears to evoke positive responses toward the government that sponsors the contest. Presumably, in the historical periods that preceded the advent of mass participation, the ceremonies surrounding coronations and other transfers of power were designed to stimulate similar positive reactions to the legitimacy of the succession.

Positive response to the simple occurrence of an electoral contest, however, appears very much to be a function of civic training. As we saw in Chapter 2, patterns of change in popular reaction to elections are strongly associated with level of education. As educational attain-

---

[18] Some partial and limited data on the 1976 election show a similar pattern. A Gallup poll done for *Newsweek* after the election reports that 49 percent of those voting for Ford became more favorable toward Carter (19 percent became less favorable). "Great Expectations," *Newsweek*, January 24, 1977, p. 20. Similarly, a preelection/postelection telephone poll in the Champaign-Urbana area with approximately 90 respondents found that 51.9 percent of the Ford voters became more positive toward Carter while 20.9 percent became more negative (this change was somewhat less noticeable among nonvoters). This study was supervised by Professor Susan Hansen of the University of Illinois and is contained in Louis Miller *et al.*, "The Impact of Elections on Political Attitudes," unpublished research paper, University of Illinois, Urbana-Champaign, 1977.

ment increases, so does the proportion of respondents shifting from negative to positive positions following the election. What is striking, though, is that it is particularly among those respondents with relatively high levels of education that actual voting participation does not seem to be a necessary correlate of positive postelection attitude change. In 1968, for example, positive shifts were of a considerably greater magnitude than negative shifts among both *participants* and *nonparticipants* with high school or college educations. The stimulus of the election itself seems capable of evoking positive responses among citizens who have previously been taught to place a high value on the electoral process. Among respondents with a grade school education or less, however, the results were markedly different. Within this group of respondents the patterns of change among voters and nonvoters differed sharply. Among voters the proportion of positive changes was comfortably larger than the proportion becoming negative after the election. Among nonvoters, though, the results were reversed, with a larger proportion becoming negative after the election (see Table 5.8).

A similar pattern of responses is evident in the 1972 data reported in Table 5.9. Here respondents with no more than a grade school or high school education differed markedly from those who had attended college. These findings suggest that the propensity to respond positively to the occurrence of an election, what might be called a "democratic coronation effect," is instilled during the educational process. For citizens who have been taught to believe in the virtues of the electoral process, the mere occurrence of an election may evoke positive responses toward the regime. Actual participation, however, is critical for those individuals who have not previously received adequate civic training.

The particular importance of participation for the most poorly "trained" or socialized segments of the electorate offers an interesting commentary on the consequences of nonvoting in general and legal barriers to voting in particular. For it is precisely those segments of the mass public with the least exposure to civic training through the educational system that, as we saw earlier, are most easily discouraged from voting. Governmental policies that create impediments to voting, such as registration requirements, are likely to discourage precisely

TABLE 5.8 *Changes in popular perceptions of "say" in government following the 1968 presidential election.*

	Level of Education					
	8 Years or Less		9 to 12 Years		College	
	Voted	Did not vote	Voted	Did not vote	Voted	Did not vote
Percentage of respondents with negative preelection perceptions who became positive following the election	37.1 (N = 143)	17.8 (N = 101)	53.3 (N = 368)	40.9 (N = 115)	72.0 (N = 189)	55.3 (N = 47)
Percentage of respondents with positive preelection perceptions who became negative following the election	21.6 (N = 37)	26.7 (N = 15)	15.9 (N = 125)	19.2 (N = 26)	13.0 (N = 115)	18.2 (N = 11)

TABLE 5.9 *Changes in popular perceptions of "say" in government following the 1972 presidential election.*

	8 Years or Less		9 to 12 Years		College	
	Voted	Did not vote	Voted	Did not vote	Voted	Did not vote
Percentage of respondents with negative preelection perceptions who became positive following the election	28.6 (N = 70)	17.5 (N = 57)	41.9 (N = 129)	30.9 (N = 97)	48.2 (N = 56)	38.1 (N = 21)
Percentage of respondents with positive preelection perceptions who became negative following the election	34.0 (N = 47)	33.3 (N = 24)	16.0 (N = 237)	32.5 (N = 77)	5.5 (N = 220)	14.3 (N = 28)

Level of Education

those individuals whose actual participation must be obtained if their support for the regime is to be secured. When they do not participate, the poor and the poorly educated exhibit an overwhelmingly negative response to the occurrence of an election. Governments that erect barriers to voting do so at their own peril. Indeed, elite recognition of this peril has often been a factor behind extension of the suffrage to the lower classes. One of the most eloquent statements of the argument was made by none other than the prominent abolitionist Rev. Henry Ward Beecher, of "Beecher's Bibles" fame. In a widely circulated 1865 sermon, Beecher called for extension of the suffrage to newly freed blacks on precisely the ground that participation was essential to secure the support of the least socialized segments of the community:

I claim, again, that in a free republic, though it is manifestly dangerous to multiply ignorant voters, yet, it is far more dangerous to have a large under-class of ignorant and disfranchised men who are neither stimulated, educated, nor enobled by the exercise of the vote. The best government, the wisest laws, the discreetest institutions, and the ablest administration of them, will not save us from perils. There is danger in everything; and to have an ignorant class voting is dangerous, whether white or black; but to have an ignorant class, and not have them voting, is a great deal more dangerous. In other words, a great mass at the bottom of society that have none of the motives, none of the restraints, none of the appeals to conscience and to manliness that come with the necessity and duty of voting, are more dangerous in critical periods than they could possibly be if they were made citizens.[19]

THE SUBSTITUTION OF CONSENT FOR COERCION

Elections appear to generate a measure of popular support for leaders and to induce citizens to believe that the government is responsive to

---

[19] Rev. Henry Ward Beecher, "Universal Suffrage," speech delivered at Plymouth Church, Brooklyn, New York, February 12, 1865, and reprinted in *The Commonwealth* (February 1865).

their own needs and wishes. The opportunity to participate, as we saw, helps convince citizens that they have some "say" about the government's actions. This capacity of electoral institutions to enhance popular support and to strengthen the public's belief in its government's responsiveness is potentially quite important. For example, citizens who believe that a government is responsive to them are presumably unlikely to support or participate in attempts to undermine or overthrow the regime. And, indeed, governments that permit broad mass participation are empirically less likely to encounter popular insurrection than those that do not. Similarly, regimes that are able to maintain a measure of popular support are generally less susceptible to military coups and takeovers than those regimes that must rely more heavily on coercion as an instrument of governance.[20] One of the costs of governing through force alone is that the instrument of coercion may become too powerful to be controlled. The almost routine military coups in some portions of Latin America are cases in point. Moreover, popular support for a regime and its leaders may ease the way for a government's policy initiatives. Generalized popular support for a set of public officials can at least discourage potential foes of the government's programs. For example, in the American context, strong general popular suport for a president tends to increase the likelihood that members of Congress will respond favorably to presidential policy initiatives.[21] It is in part for this reason that presidents are so concerned with their standing in opinion polls. The appearance of popular support tends to reduce opposition to a president's legislative programs.

The importance of the support generated by democratic elections, however, comes into particularly sharp focus if we consider the effect of electoral participation upon the state's capacity to extract resources from its citizens. Extraction of services and resources, especially

---

[20] Extralegal seizures of power of all varieties—the *World Handbook* calls these "irregular executive transfers"—occur with overwhelmingly greater frequency among authoritarian governments than in the democratic context. See Charles Lewis Taylor and Michael C. Hudson, *World Handbook of Political and Social Indicators,* 2d ed. (New Haven, Conn.: Yale University Press, 1972), pp. 150-153.

[21] On this point, see David R. Mayhew, *Congress: The Electoral Connection* (New Haven, Conn.: Yale University Press, 1974), p. 43.

taxes, is a necessary condition for implementation of any government's programs and, indeed, for the state's very existence. It is undoubtedly the case that even governments fortunate enough to possess the enthusiastic support of their subjects must in some measure depend upon the threat of coercion to extract resources and services. At the very least, governments must have the capacity to deal with the common problem of the "free rider." Even citizens who strongly support a government and its policies may, left to themselves, be happy to allow others to bear the costs of these programs. Without some threat of coercion, it might be perfectly reasonable for all or most individuals to seek to evade the costs of acquiring even the public goods they most strongly desire.[22]

But nonetheless, the extent to which governments must rely upon coercion to secure popular acquiescence varies greatly. Some regimes appear to rule very nearly by force alone. The capacity of what have been called "authoritarian regimes without authority" to extract resources and services or, indeed, to prevent their own overthrow, depends mainly upon the size, efficiency, and loyalty of their armed forces. As in the recent cases of Iran, Uganda, Ethiopia, and Nicaragua, the defeat or defection of the government's military and police forces leaves it with no capacity to rule. The subjects of some regimes, on the other hand, appear willing enough to obey that little direct coercion is necessary. In the United States, for example, surprisingly little threat of force is needed to induce citizens to pay taxes. Certainly, as those who have dealt with the Internal Revenue Service will attest, tax payment is not entirely voluntary. Yet America's tax system relies to a greater extent than that of most nations upon its citizens' willingness to honestly report their incomes. The government of the United States is probably not prepared to deal with tax evasion on a massive scale.[23]

---

[22] The problem of the free rider is discussed in Mancur Olson, Jr., *The Logic of Collective Action* (New York: Schocken, 1968).

[23] One fascinating experimental study suggests that appeals to conscience are more effective spurs to tax law compliance than are threats of sanctions. Richard D. Schwartz and Sonya Orleans, "On Legal Sanctions," *University of Chicago Law Review* 34 (1967): 282-300.

In general, it might be expected that a government's capacity to extract taxes and services from its citizens is enhanced if the public believes that the regime is responsive to its own needs and preferences. If citizens believe that the government is responsive to them—that they have some "say" about what the government does—they are also likely to believe that the resources they provide will be used for their own benefit. By contributing to a popular belief in governmental responsiveness, democratic elections can also contribute to the government's capacity to extract taxes and services with a minimum of force. Electoral participation, in other words, may at least help to partially substitute popular consent for coercion as the basis for the state's capacity to govern.

An empirical illustration of the significance of electoral processes can be obtained by comparing the effects of participation and coercion upon the capacity of democratic and authoritarian regimes to extract revenues from their citizens. With the assistance of the *World Handbook of Political and Social Indicators,* all nations for which the relevant data were available were again divided into two groups, the first group consisting again of nations that either did not permit routine elections or whose electoral processes the *World Handbook* deemed rigged or irregular, and the second group consisting of nations that routinely permit competitive elections.

First, for each of the two groups of nations a correlation was obtained between the size of national internal security forces and the share of the national per capita gross domestic product (GDP) at the government's disposal. This correlation is designed to measure the relationship between governments' capacity to coerce and their ability to extract revenues from their citizens. Second, for each of the two groups of nations a correlation was obtained between electoral participation as measured by the proportion of the adult population that voted in the most recent national election and the share of national per capita gross domestic product at the government's disposal. This correlation is designed to measure the relationship between mass participation and the government's ability to extract revenues. Third, for each group of nations a correlation was obtained between electoral participation and the size of national internal security forces. This correlation, obviously, is designed to measure the association between the extent of mass participation and governments' capacity to engage in coercion. All of these correlations are reported in Table 5.10.

The correlations reported in Table 5.10 provide a fascinating view of the effects of democratic elections upon governments' abilities to extract revenues from their citizens. First, among those nations that *do not* permit routine competitive elections, there appears to be a strong relationship between the size of national internal security forces and governments' shares of the national per capita gross domestic product. This relationship suggests, at least, that within this group of nations the extraction of revenues is closely linked to governments' capacity to engage in coercion. Mass participation, by contrast, seems not to be correlated with governments' shares of the gross domestic product.

Among those nations, on the other hand, that *do* permit routine competitive elections, there appears to be no relationship between the size of national internal security forces and governments' shares of the per capita gross domestic product. This group of nations, however, does appear to exhibit a strong relationship between rates of electoral participation and governments' shares of the gross domestic product. Among the democracies, it would seem, governments' ability to extract revenues is more closely linked to electoral participation than to the amount of force at the state's disposal.

We must, of course, recognize that these findings are not conclusive. The data were drawn from a limited time period, and as always,

TABLE 5.10 *Participation and coercion as sources of revenues—Pearson correlation coefficients.*

	Size of national internal security apparatus	Voters as a percentage of the adult population
Government consumption as a percentage of the GDP in nations lacking democratic elections	.36 (N = 24)	.06 (N = 8)
Government consumption as a percentage of the GDP in nations with competitive electoral processes	−.12 (N = 35)	.49 (N = 29)

some alternative explanation for the pattern of relationships is possible. Nevertheless, these patterns of association are at least consistent with the view that the popular support generated by democratic electoral procedures can substitute for coercion as a means of extracting revenues from a populace. Democratic elections may help to persuade citizens to contribute what the state might otherwise have been forced to attempt to seize from them.

Democratic electoral participation clearly is no guarantee of popular acquiescence to taxation, military service, or any other form of governmental extraction. Violent opposition to taxation has occurred in the United States—the Whiskey Rebellion is an example. Violent opposition to military conscription was important during both the Civil War and the Vietnam war. And, of course, the idea of "tax revolt" became quite popular in the United States during the 1970s. But even though elections do not guarantee popular consent to taxation and service, electoral participation does appear at least to create a more favorable climate for government.

THE LIMITS OF ACQUIESCENCE

Despite the advantages that governments can derive from democratic elections, electoral participation does not evoke positive beliefs about leaders or the regime among all citizens. Indeed, electorates can upon occasion respond unfavorably to electoral outcomes. It is not difficult to find instances of elections that have estranged segments of a nation's public. In the United States, for example, most of the individuals who voted for George Wallace in 1968 appeared to conceive their candidate's defeat to indicate some more general defect in the American political process (see Table 5.11). Among Wallace voters and nonvoters who favored Wallace in 1968, belief in the government's responsiveness declined precipitously after the election.

There are obviously limits to the ability of elections to generate citizen support for leaders and the regime. These limits appear mainly to be a function of the salience of issues and intensity of conflicts surrounding electoral contests. At some point, conflicts can

TABLE 5.11   *Changes in perceptions of whether or not public officials care among Wallace supporters following the 1968 presidential election.*

	Voted for Wallace	Preferred Wallace but did not vote
Percentage of respondents with negative preelection perceptions who became positive following the election	27.1 (N = 59)	25.0 (N = 20)
Percentage of respondents with positive preelection perceptions who became negative following the election	50.0 (N = 38)	42.9 (N = 14)

become sufficiently intense that participation will exacerbate rather than diminish hostilities. We can see something of this by examining the impact of one extremely salient issue upon citizens' reactions to the outcome of an election. In 1972, respondents' positions on the Vietnam war issue appear to have had considerable relevance for postelection changes in beliefs about the regime. What is apparent with regard to this issue is an "alienation of the extremes" effect. As Table 5.12 indicates, respondents placing themselves both at the extremely dovish *and* extremely hawkish ends of the scale exhibited a markedly less positive pattern of responses to the election's outcome than those with more moderate points of view. It would indeed appear that highly salient issues and controversies can limit the ability of participation to generate acquiescence. For this very reason, governments have typically sought to reduce the possibility of divisive conflict, for example through electoral arrangements that minimized the extent to which hostile groups were directly pitted against one another in a single electoral arena. Federal and consociational arrangements in a number of nations are examples.[24] And occasionally, collusion among competing partisan elites stems from an interest in avoiding divisive electoral conflicts. When all is said and done, however, some potential for divisive conflict is inherent in competitive

---

[24] On consociational arrangements, see Arend Lijphart, *The Politics of Accommodation* (Berkeley and Los Angeles: University of California Press, 1968).

TABLE 5.12 *Changes in popular perceptions of "say" in government following the 1972 presidential election.*

	Vietnam Issue Position*						
	1	2	3	4	5	6	7
Percentage of respondents with positive preelection perceptions who became negative following the election	28.6 (N = 98)	17.9 (N = 56)	11.7 (N = 94)	15.0 (N = 167)	6.0 (N = 83)	9.3 (N = 43)	17.9 (N = 67)

* Scale position 1 indicates a preference for an "immediate withdrawal" of American troops from Vietnam. Scale position 7 indicates a preference for a "complete military victory."

elections. And at least upon occasion, the realization of this possibility may rob those who rule of the popular consent that electoral participation can engender. Indeed, in some societies ethnic, religious, economic, and cultural divisions may be so deep that electoral competition would almost surely exacerbate conflict rather than promote consent. It does not seem reasonable to presume that an election in, say, Northern Ireland would secure the losers' acquiescence.

Thus the intensity of underlying cleavages may serve as a limit upon the capacity of electoral participation to generate mass support. It is, in a sense, when the decisions to be made are not especially significant that electoral choice promotes popular acquiescence. But is already a commentary upon the character of the decisions normally made by democratic electorates that the opportunity to choose seems generally to increase the likelihood that they will obey.[25]

---

[25] It should be noted that participation is not the only mechanism that governments may use to maintain or increase popular acquiescence. Other techniques have included the manipulation of religion, property ownership, and nationalism. See Lowi's list of "deadly virtues." Theodore J. Lowi, *American Government: Incomplete Conquest* (Hinsdale, Ill.: Dryden Press, 1976), ch. 3.

ELECTIONS
AND THE
STATE'S POWERS

At the same time that they enhance governments' authority, elections facilitate expansion of states' powers. Democratic elections can help induce citizens to freely grant their rulers power that authoritarian regimes often can acquire only by forcibly suppressing popular opposition. Over time, the state's expansion diminishes its vulnerability to electoral intervention while opening the way for increased governmental intervention into electoral processes. Thus, by helping to reconcile citizens to "big government," elections fuel the very processes that erode their own significance as instruments of popular control.

The size and scope of government are among the most striking features of contemporary political life. Over the past century, the governments of all the industrial nations have grown substantially in size and complexity. For example, governmental expenditures in the United Kingdom at the turn of the century represented a mere 11 percent of the gross national product. By the 1970s this percentage had more than quadrupled to almost 50 percent of the gross national product. During the same period in France, governmental expenditures increased from 14 percent to 37 percent of the gross national product. Similarly, in the United States, governmental expenditures more than tripled as a percentage of the gross national product, increasing from an average of 10 percent at the turn of the century to an average of 35 percent in the 1970s. In Germany, governmental expenditures expressed as a percentage of the gross national product quintupled during the twentieth century, increasing from 8 percent at the beginning of the century to an average of 42 percent in the 1970s. At the same time, the percentage of the labor force employed by government has also increased sharply. In the United States, for example, federal, state, and local governments together accounted for more than 13 million civilian employees—approximately 10 percent of the civilian labor force—during the 1970s. As recently as 1940, the comparable total was only 4.5 million.[1]

---

[1] The source of expenditure data was William W. Lammers and Joseph L. Nyomarkay, "Cabinet Level Recruitment and the Rise of the Administrative State: The Past 100 Years in France, Germany, the United Kingdom and the United States," paper presented at the Annual Meeting of the American Political Science Association, New

Accompanying this increase in the state's size has been a marked growth in the scope of its activities. Twentieth-century dictatorships and democracies alike intervene in every facet of economic, social, and political life. De Tocqueville was probably the first to perceive this distinguishing characteristic of the modern state. The power wielded by the sovereigns of earlier eras, according to de Tocqueville, was often absolute but was also limited in its scope. For example:

> *the whole government of the [Roman] empire was centered in the hands of the emperor alone . . . yet the details of social life and private occupations lay beyond his control. The emperor possessed an immense and unchecked power . . . but [that power] did not reach the many; it was confined to some few main objects and neglected the rest; it was violent, but its range was limited.* [2]

Government in the twentieth century, by contrast, penetrates every corner of its citizens' lives. Even in the United States, which, of course, has a strong tradition of limited governmental authority, the contemporary state has come to regulate almost all economic activity, to provide a vast array of services, and to engage in enterprises ranging from the exploration of space to the management of a less than reputable Washington nightclub.

Particularly in the democracies, this expansion of the state has been facilitated by electoral processes. The opportunity to participate,

---

York, New York, September 1978. The number of government employees in the United States is reported in U.S. Department of Commerce, Bureau of the Census, *Historical Statistics of the United States* (Washington, D.C.: U.S. Government Printing Office, 1971). In 1970, the number of federal civilian employees was 2,881,000—a figure dwarfed by the more than 10 million state and local government employees. However, not only do federal funds help to pay the salaries of many state and local employees, but to some extent the size of state and local government is a response to federal mandates and programs. Of course, in addition, the federal government employs over 3 million military personnel. Time-series data that describe changes in the size of the state sector in all the Western democracies since the mid-nineteenth century are presently becoming available. See Peter Flora *et al.,* "Historical Indicators of the Western European Democracies," University of Mannheim, mimeo, 1975.

[2] Alexis de Tocqueville, *Democracy in America* (New York: Random House, Vintage Books, 1945), vol. 2, p. 334.

as we saw, helps to convince citizens that they have some "say" about what their government does. This sense of influence indeed has considerable basis in fact. Democratic electoral institutions formalize mass influence in political life and do allow citizens some "say" in public affairs. But precisely because they encourage citizens to believe that the government is formally obliged to respond to their wishes, elections also help to convince the public that expansion of the scope and magnitude of governmental powers can be to its advantage. Democratic elections help to persuade citizens that expansion of the state's powers represents an increase in the state's capacity to serve them. As a result, democratic elections help to establish a climate of opinion conducive to the state's growth.

Mass electoral participation can hardly be considered the sole cause of the expansion of governmental power in the twentieth century. Obviously, a large number of economic, social, and political factors have helped spur the emergence and development of the modern state. But whatever the precise extent of elections' contribution, the state's growth in its turn has had the most profound implications for democratic electoral politics.

First, expansion of the state's powers inevitably diminishes the vulnerability of policymaking processes to electoral intervention. The enormous scope of national programs and involvements in the twentieth century has required the construction of a large and elaborate state apparatus and the transfer of considerable decision-making power from political to administrative agencies. As a consequence, the development and implementation of contemporary public policies is increasingly dominated by bureaucratic institutions, rules, and procedures that are not so easily affected by the vicissitudes of mass electoral politics.

Second, expansion of the state's role in the economy and in society tends to feed back upon the political process itself to result in additional national regulation of competitive electoral practices. Ironically, increased governmental intrusion into political processes is, in large measure, a response to the political problems caused by the twentieth-century state's expanded social and economic involvements. Modern governments' extensive economic and social programs have powerful politicizing effects, often sparking the organization of a host of new interests, groups, and forces. This explosion of interest-group activity can impose enormous pressure upon electoral and legislative processes—pressure that almost inevitably leads to problems of bias and corruption and fears of special-interest domination of political mechanisms. And, indeed, the Watergate revelations in the United States underscored the real threat to the equity and integrity of political processes posed particularly by interest groups' financial involvements in electoral politics. Increased pressure-group activity during the 1960s and 1970s was among the chief factors prompting several of the Western democracies to attempt to limit the role of private financial resources in the electoral process. Legislation enacted in the United States during the 1970s placed restrictions on interest groups' contributions to political candidates, introduced public funding of presidential races, and established the Federal Election Commission to supervise campaign funding.

This type of campaign finance regulation may help to enhance the honesty and equity of political practices. However, such regulation also represents a significant governmental encroachment upon competitive electoral processes. Money is a key political resource. Campaign finance legislation in the United States, despite its many loopholes, meant that the ability of groups and individuals to compete for public office, or to influence the results of such competition, would now be a question of national policy rather than simply a matter of private choice.

In effect, campaign finance reform entailed a substitution of government for politics—a substitution of formal rules and administrative procedures for competitive electoral practices. This substitution marked a significant shift toward greater governmental oversight of the competitive processes through which control of the government is ostensibly determined. Thus, as a political repercussion of government's expanded role in the economy and in society, competition for control of the state gave way to state control of competition.

VOTING AND THE STATE'S EXPANSION

In the absence of elections or other institutional mechanisms for mass involvement in political life, there is at least an implicit adversary relationship between rulers and those they rule. As we saw earlier, when formal means of popular consultation are lacking, rulers' concern with their subjects' wishes and welfare tends to be an inverse function of the regime's capacity to compel popular obedience and quiescence. This adversary relationship gives subjects a stake in seeking to check the expansion of their rulers' administrative and military capabilities. So long as rulers' attention to their subjects' welfare is perceived, in some measure, to depend upon the regime's weakness, efforts to expand or enhance the state's powers pose an obvious threat to its citizens' interests. The perception of an adversary relationship between rulers and ruled is, for example, at the heart of the familiar seventeenth- and eighteenth-century concerns with separation of powers, checks and balances, and other constitutional devices to limit the concentration of governmental power. The greater the state's power, it was assumed, the greater the potential threat to its citizens' liberty and well-being.[3]

Perhaps the finer points of constitutional theory have not always been fully grasped by ordinary citizens. But ordinary citizens do not necessarily require an abstract conception of the adversary relationship between themselves and their rulers to be troubled by the state's growth. The masses, as we saw, have typically been asked to bear the concrete costs of state building, especially in the form of increased taxation and military service. Attempts by rulers to impose these burdens have usually been sufficient to arouse opposition even among those of their subjects who lacked a firm understanding of the important issues of political theory that were at stake. The efforts, for example, of sixteenth- and seventeenth-century European monarchs to centralize national authority, subordinate rival institutions such as the church and Estates, and to build bureaucracies and standing armies almost invariably encountered intense, often violent, and

---

[3] This is, of course, one of James Madison's major themes. See, for example, E.M. Earle (ed.), *The Federalist* (New York: Modern Library, 1937), no. 47. See also G.N. Clark, *The Seventeenth Century* (Oxford: Oxford University Press, 1929), p. 94. Clark observes, "Contemporaries knew that the dynastic system meant that the interests of rulers and their subjects must be more or less widely divergent."

sometimes successful popular resistance.[4] Indeed, collective violence was among the chief obstacles to the construction of the modern state. Traditionally, rulers were best able to expand and centralize national power either when their subjects lacked the capacity to resist or when some exogenous factor such as a foreign foe appeared to pose an even greater threat to the public's welfare. It is in part for this latter reason that war has often eased the way for expansion of the state's role.[5]

Democratic elections fundamentally alter the relationship between rulers and those they rule. With the availability of electoral mechanisms, popular influence need not have an inverse relationship to rulers' power. Karl Mannheim, for example, argued, "In a democratic state, sovereignty can be boundlessly strengthened by plenary powers without renouncing democratic control."[6] Because elections formalize and institutionalize citizens' influence over their leaders' conduct, mass influence need not decline when rulers' power increases. Not even the most powerful elected official, after all, is immune to reprisal at the polls.

It is, however, this apparent erosion of the adversary relationship between rulers and ruled that converts mass political activity from a limit upon to a catalyst for the growth of government. Given a formal electoral means of affecting their rulers' actions, citizens potentially stand to benefit from rulers' power rather than from their weakness. The democratic election opens the possibility that citizens can use rulers' administrative and military capabilities for their own benefit,

---

[4] Charles Tilly, "Reflections on the History of European State-Making," in Charles Tilly (ed.), *The Formation of National States in Western Europe* (Princeton, N.J.: Princeton University Press, 1975), p. 22.

[5] The effects of war on the government's expansion in the United States is discussed in Bruce D. Porter, "Parkinson's Law Revisited: War and the Growth of Government," *The Public Interest* 60 (Summer 1980): 50-68. See also Robert A. Dahl and Charles Lindblom, *Politics, Economics and Welfare* (New York: Harper, 1953), pp. 402-412, for an analysis of the subordination of individual market choices that may appear to be necessary in wartime.

[6] Karl Mannheim, *Man and Society in an Age of Reconstruction* (London: Kegan Paul, Trench, Trubner and Co., 1940), p. 341.

rather than simply benefit from rulers' inability to construct a governmental apparatus sufficiently powerful to compel popular quiescence. Democratic elections help to persuade the public that expansion of the state's powers is equivalent to expansion of its own.

The public's belief in its capacity to control the state's actions is only one of the many factors responsible for the state's extraordinary growth in the twentieth century. But at the very least, citizens' sense of influence helps to create an environment of opinion conducive to increased governmental intrusion into social and economic affairs. In the United States, for example, individuals who believe that they influence the government's actions are also more likely to believe, in turn, that the government should have more power. Such individuals are also relatively more supportive of a greater degree of governmental intervention in the economy and society and are more likely than others to express a lack of concern with the implications for civil liberties of governmental intervention (see Table 6.1). To the extent that they contribute to the public's sense of influence, democratic elections help to create a more permissive climate for the state's expansion.

Permissive public attitudes can, of course, ease the way for elites seeking to use the state's power for their own purposes—the Progressive era in the United States is a prime example. At the same time, public beliefs generally congenial to governmental intervention can increase the likelihood that the mass public itself will seek expanded state action as a means of dealing with social and economic problems. The electorate's demands for services, for example, have been important factors in increasing the role of the American national government over the past 40 years. For example, in the United States, what Huntington calls the "welfare shift" during the 1960s was a drastic increase in domestic spending—$184 billion between 1960 and 1971 for education, social security, health, hospitals, and welfare—that resulted almost directly from citizens' demands for such services.[7]

---

[7] Samuel Huntington, "The United States," in Michel J. Crozier, Samuel Huntington, and Joji Watanuki, *The Crisis of Democracy* (New York: New York University Press, 1975), ch. 3, part 2.

TABLE 6.1 *Belief in influence as a source of mass support for state intervention.*

	Government should have more power	Government should be able to limit gas use	Government should be able to require national I.D. card	Government should be able to investigate backgrounds	Government should be able to require pollution equipment	Government should be able to wiretap
Government listens to people:						
A great deal	63.1%* (N = 236)	74.8% (N = 246)	41.1% (N = 237)	79.8% (N = 242)	71.4% (N = 233)	52.4% (N = 241)
Sometimes	49.1% (N = 1213)	68.1% (N = 1270)	39.5% (N = 1220)	75.2% (N = 1248)	70.6% (N = 1205)	49.3% (N = 1213)
Never	40.1% (N = 691)	58.1% (N = 736)	38.7% (N = 727)	71.5% (N = 747)	53.9% (N = 697)	41.9% (N = 708)
Elections affect government policy:						
A great deal	50.5% (N = 1164)	68.6% (N = 1205)	41.8% (N = 1176)	77.3% (N = 1190)	70.0% (N = 1156)	49.3% (N = 1161)
Sometimes	45.2% (N = 774)	65.1% (N = 819)	35.8% (N = 819)	73.1% (N = 791)	61.0% (N = 771)	45.9% (N = 786)
Not at all	44.3% (N = 210)	53.5% (N = 229)	43.3% (N = 222)	66.9% (N = 239)	55.6% (N = 207)	42.3% (N = 221)

* That is, 63.1 percent of those respondents who believe that government listens to the people a great deal also think that the government should be given more power.

Over the course of American political history, the state's growth has been closely linked to electoral preferences. At no time, of course, has the mass electorate specifically voted in favor of a larger and more powerful government. However, such a government emerged from decisions that were, in part, made by the mass electorate. Historically, three of the sharpest increases in the size of the American state—at least as measured by its budgetary outlays—occurred as elected officials sought to build a state apparatus sufficiently large and powerful to implement the courses of action endorsed by the electorate during periods of critical realignment. Indeed, with the understandable exception of Jefferson's victory in 1801, the points of policy change following critical elections that we observed in Chapter 4 are also the most important periods of transition for the size of the American national government. A T-test comparing successive five-year periods in the same manner described in Chapter 4 suggests that the largest points of permanent growth in the size of the American national budget took place during these critical periods. In essence, the increases in budgetary outlays that occurred at these points in time marked new plateaus in the size of the state (see Fig. 6.1).

The permanence of increases in the size of the state during critical electoral periods is largely a function of the fact that it is mainly during these periods that national governmental institutions have been constructed in the United States. In the 1860s, for example, aside from the enormous costs of conducting the Civil War, there also occurred more permanent increases in the size and scope of governmental activity that were not directly related to the war effort. In 1862, the federal government established the Department of Agriculture and the National Banking System. During the same period, the federal government created an immigration bureau, inaugurated a program of grants and loans to railroads (beginning with the Union Pacific in 1862), expanded the national credit base through bond flotations and loans, and established income tax and internal revenue administrations. In the 1880s, the United States began the construction of the institutions, such as the Interstate Commerce Commission, through which the national government came to play a major role in regulating, rationalizing, and expanding economic activity. Much of this process of institution building was, to be sure, aimed at bolstering

FIG. 6.1 *Change over time in the size of the U.S. budget.*

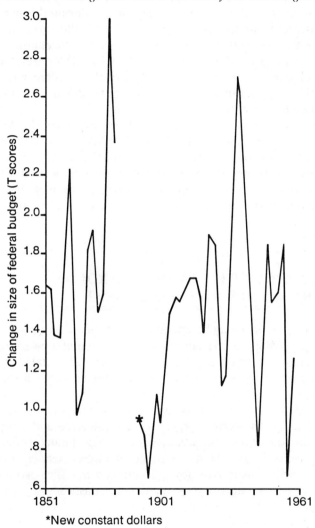

*New constant dollars

the foundations of industrial capitalism.[8] Yet at the same time, the character of the federal government's growth during this period was fully consistent with the electorate's decisions in the period 1876-80— decisions that were, after all, reaffirmed in 1896. The character of the state's growth during the period of the New Deal is too well-known to require elaboration here. The beginning of the "welfare state" was a direct, if initially halting, response to popular demands for national services and intervention into the economy.

Thus the points of the state's greatest expansion in American history were, at least in some measure, linked to the wishes of the electorate. These ties between electoral participation and the state's expansion underline the irony. Though it is associated with and facilitated by democratic electoral processes, ultimately the growth of the state erodes the significance of elections as institutions of popular control.

THE EROSION OF POPULAR CONTROL— GOVERNORS VERSUS GOVERNMENT

However much they may be linked to the implementation of citizens' wishes, expansion of the scope of governmental powers and the concomitant construction of a large and complex state apparatus inevitably diminish the possibility of popular control via the ballot box.

The idea that elections facilitate citizen control over the activities of the state is derived largely from eighteenth- and nineteenth-century theories of representation. Eighteenth- and nineteenth-century theorists argued that the dependence of elected leaders upon the favor of their constituents for continuance in office would force leaders to rule in accordance with their constituents' wishes and

---

[8] A good summary can be found in Edward S. Greenberg, *Understanding Modern Government* (New York: Wiley, 1979), ch. 3. A provocative analysis of the most important pieces of legislation of this period is presented by Gabriel Kolko, *The Triumph of Conservatism* (Chicago: Quadrangle, 1963).

interests. James Madison, for example, argued that "they will be compelled to anticipate the moment when their power is to cease, when their exercise of it is to be reviewed, and when they must descend to the level from which they were raised; there forever to remain unless a faithful discharge of their trust shall have established their title to a renewal of it."[9]

Classical theories of representation were concerned primarily with the question of how the governed could control the individuals who governed them. They were not intended, however, to answer the much more complex question of how the governed might control a *government*. At the time when most popular governments were founded, many theorists recognized the importance of that distinction. Rousseau, for example, argued that to prevent "usurpations" citizens not only must have the opportunity to select their governors but must also be regularly asked whether they wished to preserve the existing form of government.[10] But despite the sensitivity of the founding theorists to the difference between electing governors and controlling government, the distinction has largely been ignored in more recent years. At some point after popular governments became old hat, we apparently began to assume that true popular control of the individuals in office would be tantamount to a significant degree of popular influence in government.

The distinction, however, between control of governors and influence in government is critically important. For every office-holder there is an office—and the office is part of a vast fabric of laws, institutions, and processes that can be quite resistant to popular influence despite the electorate's ability to install and remove office-holders. Particularly in the twentieth century, autocratic rule has to a significant extent given way to a routinized and institutionalized governmental process. The more rule becomes institutionalized and the governmental process routinized, the more the significance of popular control of the individuals in office is likely to be diminished.

---

[9] Earle, *The Federalist*, no. 57, p. 372.

[10] Jean Jacques Rousseau, *The Social Contract*, trans. and ed. by G.D.H. Cole (New York: E.P. Dutton, 1950), p. 101.

In the United States, the institutional arrangements mandated by the Constitution have, to some degree, always served to limit the direct impact upon the government of popular election of public officials. Staggered terms in the Senate, for example, leave individual senators vulnerable to the electorate while partially insulating the Senate as an institution from the impact of changes in electoral behavior. The separation of powers, bicameralism, and the extraordinary legislative majorities required for passage of some types of measures are only among the most obvious examples of institutional arrangements that can partially insulate the behavior of the government from the impact of popular election of governors.

Despite the continuity of basic constitutional arrangements, however, if we compare nineteenth- to twentieth-century American government, what is particularly impressive is the extent to which the nineteenth-century governmental process, particularly after the advent of the mass party, was a direct outgrowth of the electoral process. In the nineteenth century, within broad limits, what the national government did was dependent upon prevailing community sentiment. Governments behaved as though they were the sum of the actions of the individuals placed in office by the electorate. The striking continuity between the electoral process and the governmental process in nineteenth-century America is best described by de Tocqueville: "In America the people appoint the legislative and the executive power and furnish the jurors who punish all infractions of the laws. The institutions are democratic not only in their principle but in their consequences. . . . It is evident that the opinions, the prejudices, the interests and even the passions of the people are hindered by no permanent obstacles from exercising a perpetual influence on the daily conduct of affairs."[11] Further, "The great political agitation of American legislative bodies . . . is a mere episode or a sort of continuation, of that universal movement which originates in the lowest classes of the people and extends successively to all the ranks of society."[12]

---

[11] De Tocqueville, *Democracy in America,* vol. 1, p. 18.

[12] *Ibid.,* p. 259.

In the nineteenth century there were few boundaries between the electoral process and the behavior of the government. By the mid-twentieth century, however, three fundamental changes in the character of the regime had given the governmental process a considerable degree of insulation from electoral politics. These changes were: (1) the expansion of rule through law; (2) the growth of administration; and (3) the conversion of policymaking to an institutional process.

THE FORCES OF INSULATION

The expansion of rule through law

Until the Civil War, American public policy at the national level was largely *ad hoc* and particularistic. With a few important exceptions, national policy consisted of discrete grants of subsidy or aid to specific groups or interests. Among the more important examples are grants of lands to railroad corporations, disposition of the public lands to settlers, piecemeal manipulation of tariff schedules, subsidies to steamship lines, and public subscriptions in canal companies.

The characteristic shared by all these policies is that they required little, if any, continuing activity or even commitment to future action on the part of the government. Disposition of the public lands to settlers was, as White notes, a "once for all operation."[13] The tariff was simply a set of subsidies determined by processes of bargaining and log rolling that began virtually from scratch during each congressional session. Prior to the Civil War, the post office was virtually the only ongoing public service. The *ad hoc* character of national policy in the nineteenth century meant that virtually all public programs were a direct function of who happened to hold public office that year. And since the question of public office was determined by the electorate, the *ad hoc* character of national policy meant that the

---

[13] Leonard White, *The Jacksonians* (New York: Free Press, 1954), p. 436.

behavior of the government was directly linked with the behavior of the electorate.

In the twentieth century, on the other hand, a predominant portion of the government's actions each year is based upon rules and laws previously enacted. Beginning in the 1880s and increasing after the 1930s, national policy began to incorporate rules of law that required ongoing activity on the part of the government—rules that committed the government to specified courses of action over time.

Thus in the nineteenth century national economic policy consisted principally of *ad hoc* subsidies to particular interests. This pattern continued to an extent in the twentieth century—loan guarantees to the Lockheed Corporation serve as an obvious recent example. But the bulk of national economic policy in the twentieth century consists of ongoing and only partially discretionary regulation of business conduct and manipulation of taxes, credit, and the supply of money. These programs, such as antitrust, regulation of a variety of business practices, and tax policy, commit the government to specified courses of action over time whenever some type of conduct or state of affairs occurs.

Similarly, in the area of agricultural policy, price supports and credit and acreage allotments determined by statutory formulas that have standing over time have largely replaced *ad hoc* aid via tariffs on specific commodities. In the areas of welfare, civil rights, education, housing, labor, and so on, national policy consists principally of rules and entitlements that continue to operate over time.

If we examine the allocation of federal expenditures during any given year as a rough indicator of governmental activity, what is of course striking is the incremental nature of changes in outlays. As Wildavsky notes, "most of the budget is a product of previous decisions." Because of the continuing nature of most governmental programs and outlays, "the greatest part of a government budget represents expenditures which are mandated by previous programs."[14]

---

[14] Aaron Wildavsky, *The Politics of the Budgetary Process* (Boston: Little, Brown, 1974), p. 216.

This change from governmental behavior based upon *ad hoc* enactments in the nineteenth century to behavior based upon ongoing rules of law in the twentieth, is critically important for the consequences of elections. This change means that a significant portion of the government's activities can persist over time despite changes in the individuals in office. And in turn, this means that the direct link between electoral selection of those individuals and governmental behavior is broken. So long as a law is in effect, the behavior of the government in that area is not directly sensitive to the behavior of the electorate. Even if passage of a law initially results from the pressure of "public opinion," so long as the law continues in force, the government's behavior can but need not be affected by subsequent changes in public opinion.

Of course, rules of law can be altered or abolished. But quite frequently, once a rule is enacted it creates vested interests prepared to defend it.[15] The reaction of the airline industry to proposed deregulation is one recent example. Moreover, as we shall see, rules of law have an impact upon the organization of the government itself that can make change through the electoral process difficult.

From execution to administration

The nucleus of the national administration was built during the very earliest years of the republic. The Treasury, State, War, and Navy departments as well as the Office of the Attorney General and the Post Office were established by the very first American congresses.

Despite this wave of institution building, early congresses engaged in a good deal of direct governing through special committees and required all major and many minor administrative decisions to be made by the president himself, even to the extent of personally signing patents for inventions and personally approving each contract for lighthouse construction. Through the Civil War, presidents personally supervised administrative details. Jefferson, for example,

---

[15] See Theodore J. Lowi, *The End of Liberalism*, rev. ed. (New York: Norton, 1979).

personally gave instructions on post-road river crossings.[16] Van Buren personally had to decide who would purchase a fire engine authorized by Congress.[17] Fillmore personally was required to approve a plan to supply the New York Navy yard with water from a spring.[18]

Obviously, the president could not supervise every administrative detail even in the nineteenth century, but administrative agencies were very much the servants of the president and the Congress. The nineteenth century is, of course, famous for the spoils system and the principle of rotation in office. But a much more important limit on administrative independence and discretion was the fact that most national policies were executed rather than administered. Given the *ad hoc,* "once for all" character of most nineteenth-century legislation, there was little room for administrative modification of the decisions of the president and the Congress.

The importance of administration began to increase at the turn of the century with the creation of four new governmental departments and three independent regulatory commissions. This growth of administration, which accelerated after the 1930s, was, of course, a direct result of national programs intended to continue in effect over time. Laws regulating business conduct or manipulating the tax structure or providing relief for different classes of indigent persons could no longer simply be executed but instead required large and specialized staffs of administrators for their implementation on an ongoing basis.

In principle, administrative agencies were created to put into practical and routine effect the laws promulgated by Congress. In practice, of course, administrative agencies operating typically, and to some degree necessarily, under broad delegations of congressional power make important policy decisions and effectively exercise a variety of executive, legislative, and judicial powers. Bureaucratic rule making is often far more important to affected groups and interests than is congressional legislation.[19]

---

[16] Leonard White, *The Jeffersonians* (New York: Free Press, 1951), p. 71.

[17] White, *The Jacksonians,* p. 71.

[18] *Ibid.,* p. 70.

[19] Lowi, *The End of Liberalism.*

Public administration in many areas of policy has become, in effect, the permanent government, substantially independent of congressional and presidential control. Congress, of course, has the ultimate authority to create and destroy, structure and restructure, agencies. But Congress often lacks the more mundane information, staff, expertise, and time to oversee the daily operations of the administrative branch.[20]

The president's control over administration, particularly but not exclusively in domestic policy areas, is also limited. Some agencies have independent statutory authority. The president's powers of appointment and removal are limited. The president, like Congress, is hampered by lack of time, information, and expertise. In many instances the best presidents can do is to attempt to persuade administrators to cooperate with their programs. Of course, many agencies have protected themselves from undue presidential interference by forming stable relationships with key congressional commmittees and subcommittees.[21]

In recent years presidential decision making has itself become a corporate rather than an individualistic product.[22] The office of the president has come to include a number of specialized staffs and agencies with important roles in domestic and foreign affairs. The

---

[20] See, for example, Samuel P. Huntington, "Congressional Responses to the 20th Century," in David Truman (ed.), *Congress and America's Future* (Englewood Cliffs, N.J.: Prentice-Hall, 1965), pp. 5-31. On the problem of congressional oversight see the excellent discussion in Lawrence C. Dodd and Richard L. Schott, *Congress and the Administrative State* (New York: Wiley, 1979). See also Theodore J. Lowi and Margaret Stapleton, "Congress, the Atom, and Civil Rights: A Case Study in Civil Wrongs," in Theodore J. Lowi and Randall Ripley (eds.), *Legislative Politics, USA* (Boston: Little, Brown, 1973), pp. 290-312.

[21] The inability of presidents to control the bureaucracy is a major theme of every text on the subject. See, for example, Grant McConnell, *The Modern Presidency* (New York: St. Martin's Press, 1967), ch. 4. Nixon's efforts to bring the bureaucracy under some measure of control is described in Robert Nathan, *The Plot That Failed* (New York: Wiley, 1975).

[22] See, for example, Thomas Cronin, "The Swelling of the Presidency," in Stanley Bach and George T. Sulzner, *Perspectives on the Presidency* (Lexington, Mass.: Heath, 1974), pp. 179-189.

National Security Council with its staff arm, the Central Intelligence Agency, and the Office of Management and Budget are the two most important examples.

Thus, in short, the day-to-day management of national affairs in the twentieth century is principally in the hands of a number of semi-autonomous bureaucratic agencies. While congressional statutes in the nineteenth century generally required only execution on a "once for all" basis, often by the president himself, twentieth-century legislation must be interpreted and administered over long periods of time. In the process, bureaucratic agencies in effect make law with only sporadic interference from their elected overseers.[23]

Policymaking as an institutional process

In the early nineteenth century, the legislative process was relatively simple, undifferentiated, and unspecialized. Legislative proposals usually originated in the Congress, and the House and Senate both functioned as genuine deliberative assemblies. In the House, many important matters of business were conducted in the Committee of the Whole. According to Galloway, the principles of all the major measures of the first five congresses were formulated first in the Committee of the Whole and then referred to select committees for detail and drafting.[24] In the early years, even though standing committees did begin to emerge in 1816, Congress as a whole generally retained authority over the legislative process either by establishing only temporary and carefully instructed select committees for individual bills or by considering the details of legislation in the Committee of the Whole.[25]

The organization of the nineteenth-century Congress was partisan. In the House, the majority party caucus elected the Speaker, who,

---

[23] This is, of course, one of the major points of Lowi, *The End of Liberalism*. See also David Nachmias and David H. Rosenbloom, *Bureaucratic Government USA* (New York: St. Martin's Press, 1980).

[24] George Galloway, *History of the United States House of Representatives* (New York: Crowell, 1962), ch. 2, especially pp. 10-13.

[25] *Ibid.*, pp. 64-71.

even after the development of standing committees, exercised a substantial degree of influence over legislative proceedings. The Speaker chaired the Rules Committee and controlled other committee assignments and chairmanships. Leadership and influence in the nineteenth-century Congress was, to a substantial extent, won outside Congress itself. National party leaders could become congressional leaders with little or no prior congressional service. Henry Clay, for example, was elected Speaker during his first term in Congress in 1811. Committee chairmen were selected on the basis of their value to the party. Seniority in Congress and on the committee itself did not become important until the late nineteenth century and did not come to be a virtually unbroken rule of selection until the twentieth century.[26]

The nineteenth-century legislative process was directly linked with elections. The partisan organization and leadership of both House and Senate meant that they were, in essence, externally imposed upon the Congress. The party that won the most seats in House elections dominated the legislative process. For indirectly elected senators the case is, of course, more complex. But again, external rather than institutional criteria determined organization and leadership. Especially in the case of the House, decisions made by the national electorate could, in the nineteenth century, have a clear and direct impact on both the organization of and the distribution of influence in Congress. Particularly given high rates of congressional turnover in the nineteenth century, electoral politics could have an immediate impact on the legislative process.[27]

In the modern Congress, the links between the electoral process and the legislative process are neither clear nor direct. The modern Congress continues to be organized by the major parties. But parties

---

[26] See Nelson Polsby, Miriam Gallaher, and Barry Spencer Rundquist, "The Growth of the Seniority System in the U.S. House of Representatives," *American Political Science Review* 63 (September 1969): 787-807.

[27] See *ibid.* See also Nelson W. Polsby, "Institutionalization in the U.S. House of Representatives," *American Political Science Review* 62 (1968): 144-168; and Hugh Douglas Price, "The Congressional Career—Then and Now," in Nelson Polsby (ed.), *Congressional Behavior* (New York: Random House, 1971), pp. 14-27.

are clearly overshadowed in organizational importance by the standing committees and subcommittees.[28] Within their subject matter jurisdictions, committees and subcommittees have a substantial degree of autonomy in the House, and to a slightly lesser degree in the Senate. The procedural rules of Congress make it extremely difficult for a bill to come to the floor without the appropriate committee and subcommittee approvals. And although in both House and Senate the party leadership controls the legislative calendars, legislative action on the floor is primarily influenced by the committees.

Committee leadership is, of course, based on committee seniority. In recent years, seniority has come under attack but nevertheless remains the key principle. Seniority as a criterion for promotion means that leadership in Congress in the twentieth century is not directly tied to electoral politics. Indeed, leadership is almost automatically awarded by the seniority system to those members who have proven to be least vulnerable to the electorate.

With organization and leadership based on internal, institutional criteria rather than external, political criteria, the legislative process in Congress is no longer as closely linked to elections as it was in the nineteenth century. Legislation has become an institutional process in which many, if not most, domestic legislative areas are dominated by "subgovernments" composed of a congressional subcommittee and its subject matter counterpart in the bureaucracy. Given seniority as a key criterion for committee leadership, these institutional alliances can be extremely stable and only marginally affected by electoral politics. The twentieth-century legislative process may respond, at times, to citizens' needs but is to a considerable degree insulated from the impact of their behavior at the polls.[29]

---

[28] For an analysis of the transformation, see, for example, David W. Brady, "Congressional Leadership Then and Now," in Robert L. Peabody and Nelson W. Polsby (eds.), *New Perspectives on the House of Representatives* (Chicago: Rand McNally, 1977), pp. 389-408.

[29] This emerges as the most important implication of the "institutionalization" of Congress. See Ripley's summary. Randall B. Ripley, *Congress: Process and Policy* (New York: Norton, 1975), ch. 2.

GOVERNORS AND GOVERNMENT

As a consequence of these changes in the character of the regime, the twentieth-century governmental process is significantly insulated from the effects of mass electoral politics. Voters may continue to select and depose some public officials, but the behavior of the government is not necessarily, as a result, vulnerable to changes in electoral behavior. Indeed, popular selection of the individuals in office can help to protect the authority and autonomy of the regime by channeling mass disaffection and discontent away from governmental processes and institutional arrangements. The electoral vulnerability of the individuals in office may serve as a safety valve for the regime, with the same sort of diversionary effect that monarchs often sought to create by dismissing unpopular ministers and blaming them for the regime's shortcomings. In a modern democracy, the ease with which rulers can be deposed can lessen the likelihood that pressure will mount for changes in rule. This has virtually become the key function of the American presidency in the twentieth century. In a twentieth-century democracy, rulers can be deposed without significant changes in rule.

STATE INTERVENTION AND ELECTORAL PROCESSES

Expansion of the state's powers not only entails the construction of a complex state apparatus that can diminish governments' vulnerability to electoral intervention but also paves the way for increased governmental regulation of political mechanisms themselves. State intervention into economy and society tends eventually to spill over into the electoral process. The most important example of such spillover in recent American history is the campaign finance reform instituted during the 1970s. This legislation represented a significant expansion of the national government's capacity to regulate electoral processes. Indeed, these campaign finance enactments substantially increased the potential for state control of the possibilities for access and influence through democratic electoral means.

Much of the impetus for expanded state regulation of political processes, as we noted earlier, derives from the explosive politicizing effects of modern governments' vast economic and social programs. The activities of organized groups are generally viewed in terms of their effects upon governmental action. But interest-group activity is often more a consequence than an antecedent of the state's programs. Even when national policies are initially responses to the appeals of pressure groups and the like, government involvement in a given area is a powerful stimulus for political organization and action, or increases in political action, by those whose interests are affected. A recent *New York Times* report, for example, noted that in the past several years expanded federal regulation of the automobile, oil, gas, education, and health-care industries impelled each of these interests to substantially increase its efforts to influence the government's behavior. These efforts, in turn, had the effect of spurring the organization of other groups to augment or oppose the activities of the first.[30] Similarly, federal social programs have often sparked political organization and action on the part of clientele groups seeking to influence the distribution of benefits and, in turn, the organization of groups opposed to the character of the benefits or cost of the programs in question.[31] Substantially increased political organization and activity by fundamentalist religious groups in recent

---

[30] John Herbers, "Special Interests Gaining Power as Voter Disillusionment Grows," *New York Times,* November 14, 1978. One PAC director observes: "It was not the Federal Election Campaign Act and the Federal Election Commission that promoted the PAC movement; it was every other law and every other regulatory body that began intruding into the business of business. A clear pattern emerges when reviewing one who does and who does not have a PAC—the more regulated an industry and the more obvious an industry is as a congressional target, the more likely it is to have a political action committee." Bernadette A. Budde, "Business Political Action Committees," in Michael J. Malbin (ed.), *Parties, Interest Groups and Campaign Finance Laws* (Washington, D.C.: American Enterprise Institute, 1980), p. 11.

[31] One example of a pressure group "caused" by a federal program is the National Welfare Rights Organization (NWRO), whose formation during the 1960s was a response to federal and local welfare policies. See Frances Fox Piven and Richard A. Cloward, *Poor People's Movements* (New York: Random House, Vintage Books, 1979), ch. 5; and Frances Fox Piven and Richard A. Cloward, *Regulating the Poor* (New York:

years obviously came in response to federal legislative programs and judicial actions relating to such matters as abortion.

From the public's pespective, this explosion of interest-group activity poses an obvious threat to the equity and integrity of the political process. And for their part, incumbent elites are only too happy to respond to the public's concerns. At the same time that it evokes public apprehension, rapid politicization of new groups and forces can also be quite consternating to established interests and elites. Elected officials, in particular, may suffer increased pressure and harassment. In recent years, for example, a host of new "single-issue groups" organized around matters ranging from abortion to trade regulation have subjected Congress to enormous pressures and cross-pressures on behalf of their various causes. These groups often threaten severe reprisals against their congressional opponents. For example, in the 1970s the National Conservative Political Action Committee (NCPAC) promised to spend millions of dollars to unseat opponents of its stands on gun control and abortion. NCPAC funds, indeed, came to play important roles in the defeat of liberal Democrats such as Frank Church in the 1980 Senate races.[32] A particular target of conservative political action groups was George McGovern, who was, of course, defeated in his 1980 senatorial reelection bid. Groups opposing McGovern included the National Right-to-Life Committee, the Life Amendment Political Action Committee, the Committee for the Survival of a Free Congress, the National Conservative Caucus, the American Conservative Union, the Fund for a Conservative Majority, the Young Americans for Freedom, the John Birch Society, the Citizens for the Republic, the National Right to Work Committee,

---

Pantheon, 1971), pp. 320-338. The "War on Poverty" obviously also had a major politicizing effect. See, for example, Daniel P. Moynihan, *Maximum Feasible Misunderstanding* (New York: Free Press, 1970).

[32] Bernard Weinraub, "Oust-Church Drive in Idaho Stirs Smear-Tactic Charges," *New York Times*, May 11, 1980. Not to be outdone, the liberal "National Committee for an Effective Congress" promised to seek the defeat of five conservative senators and 66 conservative representatives in the 1982 election. The list incuded several 1980 winners who had not yet even taken office. See "Progressives' Target List Names 71 Conservatives," *New York Times*, December 4, 1980.

the Eagle Forum, the Citizens' Committee for the Right to Keep and Bear Arms, the Gun Owners of America, the Tax Limitation Committee, the Committee to Defeat the Union Bosses, and the Committee to Save the Panama Canal.[33]

The campaign finance regulations enacted in the United States during the 1970s resulted at least in part from this conjunction of public apprehension and elite discomfiture. The initial demand for reform, of course, came from groups comprising the "New Politics" movement—Common Cause in particular—which sought a variety of political reforms designed to weaken their opponents within the Democratic party. Once proposed, however, campaign finance regulation attracted widespread public support and, in addition, came to be viewed favorably by incumbent legislators. Indeed, many members of Congress pointed specifically to the baneful effects of "special-interest intimidation," by which they presumably meant interest groups' threats to support challengers to their reelection bids, as a chief justification for the imposition of legal limits upon campaign contributions and other political activities by such groups.[34]

The broad outlines of American campaign finance legislation are well-known. The Federal Elections Campaign Act of 1971, as amended in 1974 and subsequently, set dollar limits upon private contributions to candidates for national office and established the Federal Election Commission (FEC) to supervise funding and campaign practices.[35] Under the terms of the 1976 amendments, individuals were limited to contributions of $1000 to any single candidate in any election, and political action committees (PACs) were limited to contributions of $5000 to any single candidate in any election. The 1974 amendments, coupled with earlier legislation, also entitled qualifying candidates in

[33] Leslie Bennetts, "National Anti-Liberal Crusade Zeroing in on McGovern in South Dakota," *New York Times*, June 2, 1980.

[34] Steven V. Roberts, "Problem of Campaign Funds," *New York Times*, October 18, 1979. Campaign finance reform and the New Politics movement is discussed in Martin Shefter, "Party, Bureaucracy, and Political Change in the United States," in Louis Maisel and Joseph Cooper (eds.), *Political Parties: Development and Decay* (Beverly Hills, Calif.: Sage, 1978), pp. 211-266.

[35] The 1971 act is P.L. 92-225, 86 Stat. 3 (1972). The 1974 act is P.L. 93-443, 88 Stat. 1263.

presidential primary elections to receive federal matching grants in support of their campaign efforts and, in addition, provided for full public funding of major party candidates in the general presidential election. The 1974 amendments, of course, also mandated spending limits for federal candidates. Such limits were, however, struck down by the United States Supreme Court in the 1976 case of *Buckley* v. *Valeo,* except as applied to presidential candidates who agreed to accept federal funds.[36] Several excellent summaries of the principal provisions of the various pieces of legislation are available elsewhere.[37]

Campaign finance reforms were ostensibly designed to reduce the inequities resulting from candidates' unequal access to private campaign funds and, more important, from the ability of well-financed groups and wealthy individuals to use their resources to acquire a disproportionate share of influence over electoral and policymaking processes. And perhaps, despite its many loopholes, the Federal Elections Act does represent a step in the direction of greater political equality. But what is even more significant about the 1971 act and subsequent amendments is the extent to which they fundamentally enhance the national government's role in the political process.

Money is a key political resource. Particularly given the demise of party organization in the United States, candidates for office must rely heavily upon media advertising, salaried staffs, professional opinion polling, and a variety of other costly mechanisms to make an impression upon the electorate. As a result, candidates' electoral fortunes—those of insurgents, in particular—are closely linked to their capacity to raise funds. At the same time, the ability of individuals or groups to contribute funds to political campaigns can be a significant source of influence in electoral and subsequent policymaking processes. The imposition of statutory limits upon campaign contributions, coupled with public funding of presidential races, thus gave the federal government a potentially critical source of control over

---

[36] *Buckley* v. *Valeo.* 424 U.S. 1 (1976).

[37] For example, see Bruce F. Freed, "Political Money and Campaign Finance Reform, 1971-1976," in Jeff Fishel (ed.), *Parties and Elections in an Anti-Party Age* (Bloomington: Indiana University Press, 1978), pp. 242-243.

competitive electoral practices. On the one hand, even voluntary public funding of presidential races meant that a formula set by the national government would greatly affect both the quantity of financial support available to presidential candidates and the state-by-state pattern in which candidates were entitled to spend those funds. At the same time, statutory control of campaign contributions meant that national policy would now greatly influence what had, theretofore, been an important means through which private groups might influence national policy.

American campaign finance regulation remains, to be sure, in a preliminary stage. Thus far, candidates and contributors have been able to find enough loopholes, exceptions, and unanticipated statutory interpretations so that many of the possibilities inherent in the regulations have not yet been realized. Nevertheless, the introduction of this campaign finance legislation poses profound problems for democratic electoral processes in the United States.

First and most obvious, campaign finance legislation permits incumbent elites to set rules and conditions governing the use of the financial resources essential to effective electoral competition. The formulation of these rules affords those in power a new opportunity to control electoral access and influence and to protect their own positions. Campaign finance regulation opens an almost infinite variety of possibilities for electoral manipulation. The public funding rules set by the 1974 Federal Elections amendments, for example, clearly discriminate against third-party and independent presidential bids.[38] Neither new third parties nor independent presidential candi-

---

[38] In essence, major-party presidential candidates are automatically entitled to federal subsidies, which in 1980 amounted to more than $29 million. Minor-party candidates are entitled to retroactive awards if they win at least 5 percent of the votes cast in the November election. Though subsidies awarded after the election are not especially useful means of winning votes, candidates may borrow against these potential awards before the election. Until September 1980, independent candidates were not considered eligible for any public funds. In that month, however, the Federal Election Commission ruled that John Anderson's independent presidential campaign was entitled to the same sort of retroactive funding as a minor party. See Leslie Bennetts, "Anderson May Get Federal Funds," *New York Times,* September 5, 1980.

dates are eligible to receive any public funds prior to the election. The Democratic and Republican candidates—whose parties wrote the rules—are, of course, eligible for full subsidies from the public treasury.[39] European campaign finance laws are also typically designed to discriminate against new parties.[40]

But even in the absence of explicit bias, restrictions on campaign contributions and expenditures inevitably work to the advantage of established elites and interests. However equitable the language of the statute or evenhanded its administration, campaign finance regulation can frustrate the efforts of new groups to acquire access and influence through electoral politics. Clearly, statutory limits on campaign spending which apply equally to all candidates hurt insurgents and help incumbents. Insurgents typically must spend a

---

[39] For a lively discussion of the effects of campaign finance regulation from the perspective of an independent candidate, see Eugene McCarthy, *The Ultimate Tyranny* (New York: Harcourt Brace Jovanovich, 1980). Also quite revealing are the views of Neil O. Staebler, one of the original members of the Federal Election Commission. According to Staebler, the FEC is best served by commissioners with close ties to the two major parties. "The greatest potential hazard the FEC presents is the damage it might do to the political parties. Joan Arkens and I were the only commission members who have really had any party experience. We struggled hard and managed to avoid a lot of damage, but this area remains a dangerous one. Ignorance of party functions is characteristically present in those from an academic or a third-party background." Citizens' Research Foundation, "Neil O. Staebler on the Campaign Finance Revolution" (University of Southern California, 1979), p. 9. In 1980 the Anderson campaign was constantly plagued by shortages of funds. At one point, Anderson was forced to cancel a long-planned, four-day whistle-stop train tour across five states because of insufficient funds. At the same time, campaign staff was cut, senior staff members forced to take salary cuts, and campaign advance workers billeted in private homes to save hotel expenses. With nearly $30 million each in federal funds to spend, the Democratic and Republican candidates had somewhat less difficulty mounting campaign efforts. See "Three Aides Quit in Shake-up of Anderson Campaign Staff," *New York Times,* August 29, 1980.

[40] See Khayyam Z. Paltiel, "The Impact of Election Expenses Legislation in Canada, Western Europe, and Israel," in Herbert E. Alexander (ed.), *Political Finance,* Sage Electoral Studies Yearbook, vol. 5 (Beverly Hills, Calif.: Russell Sage Foundation, 1979), pp. 15-39. See also Khayyam Z. Paltiel, "Public Financing Abroad: Contrasts and Effects," in Malbin, *Parties,* especially pp. 366-369.

good deal more than their incumbent opponents to have any chance of electoral success.[41]

Perhaps even more important, however, restrictions on group or individual campaign contributions work to the advantage of established interests and against the political aspirations of new groups. The opportunity to contribute to political campaigns is generally a more important source of influence for new groups and forces than for more established economic or social interests. As a result, though applied in the most evenhanded manner, limits on campaign contributions tend to bolster the political status quo.

An interesting picture of this conservative consequence emerges from empirical analysis of the relationship between campaign contributions and congressional roll call voting. Examination of the effects of campaign contributions upon congressional voting indicates that such contributions do, indeed, have an impact upon representatives' actions. Roll call voting by at least some United States representatives in both the 93rd and 94th congresses appears to be significantly associated with interest groups' campaign contributions in the preceding elections. At the same time, the pattern of the relationships between campaign contributions and representatives' roll call voting indicates that these contributions tend to be far more important to groups seeking to change legislative outcomes than to interests satisfied to preserve established patterns of power and policy.[42]

CAMPAIGN CONTRIBUTIONS AND CONGRESSIONAL BEHAVIOR

Using the reports filed with the FEC by all congressional candidates after the 1972 and 1974 congressional elections, we may obtain a view

---

[41] See Gary Jacobson, "The Effects of Campaign Spending in Congressional Elections," *American Political Science Review* 72 (June 1978): 469-491.

[42] For a fuller account, see Benjamin Ginsberg and John Green, "The Best Congress Money Can Buy: Campaign Contributions and Congressional Behavior," paper

of the effect of campaign contributions upon congressional behavior.[43] These reports include the amount each congressional candidate received from any PAC as well as from any individual contributor donating more than $100. Though it is possible that some candidates may have received illicit contributions that were not reported to the FEC, we must assume that these were randomly distributed. We shall take account only of campaign contributions made by PACs. Preliminary tests, however, indicate that the results would not have been materially affected by the inclusion of contributions from individuals.

For purposes of analysis, the more than 500 PACs that made contributions in one or both elections were grouped into 14 categories. The contribution received by any individual congressional candidate from an "interest" is defined as the sum of the total dollar amounts the candidate received from all the PACs in the particular category. The categories are a simple nominal classification of economic and social interests that accords with most conventional classifications of the patterns of interest-group alliances in American domestic politics. Table 6.2 lists the 14 categories and the total dollar amount each contributed to all candidates in the two elections.

Though the amounts contributed by these groups of interests vary considerably, these variations should not unduly affect the empirical analysis. In general, groups that contributed more money also made contributions to a larger number of candidates so that the average contribution size does not vary greatly across the 14 interests. Moreover, our concern is with the impact of each interest upon the representatives to whom it contributed rather than with the relative success of the interests in acquiring congressional support.

---

presented at the Annual Meeting of the American Political Science Association, Washington, D.C., September 1979. Some of the same data, viewed from a different perspective, can be seen in John Green's excellent doctoral dissertation. John Green, "Federal Campaign Finance: Money, Representation and Congressional Behavior," Cornell University, in preparation. I must assume sole responsibility for the interpretation presented in the present context.

[43] Common Cause, *1972 Congressional Campaign Finances* and *1974 Congressional Campaign Finances* (Washington, D.C.: Common Cause, 1972 and 1974)

TABLE 6.2   *The total dollar amounts contributed to congressional candidates by 14 categories of interests in 1972 and 1974.*

	1972	1974
Agriculture	$ 35,000	$ 65,230
Dairy	592,075	195,950
Aerospace	41,422	35,232
Trucking	24,000	121,225
Oil	22,650	99,395
Chemicals	7,525	27,895
Food processing	26,000	62,429
Banking	199,893	191,000
Law	-----	12,957
Medicine	828,464	1,504,220
Labor	3,653,000	3,884,720
Business	1,781,000	1,784,000
Liberals	166,000	242,559
Conservatives	149,000	252,805

So that congressional behavior might be compared with campaign contributions, I analyzed roll call votes in the 92nd, 93rd, and 94th congresses, that is, the congresses immediately preceding, intervening between, and immediately following the 1972 and 1974 congressional elections. For each of the 14 interest categories, I collected all the roll call votes in each congress on which the interests in question appeared to take a position. Any issue that seemed to divide the constituent components of an interest category was excluded, thus leaving for each category of interests the roll call votes in each congress on which all the members of the category appeared to share a common position. These determinations were based upon a time-consuming and labor-intensive review of the materials published by the relevant interest groups as well as an examination of reliable secondary sources such as *Congressional Quarterly* reports. No doubt, exclusion of the issues that divided particular interest categories meant that some important votes were omitted from the analysis. Yet this procedure was essential to allow each category to be treated as an entity. It is not likely that an alternative system of classification could resolve this problem. Any group larger than one member is likely to exhibit divisions on some matters. Psychologists might wish to take this argument even a step further.

Using the roll call votes on which all the members of an interest category shared a common position as a base, interest-group support scores were calculated for each representative in each of the three congresses. The interest-group support score is simply the proportion of roll calls in a given congress in which the particular representative voted in accord with the interest's position. For example, a representative whose vote supported the position held by dairy interests in 70 percent of the relevant roll call votes in the 93rd Congress simply received a dairy support score of 0.7 for that congress.

Our procedure for measuring the impact of campaign contributions upon representatives' roll call voting behavior is quite simple. The data include each representative's support score for each of the 14 interest groups in the 92nd, 93rd, and 94th congresses. These data can be used to calculate the degree of change in each representative's support for each interest between successive congresses. The degree of change in the support shown by any representative for any interest between any two successive congresses is given by the formula

$$\frac{C_2 - C_1}{C_1}$$

where C_2 is the representative's support for the interest in the second congress of a pair and C_1 is the same representative's support for the identical interest in the first congress of the pair.[44]

---

[44] This mode of analysis takes account of only one of the possible pathways through which campaign contributions can affect legislative policy outcomes. Studies of the policy implications of popular voting typically assume two broad pathways through which the behavior of the mass electorate can influence the actions of the government. First, the threat of electoral reprisal or hope of electoral reward may induce public officials to take account of their constituents' wishes even when these conflict with their own views. Second, voters' capacity to select leaders who share their own interests and preferences may mean that officials' actions will accord with the popular will even when public officials make no conscious effort to heed the view of their

To measure the impact of campaign contributions, I have correlated the degree of change in each representative's support for each interest group with the dollar amount the representative received from the interest group in the intervening congressional election.[45] Obviously, only representatives who served in both of a given pair of congresses could be included in the analysis.[46] It should be noted that

---

constituents. Thus, in the case of legislative representation, elections may permit citizens to influence congressional policymaking through their effort upon both the behavior of representatives and the composition of Congress. Interest groups do not cast ballots. But these two pathways correspond roughly to the two broad avenues through which their campaign contributions may potentially influence legislative outcomes. First, campaign contributions may affect the behavior of representatives, possibly inducing them to shift their support in one or another direction. Second, through campaign contributions interest groups may potentially influence the composition of Congress, for example, by helping to secure the election of a group's supporters and the defeat of its opponents. A full assessment of the impact of campaign contributions upon congressional policymaking would require examination of both of these avenues of infuence. However, the capacity of any particular interest group to affect the composition of Congress materially is usually very limited. Most congressional races are won handily by incumbent representatives. Only a relative handful of races during a given year are sufficiently close to allow any particular interest group's contribution to determine the outcome. Though there are significant exceptions, for most campaign contributors the more viable avenue of influence is through the behavior of representatives rather than through the composition of Congress. It is probably for this reason that the bulk of interest-group campaign contributions are given to relatively secure incumbents even though contributions would generally have a greater potential impact upon the electoral fortunes of congressional challengers.

[45] Hypothetically, contributions made to the opponents of successful candidates might also influence representatives' behavior either by inducing them to diminish their support for the interests that opposed them or by convincing them to increase their support for those interests to discourage future opposition. Tests for both of these possibilities revealed no evidence that either obtained. Unfortunately, in the context of the present analysis it is not possible to examine the impact that interest-group opposition to one candidate might have upon another. It could be the case, for example, that interest-group contributions that helped to defeat one representative might persuade others of the wisdom of supporting the interest. Eventually, perhaps, we shall be able to search for empirical evidence of this phenomenon.

[46] An alternative procedure might be to include all representatives present in C_2 even when the particular representative was not present in C_1, and ask whether interest-group contributions altered the degree of support obtained from congressional seats rather than individual representatives. Unfortunately, this alternative becomes enmeshed in the problem of the impact of campaign contributions upon electoral outcomes.

definition of the dependent variable as change in interest-group support between two successive congresses may result in some degree of underestimation of the effects of campaign contributions. However, if we were to define the dependent variable as amount of interest-group support in the single congress following an election we would be unable to distinguish between consequences and prior correlates of campaign contributions such as, for example, representatives' preexisting propensities to support a particular interest.

Table 6.3 reports the correlations between changes in representatives' interest-group support scores from the 92nd Congress to the 93rd Congress with campaign contributions received during the intervening 1972 congressional election, as well as these same correlations for change in interest-group support from the 93rd Congress to the 94th Congress with contributions received in the intervening 1974 congressional elections.

In both years the correlations, though sometimes modest, are generally positive and significant. Taken as a whole, this pattern of associations does suggest that campaign contributions are associated with shifts in congressional support toward positions more favorable to the contributor. These patterns of association can by no means be taken to prove that interest groups directly purchase congressional votes with their campaign contributions. It may be that campaign contributions simply create favorable dispositions toward the contributor. Or, perhaps contributions pave the way for other forms of persuasion by the contributor. Presumably this latter possibility is what is conventionally denoted by the phrase "buying access."[47] Yet whatever the precise mechanisms involved, there do appear to exist significant patterns of association between interest groups' campaign contributions and congressional roll call voting.

The relatively modest strength of the aggregate associations between campaign contributions and changes in congressional support is not particularly surprising. Undoubtedly, there exist a variety of factors that can inhibit the responsiveness of at least some representatives to interest groups' blandishments. Many representatives, for

---

[47] The concept of "buying access" is discussed in Harmon Zeigler, *Interest Groups in American Society* (Englewood Cliffs, N.J.: Prentice-Hall, 1964).

TABLE 6.3 *The correlations between interest-group contributions in 1972 and 1974 congressional races and changes in roll call voting behavior from the congress preceding to the congress following each election.*

	1972	1974
Agriculture	.17 (66)*	.16 (109)
Dairy	−.12 (89)	.15 (88)
Aerospace	.28 (53)	.21 (61)
Trucking	−.11 (39)	.09 (80)
Oil	.18 (56)	−.08 (110)
Chemicals	.09 (52)	.10 (71)
Food processing	−.11 (56)	.11 (106)
Banking	.09 (108)	.16 (116)
Law	------	−.07 (49)
Medicine	.05 (229)	.12 (260)
Labor	.17 (261)	.16 (270)
Business	.23 (226)	.18 (231)
Liberals	.24 (81)	.26 (96)
Conservatives	.25 (46)	.21 (58)

* The number of cases is given in parentheses. All coefficients are significant at the .05 level or better.

example, might refuse to be swayed by contributions from groups they conceived to be pursuing goals incompatible with some broader definition of the public interest. We could not, for example, expect that contributions from nuclear energy producers would have much impact upon the votes of representatives strongly concerned with the environmental and health hazards possibly posed by atomic power. Alternatively, those representatives already firmly convinced of the merits of an interest group's position might also exhibit little or no response to its campaign contributions. Such representatives would likely maintain a high level of support for an interest whether or not it chose to contribute to their electoral races. The most obvious examples are representatives who support a particular interest because they conceive its welfare to be synonymous with the broader well-being of their own electoral constituencies. Representatives need not be given campaign contributions to support corporate interests that are major employers in their districts.[48]

Thus, whatever the factors contributing to their predilections, it would be reasonable to presume that representatives with either a strongly favorable or strongly unfavorable view of a particular interest's aims would exhibit relatively little responsiveness to campaign contributions from that group. The impact of any interest group's campaign contributions is likely to be most marked among those representatives who lack any strong positive or negative predisposition toward the group.

I have repeated the correlations between campaign contributions and changes in interest-group support scores, this time controlling for the strength of representatives' predispositions. This control simply involved partitioning the recipients of each interest's campaign contributions into three groups in each pair of successive congresses, on the basis of the strength of their support for the interest in the first congress of the pair. Taking each interest separately, the first group of representatives consists of those who ranked in or above the 80th percentile of all representatives in terms of the degree of support given the interest's position. The second group of representatives consists of those who ranked in or below the 20th percentile of support given the interest's position. The third group of representatives consists of those ranking between the 20th and 80th percentiles. Thus, essentially, the first group of representatives consists of each interest's strongest supporters prior to the receipt of campaign contributions. The second group of representatives consists of those who exhibited the least support for the interest prior to the receipt of campaign contributions. And the third group of representatives consists of those in the middle range of support before receiving campaign contributions.

---

[48] Empirical tests indicate that representatives exhibit quite high levels of support for interests that are major employers in their districts whether or not they receive campaign contributions from those interests and, moreover, exhibit no changes in roll call support in response to campaign contributions.

Table 6.4 reports the correlations between the dollar amounts of campaign contributions and changes in the interest support scores of the recipients for each of the three groups of representatives.

Examination of Table 6.4 indicates quite clearly that there is little or no association between campaign contributions and the roll call voting behavior of those representatives who gave each interest either the highest or lowest degree of support prior to each election. An interest's campaign contributions would appear to have little or no impact upon the roll call voting behavior of representatives with either strong positive or strong negative predispositions toward its legislative aims.

The correlations reported for the third group, on the other hand, appear to indicate a very marked pattern of associations between campaign contributions and changes in roll call voting behavior. It would, indeed, appear that the impact of campaign contributions is felt most by representatives with neither a strong positive nor a strong negative predisposition toward the contributor. It is essentially among these "uncommitted" representatives that interest groups can build support through contributions to congressional campaigns.

To put these correlations in some perspective, on the average, each $650 received from an interest by an uncommitted representative was associated with an additional roll call vote in support of the interest's position by that representative. Again, this finding does not indicate that interest groups can purchase representatives' votes. The mechanisms through which campaign contributions are actually translated into congressional support are likely more indirect and subtle. Yet despite the possibly misleading implications of the observation, it is impossible to resist noting that some representatives' roll call votes can sometimes be quite inexpensive.

CAMPAIGN CONTRIBUTIONS AND THE POLITICAL PROCESS

Among the most interesting implications of these findings is that campaign contributions are considerably more important to groups seeking to change existing patterns of congressional support than

TABLE 6.4 Correlations between interest-group contributions in 1972 and 1974 congressional races and changes in roll call voting behavior, controlled for representatives' support of the interest prior to the elections.

	Representatives Exhibiting Most Support in C_1		Representatives Exhibiting Least Support in C_1		Representatives "Uncommitted" in C_1	
	1972	1974	1972	1974	1972	1974
Agriculture	-.23 (22)*	-.13 (31)	-.01 (26)	-.03 (27)	.26 (18)	.21 (51)
Dairy	.03 (41)	-.02 (46)	-.07 (11)	.00 (12)	.23 (37)	.26 (29)
Aerospace	-.18 (12)	-.09 (18)	.02 (16)	-.04 (21)	.32 (25)	.29 (22)
Trucking	-.17 (20)	-.06 (22)	-.02 (10)	-.08 (10)	.14 (19)	.16 (38)
Oil	-.04 (21)	-.10 (24)	-.02 (12)	-.01 (26)	.27 (23)	.26 (60)
Chemicals	.11 (35)	-.06 (38)	-.02 (13)	-.10 (12)	.29 (20)	.30 (21)
Food processing	-.13 (26)	-.14 (46)	-.01 (9)	-.06 (12)	.12 (17)	.18 (48)
Banking	.00 (51)	-.08 (62)	-.06 (6)	.04 (8)	.13 (51)	.17 (46)
Law	----	-.09 (26)	----	-.06 (10)	----	.14 (13)
Medicine	-.06 (110)	-.05 (126)	-.05 (21)	.06 (27)	.21 (98)	.22 (107)
Labor	-.11 (144)	-.07 (161)	-.12 (69)	-.10 (63)	.26 (48)	.28 (46)
Business	-.02 (112)	-.03 (126)	-.14 (56)	-.11 (65)	.28 (58)	.21 (40)
Liberals	-.10 (40)	.00 (46)	----	----	.39 (41)	.30 (50)
Conservatives	-.09 (21)	-.06 (30)	----	----	.42 (25)	.31 (28)

* The number of cases is given in parentheses. All coefficients are significant at the .05 level or better.

they are to groups satisfied with the legislative status quo. Campaign contributions appear to have little effect upon the voting behavior of representatives who already exhibit a strong positive or a strong negative predisposition toward a given interest. Thus interest groups relatively well satisfied with established levels of congressional support may have less need of campaign contributions than interests wishing to increase congressional backing for their legislative objectives.

The greater importance of campaign contributions for groups seeking to change than for those wishing merely to maintain the legislative status quo can be even more clearly illustrated by a series of simple comparisons. Taking each interest separately, I correlated representatives' postelection interest-group support scores with their preelection support scores, controlling for representatives' receipt of campaign contributions.

To the extent that campaign contributions help to maintain established patterns of congressional voting, we would expect postelection support scores to be more strongly associated with preelection support as representatives receive more campaign funds from a given interest. In other words, if campaign contributions mainly helped to preserve existing patterns of support, we would expect that the more funds representatives' received, the less their support scores would change.

If, on the other hand, contributions largely have the effect of altering established patterns of congressional voting, we would expect preelection support scores to be better predictors of postelection support on the part of representatives who received little or no money from the interest in question. In other words, if campaign contributions mainly have the effect of changing patterns of support, then the more funds representatives receive from an interest, the more their level of support for the interest should be altered.

Table 6.5 reports the coefficients obtained from the correlation of representatives' postelection support scores with preelection support scores, controlling for the receipt of campaign contributions. These findings seem to indicate quite strongly that campaign contributions are considerably more important factors for the alteration than for the preservation of established patterns of congressional support. Among representatives who received no contributions from a given

TABLE 6.5 Correlations between preelection and postelection congressional support for 14 interest groups, controlling for receipt of contributions.

	Representatives Who Received No Contribution		Representatives Who Received a Contribution between $0 and $500		Representatives Who Received a Contribution of $500 or More	
	1972	1974	1972	1974	1972	1974
Agriculture	.31 (319)*	.30 (263)	.20 (34)	.26 (48)	.09 (32)	.14 (61)
Dairy	.36 (296)	.26 (284)	.18 (38)	.17 (381)	.10 (51)	.16 (50)
Aerospace	.25 (332)	.24 (324)	.20 (21)	.13 (25)	.11 (18)	.10 (38)
Trucking	.19 (346)	.20 (292)	.09 (31)	.15 (425)	.07 (25)	.08 (38)
Oil	.16 (300)	.24 (275)	.10 (24)	.09 (51)	.07 (28)	.10 (59)
Chemicals	.29 (333)	.30 (314)	.28 (26)	.19 (33)	.12 (30)	.09 (38)
Food processing	.33 (329)	.39 (301)	.21 (62)	.20 (441)	.09 (46)	.11 (62)
Banking	.36 (277)	.30 (261)	.19 (118)	.17 (52)	.12 (111)	.06 (64)
Law	—	.25 (323)	—	.18 (24)	—	.10 (25)
Medicine	.31 (156)	.21 (112)	.20 (109)	.13 (119)	.14 (120)	.08 (141)
Labor	.22 (124)	.28 (102)	.16 (106)	.12 (110)	.06 (156)	.01 (121)
Business	.29 (159)	.21 (141)	.19 (107)	.10 (113)	.13 (119)	.07 (117)
Liberals	.39 (304)	.20 (276)	.27 (53)	.21 (49)	.16 (28)	.16 (47)
Conservatives	.40 (339)	.21 (314)	.27 (20)	.18 (26)	.20 (26)	.16 (32)

* The number of cases is given in parentheses. All coefficients are significant at the .05 level or better.

interest, postelection congressional support is considerably more strongly correlated with preelection support than is the case among representatives who did receive funds from the interest. Moreover, the more money representatives received from an interest, the weaker the association between preelection and postelection roll call voting behavior. These patterns of associations suggest that the greater the amounts of contributions received from an interest by congressional representatives, the more representatives' roll call support for that interest tends to change. Conversely, the less money representatives receive from an interest, the less their support for that interest tends to change.

These findings are based upon very simple comparisons and need to be buttressed by a much more sophisticated form of analysis than was used here. Nevertheless, the findings would appear to support the contention that campaign contributions are much more likely to be important to groups seeking to change legislative behavior than they are to interests satisfied with the legislative status quo. It is principally *in the absence* of campaign contributions that patterns of legislative support for interest groups changes least from one congress to the next.

It is very likely for just this reason that the heaviest contributors to congressional campaigns tend often to be what might be termed "insurgent interests." For example, antiwar groups were among the largest contributors to congressional campaigns in 1972.[49] Similarly, among the PACs associated with business firms in 1972 and 1974, the 40 PACs that contributed the largest total amounts to congressional races represented relatively small firms attempting to enter new markets or seeking larger shares of existing markets against the opposition of well-entrenched rivals and, sometimes, the constellation of legislative and bureaucratic forces supporting those rivals.[50]

---

[49] In 1972, antiwar groups contributed approximately $104,000 to congressional campaigns.

[50] Interestingly, not a single member of the Fortune 500 was among the major contributors to congressional campaigns in 1972 or 1974. Possibly the explosion of PAC activity in 1976 and subsequent races might have altered this pattern.

The case of one particular insurgent economic interest group is revealing. In 1972, dairy interests contributed approximately 17 times as much money to congressional campaigns as all other agricultural interest groups combined. Throughout the 1950s, dairy farmers had simply been a part of the general farm lobby, which formed one point of a well-known "iron triangle" between an interest group, a congressional committee, and a bureaucratic agency. In the 1960s, however, disputes concerning agricultural price supports led the dairy farmers to break with the farm lobby. Essentially, increased price supports for the commodities fed to cattle raised dairy farmers' costs. But other members of the farm lobby refused to back compensatory increases in milk prices. The problem that dairy farmers faced in attempting to mount an independent lobby effort was that their legislative goals were now thwarted by precisely the agricultural "iron triangle" of which they had previously been part. The response of the dairy farmers was to spend heavily, and sometimes illegally—it was dairy money that was found in Maurice Stans' safe—in political campaigns to attempt to alter patterns of political support in the agricultural sector. Though the spending practices of the dairy cooperatives may, indeed, have been reprehensible, this tactic was one of the few avenues open to them to break the stranglehold that rival farm interests held on national agricultural policy.[51] The same principle is illustrated by the explanation given by the chairman of the Ashland Oil Corporation for his company's $100,000 in illegal contributions to the Nixon campaign:

> *Were we a larger factor in our respective industries, we could expect to have access to administrative officials in the executive branch of government with ease, but being a relatively unknown corporation, despite our size, we felt we needed something . . . that would let us in the door and make our point of view heard.*[52]

---

[51] For an excellent account of the political activities of the milk producers, see James L. Guth, "The Milk Fund Scandal of 1971," *Furman Studies* 25, no. 1 (June 1978).

[52] Quoted in William J. Crotty, *Political Reform and the American Experiment* (New York: Crowell, 1977), p. 150.

REGULATION OF CAMPAIGN FINANCES

These findings indicate that interest groups' campaign contributions do influence the roll call voting behavior of congressional representatives. Members of Congress strongly committed or firmly opposed to an interest group appear unlikely to be swayed by monetary rewards. But those representatives who lack any particular predisposition toward a given interest appear susceptible to its influence via campaign contributions. Even if all representatives cannot be influenced by money all of the time, the capacity of special interests to change the behavior of some representatives some of the time through contributions to their electoral campaigns is still incompatible with democratic ideals. In particular, the impact of private campaign contributions undermines the fundamental principle of the vote as a mechanism through which each individual can exercise an equal measure of influence upon the political process. Unlike the right to vote, the capacity to make large contributions to candidates for office is surely unequally distributed.

Yet, ironically, regulations that diminish the influence of private campaign contributors and thus seem to reinforce the electoral ideal of equal opportunity can have undesirable results. First, as a number of analysts have noted, reforms eliminating private contributions from congressional campaigns might have the effect of diminishing the electoral chances of congressional challengers, although perhaps the problems of challengers could be eased through compensatory public subsidies.

The problem to which my findings point, however, is not so easily resolved. Restrictions on private campaign contributions are more damaging to the prospects of groups seeking to change legislative behavior than to groups content with the status quo. Interests that already benefit from congressional support need spend little or no money for its maintenance. Restrictions on private campaign contributions simply add to the advantage that established groups enjoy by removing a potent weapon from the arsenals of potential rivals. Electoral reforms diminishing the political impact of private dollars might appear to promote political equality. But, as de Tocqueville argued long ago, political equality can mean equality of political impotence.

STATE CONTROL OF POLITICS

Again, existing campaign statutes are filled with loopholes. One problem area, for example, was created by the Supreme Court's 1976 decision exempting independent political committees—that is, groups not formally affiliated with a candidate's campaign—from the spending limitations that apply to presidential candidates who accept public funding. During the 1980 presidential race, the formation of several nominally independent groups that sought to promote Ronald Reagan's candidacy caused considerable controversy.

But to assert that the campaign finance statutes are filled with loopholes is merely to acknowledge that many of the possibilities inherent in this type of legislation have not yet been realized. Indeed, in February 1981, the Supreme Court agreed to hear an appeal brought by the Federal Election Commission and Common Cause that could, if successful, reinstate expenditure limits for independent political committees. Whatever the remaining loopholes, however, the fact remains that through campaign finance regulation the state has assumed greater control of its own politics. Campaign finance regulation, in effect, increases the government's capacity to control citizens' putative means of controlling its actions. There is, moreover, every reason to believe that in due course many of the existing means of evading the reach of these regulations will be foreclosed. After all, it continues to serve the interests of incumbent interests and elites to bar access by new forces. And, for its part, the public certainly continues to support regulation of the pressure-group activity that it conceives to be so threatening to the integrity of the democratic process. Thus many more of the eventualities associated with increased state intervention into political life are likely to be realized in the coming years. The implications are, of course, profoundly disturbing. One example, which is so striking that it requires no commentary, suggests the possibilities. In 1978, the Federal Election Commission charged a New York conservative group with violating federal law by failing to register with the commission while spending more than $100 to publish a portion of an incumbent representative's voting record. A circular issued by a group calling itself Tax Reform Immediately (TRIM) listed Representative Jerome Ambro's votes on 25 measures and charged that 21 of the 25 votes "favored big government." The FEC, in a claim that was eventually rejected by the courts, contended that the publication of Ambro's voting record, "rather than being a form of non-partisan, issue-oriented speech was a communication which expressly advocated the defeat of a clearly identified federal candidate."[53]

EROSION OF POPULAR SUPPORT?

These effects of campaign finance regulation bring us full circle. Elections facilitate expansion of the state's powers. Over time, the state's expansion diminishes its vulnerability to electoral intervention while paving the way for governmental encroachments upon political life—encroachments that can obstruct competitive electoral processes.

Ultimately, of course, expansion of the state's powers may also lead to an erosion of popular confidence in government and politics. The public's conviction that its participation significantly influences the government's behavior facilitates expansion of the state's powers. After all, so long as the mass public controls its government's actions, expansion of the state's powers only increases government's capacity to serve. The growth of governmental power, however, diminishes

---

[53] Peter Kehos, "U.S. Says L.I. Group Broke Election Law," *New York Times,* February 19, 1978. Despite this legal setback, the FEC continues to attempt to regulate groups whose ideological perspectives lead them to oppose the reelection of incumbent lawmakers. In one case pending in 1980, the FEC cited a John Birch Society newsletter that criticized an incumbent congressional candidate for having voted for higher taxes. In another case, the FEC sought to compel a small right-wing newsletter, "The Pink Sheet on the Left," to register with the commission or face a $5000 fine because one of its subscription solicitation fliers urged readers to "combat Ted Kennedy and advance the cause of conservatism in America." See Jack Landau, "FEC Extending Its Legal Reach," *Syracuse Herald-American,* October 10, 1980. In a case stemming from the 1980 presidential primary election, the FEC charged that *Reader's Digest* had violated the Federal Election Campaign Act by purchasing television advertisements and promotions on behalf of one of its articles. The article, entitled "Chappaquidick: The Still Unanswered Questions," presumably raised doubts about Senator Edward Kennedy's character and, at least by implication, his presidential candidacy. See Edward T. Pound, "Two Publishers Accuse U.S. Election Agency of Rights Violations," *New York Times,* February 16, 1981.

the possibility of popular control and, eventually, citizen's confidence that the state is simply a servant. An ironic result of the state's expansion is a diminution of the public trust that initially helped to pave its way.

During the 1970s, the public's faith in the responsiveness of American governmental institutions, public confidence in the political process, and voter turnout exhibited sharp declines. The Watergate scandals and the Vietnam war, of course, played significant roles in reducing the public's trust in government and politics. Yet, important as they were, Vietnam and Watergate reinforced and exacerbated rather than initiated trends that had already begun to appear, as Fig. 6.2 suggests, during the early 1960s.

FIG. 6.2 *Erosion of popular confidence in government, 1958-1978.*

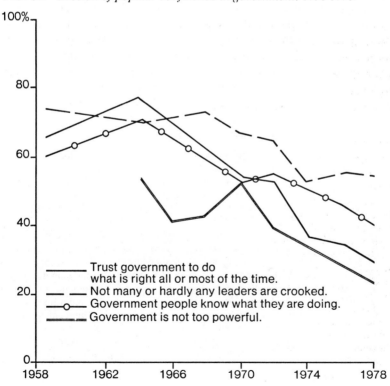

In part, at least, this erosion of public confidence in governmental institutions and the political process was a direct response to the government's steady growth in size, scope, and complexity since the New Deal. A sizable number of Americans were, with some cause, beginning to suspect that the government had become too large and powerful to concern itself with the wishes of ordinary citizens. Because of this suspicion, proposals for deregulation, tax and expenditure ceilings, and reductions in the size of the federal bureaucracy all received a fair degree of popular support during the 1970s. As the public began to doubt its capacity to control the state's actions, the state's power no longer seemed an unmitigated virtue.

This apparent increase in public sentiment for governmental retrenchment, however, does not point toward an imminent withering away of the state. On the one hand, despite the public's distrust of governmental power, most citizens continue to demand all the services now customarily provided by the welfare state.[54] Certainly, proposals for reductions in the size of the state apparatus and scope of governmental power gained some currency in the 1970s. A pledge to cut the size of the federal bureaucracy became an obligatory part of every candidate's campaign repertoire. But even though the public claimed to be losing confidence in government, Table 6.6 suggests that most

---

[54] Although, of course, most citizens would prefer lower taxes—at least for themselves—there continue to be popular majorities favoring *more* governmental spending on a variety of different sorts of programs. See Jack Citrin, "Do People Want Something for Nothing: Public Opinion on Taxes and Government Spending," *National Tax Journal* 32, no. 2, supplement (June 1979): 112-129, See also Paul Peretz, "There Was No Tax Revolt," paper presented at the Annual Meeting of the American Political Science Association, Washington, D.C.: August 29-September 1, 1980. A large majority of those responding to a national New York Times/CBS News poll conducted January 26-29. 1981, favored increasing spending or keeping spending about the same for a variety of federal programs. Eighty-nine percent favored increasing or maintaining existing levels of spending for social security. Eighty-one percent favored maintaining or increasing funding for highways, 75 percent for mass transit, 77 percent for pollution abatement, 72 percent for unemployment compensation, and 72 percent for aid to college students. Only on the question of food stamps did a sizable proportion of the survey's respondents, 47 percent, favor decreasing existing federal funding levels. See Adam Clymer, "Public Prefers a Balanced Budget to Large Cuts in Taxes, Poll Shows," *New York Times*, February 3, 1981.

TABLE 6.6 *Should the government do more to solve the nation's problems?*

The government should do:	Inflation	Energy shortage	Unemployment	Race relations	Crime/ drugs	Consumer protection	Pollution
A great deal more	80.4%*	69.0%	69.4%	46.9%	60.6%	56.9%	60.0%
Some more	18.9%	29.7%	29.4%	41.3%	37.2%	40.4%	37.8%
No more	0.8%	1.3%	1.2%	11.6%	2.2%	2.7%	2.2%
	(N = 2254)	(N = 2142)	(N = 2170)	(N = 1864)	(N = 2215)	(N = 2062)	(N = 2062)

* That is, 80 percent polled believed that the government should do a great deal more about inflation.

citizens continued to expect the same untrustworthy government to solve all of the nation's social, economic, and political problems.

Perhaps the much heralded "shift to the right" exhibited by public opinion in the 1970s and 1980s—a shift that was, of course, highlighted by the unexpected scope of Republican victory in the 1980 presidential and senatorial elections—portends at least a temporary halt to the state's growth. But despite their expressions of abhorrence for big government, "conservatives" in the 1980s differ more with their "liberal" counterparts over the proper character than the ultimate desirability of an enlarged role for the state. Many of the same individuals who urge an evisceration of the social programs that mainly benefit blacks and the poor shamelessly defend the moral equivalent of public welfare for mismanaged corporations, indolent farmers, mercenary military contractors, and rapacious tobacco growers. It should be recalled that Ronald Reagan began his successful "conservative" campaign not by promising to curtail governmental activity, but rather by vowing "to restore to the federal government the capacity to do the peoples' work." This pledge was warmly praised by another "conservative," columnist George Will, as "agreeably free of the feckless anti-government spirit that has characterized much conservatism."[55] This same absence of "anti-government spirit" characterized Reagan's inaugural address. While pledging to curb the "size and influence of the federal establishment," Reagan also declared: "Now, so there will be no misunderstanding, it is not my intention to do away with government. It is, rather, to make it work."[56]

At the same time, citizens of the democracies—Americans more than any others—retain a basic faith in the possibility of popular control of governmental powers. In the United States, the possibility of popular control, particularly through electoral mechanisms, is absolutely central to citizens' beliefs about politics. As we saw earlier, the importance of voting is a chief focus of formal civic education in

---

[55] George F. Will. "The Odds Against Carter." *Newsweek*. August 18, 1980. p. 88.

[56] "President Reagan's Inaugural Address." *New York Times*. January 21, 1981.

the United States, and is frequently reemphasized by the informal civic lessons to which most adult Americans are exposed. The idea that electoral participation means popular control of government is so deeply implanted in the psyches of most Americans that even the most overtly skeptical cannot fully free themselves from it.

Indeed, such is the power of democratic symbols that the government's most radical critics in the 1960s and 1970s were also most fervent in their belief that more participation—"participatory democracy"—was all that was necessary to ensure more popular control. This resilience of mass beliefs in control through participation, however, ensures the persistence of the fundamental electoral dilemma —the principal means through which citizens attempt to control the state's actions, indeed, the public's very belief in the possibility of such control, enhances the state's power, authority, and capacity to control its citizens.

EPILOGUE: ELECTIONS, LIBERTY, AND THE CONSEQUENCES OF CONSENT

✦✦

7

I have argued throughout this text that electoral institutions are among the most important instruments of governance available to the modern state. Elections delimit mass political activity, popular influence, and access to power. Elections transform the potentially disruptive energy of the masses into a principal source of national power and authority. Governments, as I noted earlier, rule through electoral institutions even when they are sometimes ruled by them.

But even though they may function as instruments of governance, when all is said and done, democratic electoral mechanisms do have one notable virtue. This virtue is simply that, relative to the known alternatives, democratic modes of governance appear to be most compatible with the existence of some measure of individual freedom. Though abuses occur in every nation, generally speaking, the same nations that possess democratic electoral and political institutions are also most likely to respect basic civil liberties. For example, in one 1979 survey that sought to rank all nominally independent nations on a 1 (most free) to 7 (least free) scale on the basis of citizens' civil rights and liberties, all 18 nations in the "most free" group were also democracies. No nations with competitive electoral processes ranked below the second scale position on civil liberties.[1] In another recent study, freedom of the press was found to be "complete" in 33 of 40 nations with competitive electoral systems, while only 6 of 36 electorally uncompetitive nations could boast a completely free press.[2]

Such associations, however, do not necessarily indicate that it is democracy that serves as the basis for liberty. Indeed, the history of the relationship between liberty and democratic practices suggests that democratic institutions are often consequences rather than antecedents of freedom. In some respects, the citizens of the democracies are not free because they participate. Rather, they participate because they are—or once were—free. First, a measure of liberty is a necessary condition for the functioning of democratic processes. Beyond some minimal point, governmental interference with speech, assembly,

---

[1] Raymond O. Gastil *et al.*, *Freedom in the World: Political Rights and Civil Liberties* (New York: Freedom House, 1979).

[2] Arthur S. Banks and Robert B. Textor, *A Cross-Policy Survey* (Cambridge, Mass.: MIT Press, 1963).

association, the press, and so on, precludes an open and competitive politics.[3]

But more fundamentally, democratic institutions are most likely to emerge where the public already possesses—or threatens to acquire —a modicum of freedom from governmental control. As we saw earlier, democratic elections are typically introduced where governments are unable to compel popular acquiescence. In a sense, elections are inaugurated in order to persuade a resistant populace to surrender at least some of its freedom and allow itself to be governed. Upon occasion, the opportunity to participate is accompanied by guarantees of some civil liberties. But essentially, citizens are offered the opportunity to participate only when they are already free. Essentially, participation is offered to citizens as a substitute for freedom.

In the United States, for example, the introduction of democratic institutions, as well as the adoption of formal constitutional guarantees of civil liberties, was prompted by the fact that the citizenry was free—born free, as de Tocqueville observed—and had the capacity to remain so. Even several of the framers of the Constitution who were somewhat antipathetic to the principle nevertheless urged the adoption of democratic governmental forms on the ground that the populace would otherwise refuse to accept the new government. John Dickinson, for example, asserted that limited monarchy was likely superior to any republican form of government. Unfortunately, however, limited monarchy was out of the question because of the "spirit of the times."[4] Similarly, George Mason concluded that, "notwithstanding the oppressions and injustice experienced among us from democracy, the genius of the people is in favor of it, and the genius of the people must be consulted."[5] Subsequently, the Constitu-

---

[3] Still the most powerful discussion of the requisites for a democratic politics is Madison's in *The Federalist*, no. 10. E.M. Earle (ed.), *The Federalist* (New York: Modern Library, 1937). See also Carl Cohen, *Democracy* (Athens: University of Georgia Press, 1971), ch. 10.

[4] Max Farrand (ed.), *The Records of the Federal Convention of 1787* (New Haven, Conn.: Yale University Press, 1966), vol. 1, p. 86.

[5] *Ibid.*, p. 101.

tion's proponents agreed to add the formal guarantees of civil liberties embodied in the Bill of Rights only when it appeared that the Constitution might otherwise not be ratified.[6] In effect, the public had to be persuaded to permit itself to be governed because it was, in fact, free to choose otherwise. Given especially the absence of national military forces and the virtually universal distribution of firearms and training in their use, the populace could not easily have been compelled to accept a government it did not desire. One aspect of their "genius" was, after all, that the people were heavily armed.

In general, democratic political practices are most likely to emerge and develop in "free societies"—societies in which politically relevant resources, including the capacity to employ armed force or violence, are relatively widely distributed outside the control of the central government. The importance of the distribution of military force is clear. Where at some critical historical juncture rulers lacked a preponderance of force, they tended to become much more concerned with the acquisition of voluntary compliance through participatory and representative mechanisms. In Britain and Switzerland, for example, as in the United States, the development of democratic institutions was greatly facilitated by the central government's lack of a monopoly of military force during important historical epochs. In Switzerland the military consisted of a citizen militia. In Britain the standing army was typically small, and control of police forces was in the hands of the local gentry.[7]

But simple military force is by no means the only important factor. Where other politically relevant resources and skills—wealth, education, communications, organization, and so on—are relatively widely diffused and at least partially outside the state's control, the potential for resistance or opposition to governmental authority and thus rulers' interest in their subjects' voluntary acquiescence is greatly increased. An active private press coupled with a modicum of popular literacy, as students of American history may recall, can obviously

---

[6] See, for example, Forrest McDonald, *The Formation of the American Republic* (Baltimore: Penguin, 1965), ch. 8.

[7] See Robert A. Dahl (ed.), *Political Oppositions in Western Democracies* (New Haven, Conn.: Yale University Press, 1966), p. xv.

stimulate resistance to those in power.[8] Broadly distributed reservoirs of private financial resources can expedite the formation of opposition. And, of course, the potentially countervailing role of private associations and organizations needs no elaboration. When sizable segments of the public possess financial, organizational, educational, and other resources that can be used to foment and support opposition, those in power are more likely to see the merits of seeking to persuade rather than attempting to force their subjects to accept governance.

It is in part for this very reason that economic development, as Lipset and others have attempted to demonstrate, was historically conducive to the emergence of democratic institutions.[9] Industrialization and urbanization, especially under capitalist auspices, entailed the creation and dissemination of private wealth, organizational expertise, communications, literacy, and a host of other resources that facilitated political action and increased citizens' capacities for opposition and resistance.[10] Somewhat revised and updated, Lipset's original analysis is still quite suggestive on this score. First, the societies in which the availability and dissemination of wealth, access to communications, literacy, and exposure to privately controlled media are greatest are also most likely to have developed democratic governments. According to the *World Handbook*'s data, for example, 17 of the 20 nations with the highest per capita gross national products also have competitive electoral processes, as do 16 of the 19 nations that

---

[8] See Richard Hofstadter, *The Idea of a Party System* (Berkeley and Los Angeles: University of California Press, 1969), ch. 3.

[9] Seymour Martin Lipset, *Political Man* (Garden City, N.Y.: Doubleday, Anchor Books, 1963), ch. 2. See also Phillips Cutright, "National Political Development: Measurement and Analysis," in Charles F. Cnudde and Dean Neubauer (eds.), *Empirical Democratic Theory* (Chicago: Markham, 1969), pp. 193-209; and Dean E. Neubauer, "Some Conditions of Democracy," in *ibid.*, especially p. 225.

[10] Economic development can also create attitudinal resources that facilitate mass political activity. Such activity may in turn ultimately induce elites to attempt to erect political structures that can allow the regime to accommodate sustained mass involvement. See Daniel Lerner, *The Passing of Traditional Society* (New York: Free Press, 1958), ch. 2; see also Karl W. Deutsch, "Social Mobilization and Political Development," *American Political Science Review* 55 (September 1961): 493-514.

rank highest in literacy, 19 of the 20 nations with the largest number of telephones per capita, 18 of the 20 nations with the highest per capita newspaper, radio, and television use, and 18 of the highest 20 nations in terms of percentage of labor force in professional and technical occupations.[11] On these as well as a variety of other indicators, citizens' possession of economic, technical, and educational resources seems at least to be associated with the existence of a democratic politics.

Second, consider the correlates of democratic government in Latin America. Few Latin American nations can boast a history of stable democracy. In most cases, democratic regimes have sooner or later been superseded by autocratic or military rule. Often, when more or less free elections have taken place, the results have been monitored by the military, which was willing to permit some outcomes but not others. Nevertheless, what is interesting is that the Latin American nations that have experienced the longest democratic or at least quasi-democratic interludes—even if this meant only that the generals found it expedient to step back for a time—are on the whole also those in which the availability of wealth, literacy, communications, and so on, are greatest (see Table 7.1).[12] It is, in a sense, where citizens have the means with which to maintain or acquire a measure of freedom from governmental authority that they must occasionally be governed through democratic formulas. And it is in this sense that freedom is an historical antecedent of democracy.

Whatever their origins, where they do develop, democratic institutions can undoubtedly help to protect citizens from governmental encroachments upon their rights and liberties. Democratic elections may make those in power more sensitive to their subjects' rights. Few

---

[11] Charles Lewis Taylor and Michael C. Hudson, *World Handbook of Political and Social Indicators*, 2d ed. (New Haven, Conn.: Yale University Press, 1972). See Tables 4.5, 4.7, 4.8, 5.5, and 5.10.

[12] Data pertaining to per capita gross national product, literacy, media, and occupation are drawn from Taylor and Hudson, *World Handbook*. The number of years of competitive or quasi-competitive elections are estimates based on historical accounts. See, for example, Martin C. Needler, *Political Systems of Latin America* (New York: Van Nostrand, 1970).

TABLE 7.1 *The availability of political resources and democratic politics in Latin America.*

Country	Number of years of competitive or quasi-competitive elections from 1945 to 1980	Per capita GNP rank	Literacy rank	Media availability rank	% of population in technical or professional occupations rank
Uruguay	35	3	2	1	5
Mexico	35	6	12	4	9
Chile	28	4	3	9	4
Costa Rica	27	7	4	10	8
Colombia	23	10	10	12	1
Venezuela	22	1	5	6	7
Argentina	20	2	1	3	NA
Brazil	19	12	13	13	3
Ecuador	15	16	9	14	12
Bolivia	15	19	19	7	NA
Peru	12	14	14	8	NA
Guatemala	11	11	18	17	10
Panama	11	5	7	2	6
Cuba	5	8	6	5	2
Honduras	3	17	17	18	13
Dominican Republic	1	13	11	19	6
El Salvador	0	15	16	11	15
Paraguay	0	18	8	15	11
Nicaragua	0	9	15	16	14
Haiti	0	20	20	20	NA

white elected officials in the southern United States, for example, now openly support a return to racial segregation. Democratic elections can presumably offer citizens an opportunity to reject candidates whose programs might appear to threaten basic rights and to support candidates in whose hands they believe their liberties to be more secure.

Of course, long before the advent of democratic elections, citizens possessed means of defending what they conceived to be their rights and liberties. More than one rebellion was prompted by rulers' efforts to abrogate some privilege that their subjects' held dear. Indeed, where citizens were utterly unable to protect their rights without the suffrage, they also never came to acquire the suffrage. Once introduced, however, democratic electoral mechanisms at least give the public some means of safeguarding its freedom without violence, even when, for one reason or another, violent or disorderly opposition to governmental transgressions might no longer have much chance of success.

ELECTIONS, FREEDOM, AND GOVERNMENT

While elections may offer some measure of protection for civil liberties, the public is seldom satisfied to view democratic processes only as safeguards. As we saw earlier, the availability of democratic electoral institutions tends to persuade citizens that government is simply their servant. As a result, the public comes to wish to benefit from the state's power rather than merely to be protected from it. While elections can serve as safeguards against governmental excesses and encroachments, the availability of democratic controls tends eventually to persuade citizens that they may enjoy the benefits of the state's power without risk to their freedom. Why, after all, should it be necessary to limit a servant's capacity to serve?

Unfortunately, however, despite democratic controls, freedom and government inevitably conflict. This conflict does not necessarily entail deliberate and overt governmental efforts to abridge liberties. Typically, the erosion of citizens' liberties in the democracies is a more subtle, insidious, and often unforeseen result of routine administrative processes. Federal agencies such as the Interstate Commerce Commission, the Civil Aeronautics Board, and the Federal Trade Commission, to take the most mundane examples, have considerable control over who may enter the occupations and businesses that they regulate. The Food and Drug Administration has a good deal to say about what may be eaten. The Federal Communications Commission has a measure of influence over what Americans see and hear over the air waves. The Internal Revenue Service, in the mundane course of collecting taxes, makes decisions about what is and is not a religion, whether given forms of education are or are not socially desirable, what types of philanthropy serve the public interest, and, of course, what sorts of information to acquire about every citizen. Congressional tax legislation and IRS regulations can have a critical effect upon every individual's business decisions, marital plans, childbirth and child-rearing decisions, vacation plans, and medical care.[13] Though the administration of tax policy is among the most instrusive activities of the federal government, housing policies, educational policies, welfare programs, and so on, often directed by agencies given broad, discretionary mandates by Congress, affect the most minute details of citizens' lives.[14] For the citizens of the modern state, freedom has come to mean little more than a modicum of choice about the manner in which they will accommodate themselves to the state's directives.

---

[13] A useful review of the details of U.S. tax policy and its administration can be found in Joseph A. Pechman, *Federal Tax Policy* (New York: Norton, 1971). Efforts by the IRS to distinguish, in effect, between true religion and heresy can be particularly amusing. In recent years, the agency sought to deny tax exempt status to the "All One Faith in One God State Universal Life Church" and denied tax exempt status to the "Zion Coptic Church, Inc." Curiously, the People's Temple, led by one Reverend Jim Jones, had no difficulty acquiring exemption from federal taxation. See Eugene McCarthy, *The Ultimate Tyranny* (New York: Harcourt Brace Jovanovich, 1980), p. 205.

[14] The problem of administrative discretion is discussed in Theodore J. Lowi, *The End of Liberalism,* rev. ed. (New York: Norton, 1979). See also Kenneth Culp Davis, *Discretionary Justice* (Baton Rouge: Louisiana State University Press, 1969) for a discussion of the injustices that can arise from the inevitable exercise of administrative discretion.

Despite the availability of democratic institutions, the citizens of democracies cannot expect to use the state's power without surrendering at least some of their freedom. Their failure to realize that a choice is involved simply guarantees that the state will more rapidly transform itself from servant to master. The availability of democratic electoral controls, however, tends to obscure this threat. Because of the availability of electoral controls, the public believes that big government can be perfectly compatible with personal freedom. After all, how can a government controlled by its citizens represent a threat to the rights of those citizens? The twentieth-century public believes almost as a matter of course that democratic processes somehow guarantee its liberty.[15] Indeed, as Wollheim observes, democracy has come to be seen as a form of government in which "no limit" need be placed on the governing body.[16]

This notion that democratic processes somehow reconcile personal freedom and expanded governmental authority has even crept into twentieth-century democratic theory. Eighteenth- and nineteenth-century liberal theorists, such as Jeremy Bentham and James Mill, took the relatively modest position that electoral participation could help to protect citizens' interests against tyrannical actions by their rulers.[17] Similarly, the authors of the *Federalist* acknowledged that elections might function to protect citizens' liberties, but emphasized

---

[15] Despite a general diminution of public confidence in most other aspects of government and politics, the American public continues to believe in the significance of democratic elections. Data, for example, from a recent University of Michigan poll indicate that 91 percent of those surveyed believe that it is important to vote even when their own party has no chance to win; 87 percent believe that every single vote matters though it may be only one of millions cast; 87 percent feel that everyone should vote even in apparently unimportant local elections; and 50 percent of those surveyed go so far as to assert that those who do not care about the election's outcome should vote nonetheless.

[16] Richard Wollheim, "A Paradox in the Theory of Democracy," in Peter Laslett and W.G. Runciman (eds.), *Philosophy, Politics and Society* (Oxford: Blackwell, 1962), p. 72.

[17] See James Mill, *An Essay on Government* (Cambridge: At the University Press, 1937). See also Jeremy Bentham, *Works*, ed. by J. Bowring (Edinburgh: Tait, 1843), especially vol. 9, books 1 and 2. See also Carol Pateman, *Participation and Democratic Theory* (Cambridge: At the University Press, 1970), ch. 1; and Dennis F. Thompson, *The Democratic Citizen* (Cambridge: At the University Press, 1970), ch. 3.

the importance of collateral institutional and constitutional barriers against the "unlimited government" that might result despite or even from democratic processes.[18] Many twentieth-century theorists, however, appear to see a more intimate relationship between democratic practices and liberty. Harold Laski, for example, declares that "without democracy there cannot be liberty."[19] H. B. Mayo, anticipating a point of view recently endorsed by the United States Supreme Court, avers that "democracy has a marked tendency to extend the freedoms from the political to other spheres."[20] Indeed, from the perspective of some twentieth-century writers there is no necessary contradiction between individual liberty and the most unmitigated forms of governmental authority. Karl Mannheim, for example, argues that in the ideal centrally planned society, freedom does not require antiquated institutional or constitutional restrictions on the power of the "planning authority." Instead, "democratic control" should be sufficient to compel those in power to permit a measure of personal freedom. According to Mannheim:

> *At the highest stage freedom can only exist when it is secured by planning. It cannot consist in restricting the powers of the planner, but in a conception of planning which guarantees the existence of essential forms of freedom through the plan itself. For every restriction imposed by limited authorities would destroy the unity of the plan, so that society would regress to the former stage of competition and mutual control. As we have said, at the stage of planning freedom can only be guaranteed if the planning authority incorporates it in the plan itself. Whether the sovereign authority be an individual or a group or a popular assembly, it must be compelled by democratic control to allow full scope for freedom*

---

[18] Earle, *The Federalist*, no. 53.

[19] Harold J. Laski, *Liberty in the Modern State* (London: Faber and Faber, 1930), p. 241.

[20] H.B. Mayo, *An Introduction to Democratic Theory* (New York: Oxford University Press, 1960), p. 241. See also Justice Black's opinion for the Court in *Wesberry* v. *Sanders*, 376 U.S. 1 (1964): "No right is more precious in a free country than that of having a voice in the election of those who make the laws under which, as good citizens, we must live. Other rights, even the most basic, are illusory if the right to vote is undermined."

in its plan. Once all the instruments of influencing human behavior have been co-ordinated, planning for freedom is the only logical form of freedom which remains.[21]

Logical or not, democratic institutions encourage citizens to believe that they may have both freedom and government, thus increasing the certainty that the public will choose to have government. The final irony of democratic electoral politics is that democratic institutions, the archetypes of public choice, help to mask this most fundamental of choices. The critical question is whether the public will become aware of the nature of the decision it has made. Perhaps, despite the indications to the contrary, the public's mood during the 1980 elections reflected at least the beginnings of such an awareness. The more likely eventuality, though, as de Tocqueville foresaw long ago, is that citizens will simply continue to take pride in their firm grips on what, more and more, constitute only the ends of their own chains.

---

[21] Karl Mannheim, *Man and Society in an Age of Reconstruction* (London: Kegan Paul, Trench, Trubner and Co., 1940), p. 378.

INDEX

255